HISTORY IN A CHANGING WORLD

GEOFFREY BARRACLOUGH

History in a
Changing World

OXFORD
BASIL BLACKWELL
1957

First Printed December, 1955
Reprinted May, 1956
Reprinted January, 1957

PRINTED IN GREAT BRITAIN
BY A. T. BROOME AND SON, ST. CLEMENT'S, OXFORD
AND BOUND BY THE KEMP HALL BINDERY, OXFORD

CONTENTS

PREFACE

THE experience of the last ten years has given me many reasons to know that, outside academic circles, there is a widespread demand by intelligent people of all classes and persuasions for a new view (or perhaps I should simply say for a view) of European history. I should like to think that this volume may provide some of the necessary clues for which such people are searching, and which they do not (so they aver) find in a history predicated upon those hardy perennials of text-books and examination-syllabuses, the War of Spanish Succession and the War of Austrian Succession.

I have used the words 'the necessary clues' of set purpose. Although I hope that this book will not be considered as (and, still more, will not give the impression of being) a random collection of stray essays—for not only has everything which it contains been revised and often re-written, but I have also been at pains, in selecting material for inclusion, to ensure to the best of my ability that it would lack neither coherence nor unity of theme—it does not set out to provide a self-contained account of our European past. It is neither my wish nor my purpose, nor (I believe) is it in the best interests of historical study to-day, to propound a doctrine, theory or even a particular view of European history; but I hope that what I have to say may (if only by contradiction) stimulate and provoke thought and discussion. Anyone who is going to make anything out of history will, sooner or later, have to do most of the work himself or herself. He will have to read, and consider, and re-consider, and then read some more. But where is he to begin ? Time and again, after a talk or lecture, people have approached me or written to me to ask the source of a particular view or statement, and more generally whether I can give them suggestions for further reading along the lines on which I have been speaking. It is for that reason that, after some consideration, I have appended fairly frequent bibliographical references as footnotes to the essays which follow. I am well aware that such references are unfashionable to-day ; as Mr. A. J. P. Taylor once wrote, ' if the reader does not accept my credentials, he will not be induced to do so by a display of the sources from which my plumes are borrowed '. I can only beg the reader to believe in this case that my motive is neither pedantry nor even piety towards those whose writings I have pillaged, but a genuine desire to perform a service. Whatever may be thought of the essays which follow, there are some good, lively, stimulating and even profoundly satisfying books among those I have mentioned ; and if only a few who would otherwise have missed them are drawn to them by my references, I shall be well satisfied and the purposes of history will be served.

The great German historian and philosopher, Ernst Troeltsch, once said that there are times when it is more important to make a beginning than to produce the finished article. It is in that belief that the following pages have been written. The reasons why, as it seems to me, conditions in the modern world have made a new beginning in the writing of history necessary—a proposition which, perhaps, only professional historians would be inclined to question —I have endeavoured to set out in my first chapter ; and for that reason further prefatory remarks are unnecessary. It only remains for me to express my thanks to those—the Council of the Historical Association, and the editors of *Merkur*, *The Listener*, *The Manchester Guardian*, *Past and Present*, and *Humanitas*—who have generously allowed me to reproduce material from their pages.

G.B.

September 30, 1955.

1. The Historian in a Changing World

ONE of the pressing needs of to-day is a new vision of the course of modern history. Ever since the end of the war we have laboured under a sense of the inadequacy of our inherited view of the past. As Alfred Weber wrote in 1946,[1] we feel that we stand at the end and outside of the traditional history of the schools and universities, the history which has western Europe at its centre ; and it is obvious to us, in the new constella-tion of world-affairs, that an interpretation which surveys the back-ground to the present almost exclusively from the point of view of western Europe has little relevance to our current problems. It is not here, in the painstaking examination of the diplomacy of Bismarck or of the origins of the First World War, or even in the history of international relations in the inter-war years, that we can hope to find the essential clues to the dilemmas of the present ; and we are beset by a sense of uncertainty because we feel ourselves on the threshold of a new age, to which previous experience offers no sure guide.

One result of this new situation is that history itself is losing, if it has not already lost, the hold it once exercised over the best minds as a key to present living. For a century and a half, from the time of the French Revolution, historical principles and historical conceptions dominated, shaped and determined the character of European thought. It was during this period that the underlying assumption took hold ' that the nature of anything is entirely comprehended in its development ', and that most of the spheres of intellectual, and often also of active life, are permeated by history.[2] The result was that history was raised up to a perilous eminence as the ultimate *magistra vitae*, and an imperious, self-confident Clio displaced religion and philosophy as the deity before which we bowed.

---

[1] *Abschied von der bisherigen Geschichte* (1946), 10. (An English translation of this work, under the title : *Farewell to European History*, appeared in 1947).

[2] Cf. D. E. Lee and R. N. Beck, ' The Meaning of " Historicism ",' *American Historical Review* LIX (1954), 568–9.

The cult of historicism which was thus established, meant, in the words of Guido de Ruggiero, 'the evaluation of reality as a historical process of spiritual formation '.[1] It implied the rejection of the rationalism of the eighteenth-century Enlightenment, a total break with the outlook of Voltaire and Turgot and Condorcet.[2] It substituted the concepts of development and individuality for belief in the stability of human nature and in reason; and this revaluation constituted, in the judgement of Friedrich Meinecke, 'the greatest spiritual revolution which western thought has undergone '.[3] To-day none of us, no matter where our particular interests may lie, can escape its all-pervasive influence. The reason is not merely that, before the end of the nineteenth century, history had become a principal branch of study; far more important is the fact that ' human thought in every field seemed to run to history ', and that ' it affected all other departments of mental activity '.[4] We think of ourselves as living in a scientific age; but in a profounder sense, we live—all of us, including, from Darwin's time, the natural scientists—in an historical age, or an age of historicism; and this is perhaps the ultimate reason and justification for concerning ourselves with history : it has become, whether we like it or not, an inseparable part of our mental processes and of our being.

Who would deny that the result has been to enrich our experience, to increase beyond measure our perceptions of reality, if not, indeed, our very capacity for perception? Instead of trying to constrain reality within a system, we have dismissed the ' empty figment of one linear history ' and learnt appreciation of the subtle shades of individuality, respect for irreducible particularity, acceptance of the untold ' multitude of facts ', and awareness of ' endless formation and transformation ', of ' achievement without end '; we see in history ' the most exhilarating testimony to the creative vigour, the splendid variety, of the human spirit '.[5]

[1] *Encyclopedia of the Social Sciences* VII (1932), 569. Addressing the Tenth International Congress of the Historical Sciences on 7 September, 1955, His Holiness Pope Pius XII described it as ' un système philosophique, celui qui n'aperçoit dans toute réalité spirituelle, dans le connaissance du vrai, dans la religion, la moralité et le droit, que changement et évolution, et rejette par conséquent tout ce qui est permanent, éternellement valable et absolu '.

[2] Cf. M. J. A. N. C. de Condorcet, *Sketch for a Historical Picture of the Progress of the Human Mind* (tr. J. M. Barraclough, 1955).

[3] F. Meinecke, *Die Entstehung des Historismus* I (1936), 1.

[4] H. Butterfield, *History and Human Relations* (1951), 159.

[5] Cf. below, pp. 231, 238.

And yet who, to-day, would dare to claim that historicism provides an ultimate view of reality, an adequate philosophy either for thinking or for living? 'The more we try to sound the inexhaustible meaning of the particular', it has been well said,[1] 'the more devoid everything seems to be of any meaning in particular'. That historicism is the progenitor of relativism, is too obvious a fact to require demonstration. Everything is related, judged and evaluated in relation—and far too often solely in relation—to time, place, context and environment; there are no absolutes; there is no transcendent sanction for man's action; morality itself is atomized, particularized, pulverized, until in the end it is held to be 'impossible to think one man essentially more wicked than another'.[2] The historian is taught to discover, not whether Charles I—or Hitler—was right or wrong, but 'how his action was historically conditioned', to disengage 'the structural features of a conflict which was inherent in the dialectic of events'.[3] If this is truly his function, the only function which the material to his hands permits him to undertake, then we can only conclude that his view of reality is so limited and circumscribed that it sidetracks the very problems which touch us, as individuals, most nearly. It does not abolish the moral issue; for, assuming that our knowledge is insufficient for condemnation, it is evidently by the same token insufficient for exoneration. In fact, the only conclusion we can reasonably draw is that historicism, as a key to present living, is inadequate; but who can blame the ordinary man, his modes of thought permeated through and through by unquestioned assumptions springing from historicist premises, if he acts and thinks as though historical judgements are final and sufficient in themselves, and that the criteria upon which historical judgements are based are applicable to all human problems? And who has the right to blame him if, finding as a result of an overdose of history that he has no standards left, except to judge everything in the light of circumstances, he either uses history as a comfortable pretext for cynicism, or (more likely) rejects it in disgust?

What I have tried in these few words to sketch, is, I imagine, the fundamental deficiency of the historicist myth, the direction in which—precisely because it was the dominant mode of thought of

---

[1] Cf. P. Leon, 'The Terror of History,' *The Listener* LIV (1955), 16.
[2] Butterfield, op. cit., 108.   [3] Ibid., 14, 70.

more than one generation—its effects, as they passed into wider currency under the coarsening impact of popularization, were most nefarious. But it is becoming apparent, also, that as an explanation of historical change and of historical processes the doctrine of historicism has done almost as much to obscure and bewilder as it has to enrich and enlighten our perceptions ; or at least it is clear —in terms of its own relativism—that as a theory it was *zeitgebunden*, in the sense that it expressed the appropriate outlook of one particular period, and of that period alone, and is no longer appropriate to a changing world in which conditions are radically different. It may be that Friedrich Meinecke, the leading exponent of historicism, recognized this fact when, at the end of his life, he transferred his allegiance from Ranke to Burckhardt, thereby turning away from the tradition in which he had been bred and to which he, more than any other, had given conscious shape and expression.[1] Periods of advance, security, quiet enjoyment—such as was, all in all, the nineteenth century for the professional writer of history —produce one attitude to the past ; times of defeat and collapse, as Meinecke observed, produce another, and involve the necessity of searching out new paths.[2]

In the first place, the very concentration on development and continuity, which is fundamental to historicism, may well have been natural, and seemed well founded, a century ago ; but to-day we are in a position to realize more clearly that such assumptions are at best partial views, and probably (more bluntly) deceptive half-truths. The historian who observed, over thirty years ago, that ' continuity is by no means the most conspicuous feature of history',[3] put his finger unerringly on one central fallacy of historicism ; and since that time we ourselves have experienced enough of discontinuity to feel renewed sympathy with all those historians who, from the time of Augustine and Orosius, have been more impressed by the cataclysmic than by the continuous in human affairs. Nor is it easy, any longer, to believe that ' the nature of anything is entirely comprehended in its development '. This plausible view leaves too

---

[1] F. Meinecke, *Burckhardt und Ranke* (Deutsche Akademie, Vorträge u. Schriften, no. 27, 1948) ; I cite the English translation in *German History. Some New German Views* (ed. H. Kohn, 1954), 141–156.
[2] Ibid., 155–6.
[3] F. J. C. Hearnshaw, *Mediaeval Contributions to Modern Civilisation* (1921), 18 ; cf. below, pp. 35, 230.

little room for the impact of the fortuitous and the unforeseen, for the new, the dynamic and the revolutionary, which breaks through —as I have urged elsewhere[1]—untrammelled by the past, at every great turning-point in human history. The influences and ingredients of a given age and environment—which, in earlier historical thought, were considered, too often, as an adequate explanation of the course of events—are, in fact, ' by no means sufficient in themselves to explain the next stage of the story ' ;[2] for ' no present-day issue is, or ever was, intelligible in terms of its history '.[3] In the end the historian's search for causes and origins only brings us up against the ultimate mysteries. Who would suppose, for example, after all that has been written on the ' causes ' of the French Revolution, or on the ' causes ' of the Reformation, that we are as a result really much nearer to an explanation of these two great upheavals? The doctrine of continuity is serviceable, provided that it is not pressed too far ; but development and continuity are not a total explanation of the historical process.

Furthermore they may, unduly emphasized, be misleading and dangerous because they produce in the treatment of history an evenness, an illusion of steady flow, which is both at variance with experience and detrimental to all perspective.[4] We all, in our own lives, recognize turning-points, moments of crisis, decisions which in some sense have been determinative of our future actions. For the historian, on the contrary, it is one of the cherished platitudes of historical thinking that the garment of Clio is a seamless web, that every age is an age of change, and that the world which comes within the historian's vision is in a permanent state of flux. When, long ago, the great German historian, Ranke, proclaimed that all ages are ' immediate to God ',[5] the implication was that all possess equal significance in the perspective of eternity, and that all are worthy of, and will repay, equal treatment at the hands of the historian.[6] No one will deny the element of truth in this view. We

---

[1] Below, p. 183 sq. [2] Butterfield, op. cit., 94.
[3] Below, p. 184. [4] Below, p. 157.
[5] In his famous lectures ' On the Epochs of Modern History ', delivered before king Maximilian of Bavaria in 1854, and printed in vol. IX of Ranke's *Weltgeschichte* (1888).
[6] Therefore, after the famous statement : ' I maintain that every epoch is immediate to God and that its value rests in no way upon what it produces, but upon the very fact of its existence ' (ibid., 5), Ranke specifically continues : ' before God all generations of humanity appear as having equal right, and this is the way in which the historian also must look at the matter ' (p. 6).

realize to-day, for example, that the seventh century or the ninth century has as much to tell us, and as much ultimate importance in the human story—as well as equal intrinsic interest—as the more spectacular Carolingian era which separates them. To pick out ' important ' or ' decisive ' phases or periods—' creative centuries ', they have been called,[1] as though all centuries are not creative— does not merely create the danger of false emphasis ; it also means that we shall miss the peculiar contribution which each generation makes to the problem of living, its answers to questions which are eternal. As that fine historian, A. G. Little, once observed,[2] ' the most valuable function of the historian ' is not

> to trace back the institutions and ways of thought which have survived, as though we were at the end and climax of history. It is at least as important to retrieve the treasures that have been dropped on the way and lost, which, if restored, would enrich our civilisation.

No one, to-day, would maintain that any age of the past was unproductive, a mere halting-place in time, or that at any period of the past new impulses were not stirring under the surface. We are aware, for example, that the apparent tranquillity of the years after 1815, the ' Indian summer ' following the French Revolution and the Napoleonic Wars, was illusory, and that the words ' conservatism ' or ' reaction ' only typify the most superficial aspects of the age of Metternich. Similarly the old view that Germany fell back, exhausted, into stagnation after the Thirty Years' War, until Frederick the Great of Prussia awakened it from its lethargy, has been dispelled by closer observation of the German scene after 1648. And yet who, granted all this, would deny that, at certain times, the impetus of change gathered pace, the tempo was suddenly accelerated? Troeltsch once observed that an original system of thought, a revolution in the modes of thinking, is only possible every couple of hundred years, after the preliminary stages have been thoroughly worked over.[3] The implication is that some ages are periods of preparation, others periods of fulfilment. It is not necessary (nor is it logically possible) to argue that the one is more ' important ' than the other ; it is enough to see that they are different, both in their implications and in their effects, and in their relation to us. For this

---

[1] H. J. Randall, *The Creative Centuries* (1944).
[2] The passage is cited by F. M. Powicke, *Modern Historians and the Study of History* (1955), 95.   [3] E. Troeltsch, *Gesammelte Schriften* III (1922), 110.

reason it is, I think, legitimate to describe certain periods as turning-points, when European society swung upwards, out of its existing course, on to a new plane.[1] All ages, it is true, are ages of change, all periods are transitional periods ; but we are not suffering from an illusion or hallucination when we feel, and say, that we to-day live in an age of change so great that the older preoccupations—of historians, but not of historians alone—no longer correspond to living needs, their inherited assumptions no longer fit the reality we have experienced.

An age which has undergone great upheavals—which has seen, for example, tens and hundreds of thousands of men, women and children uprooted, first by one side and then by the other, and thrust from their homes in a vast new *Völkerwanderung*—will not be impressed when it is told that history is a story of continuity, governed by a law not of revolution but of evolution. An age which has seen morality pitchforked out of politics, and has experienced the results of that experiment, will not be satisfied when it is given an historical explanation of what has taken place, and why. It is easy, at a distance of one and a half centuries, to adopt towards Napoleon I an attitude of detached relativism—and every schoolboy to-day (it would seem) has learnt to speak and write of Napoleon or Frederick the Great without falling into the vulgar error of moral approbation or disapprobation—but how many of us would adopt the same attitude towards Hitler or Mussolini? We may perhaps say—as I have ventured to say elsewhere[2]—that how a thing was accomplished, and at what cost, ' does not concern us here and now ', provided that we put due emphasis on the words ' here and now '. But ' when we are told that it is foolish to judge Charlemagne, or Napoleon, or Genghis Khan, or Hitler, or Stalin, for their mass-acres ', or that such judgements are beside the point, we can only answer that ' to accept this doctrine is to do violence to the basic notions of our morality, to misrepresent our sense of the past, and to ignore the most general concepts of normal thought '.[3] A doctrine which leads, as historicism does, in this direction, is unacceptable : it is time for reconsideration of the foundations, and of the fundamental postulates, of historical thought.

* * *

[1] Cf. below, p. 79.
[3] Cf. I. Berlin, *Historical Inevitability* (1954), 76–77.

[2] Below, p. 199.

Sooner or later, the historian returning in 1945 after a long period of service in one or other of the armed forces, found himself confronted by the kind of question, the species of doubt, I have attempted to sketch out above. Perhaps he had no greater wish than to return to his old groove, to take up again what he had unwillingly laid down, to continue the studies which had, up to 1939, seemed important to him, to build on foundations laid in the pre-war years. But where were the old grooves, and how did he fit into them? In fact, they were not totally obliterated ; but they were scored and crossed by deep furrows and channels, their course eroded by the floods of six over-full years, their outline sometimes lost, their direction diverted. If he belonged to the inter-war generation, which had grown up responding enthusiastically to the fine faith in history as *magistra vitae*, which sustained us from the days of Lord Acton into the 1930s, his mind was probably moulded by many of the implicit assumptions about history, its use and relevance, which the cult of historicism had implanted deep in him. He was satisfied with what he found existing, and took it on trust ; few of us, as we contributed in the pre-war decades to this learned periodical or that, questioned the credentials of what we were doing, or the premisses of our work. It was not that we were unaware of change and crisis in the world around us ; on the contrary, we were acutely—sometimes almost painfully—conscious of such things as the progressive failure of democratic forms of government in one European country after another, the conflict of capitalism and communism, the drastic impact of unemployment and trade depression. But as yet the tempo was not such as to disturb our inherited belief in continuity ; there seemed to be no urgent need for re-examination of our basic historical assumptions. It was not, I think, that we lived—at any rate consciously—in two watertight compartments, our left hands not knowing what our right hands were doing, but rather that it still seemed possible to fit our experiences—as other historians in an earlier generation had done[1]—into our historical scheme, instead of reconsidering and remodelling our historical assumptions in the light of our experience.

After 1945, at least for a growing number of historians, that was no longer possible. Of course we had previously all sought to refine and to define more accurately our picture of this or that phase

[1] Cf. below, p. 170.

of the past ; particularly under the impact of the great quarrying in archives which had been the mark of the previous half-century, setting in with the opening of the Vatican Archives by pope Leo XIII in 1881, and in England with the appointment of Sir Henry Maxwell Lyte to the directorship of the Public Record Office in 1886, the study of history had entered upon a period of active revision without parallel in the past. But this revision was carried out under the ban of historicism, and rarely, if ever, questioned its postulates ; it may have implied criticism of this historian or that, but it did not embody criticisms of the basic assumptions upon which the work of a generation and more of historians rested. Ideally, no doubt, there was no need to wait until 1945 for such criticism ; and already long before 1939 a few historians, such as Herbert Butterfield,[1] had begun to look at the past with a new vision. But for most of us it was the impact of war that opened our eyes to the limitations, and in some cases to the falsifications, of the history we had learnt and taught. It was not necessarily the case that this history, in detail, was wrong, but rather that it was inadequate ; but the very fact of inadequacy quickly led us to enquire whether, in that case, it must not also be wrong, at least in balance and in perspective.

Few historians, I imagine, unless the events of 1939–45 made no impact on their cloistered minds, can have escaped this sense of misgiving at some point in their contact with the past. Only the individual can say at what point doubt first crept in. In my own case, I think, the first—but thereafter by no means the only—hint of the fatal limitations of the history I had learnt was the realization that it had left me totally unprepared for a world in which the countries of eastern Europe were evidently destined to play, at the very least, a greater part than they had (or than they seemed, in the scheme of history I had inherited, to have) played in the past. In this sense it was only a pardonable exaggeration to say that, for me, it was the Russian victory at Stalingrad in 1943 that made a total revision of European history imperative.[2] I realized with consternation that three years in an English and two years in a German university had left me for all practical purposes ignorant of eastern European history, save at a few points where it caught the limelight

---

[1] I have in mind, of course, his famous essay, *The Whig Interpretation of History*, published in 1931.

[2] Cf. below, p. 181.

as a consequence of diplomatic relations with the west; and I
realized with even greater consternation that I had managed to
teach history with reasonable success (judged, at least, by examination results) to a large number of gifted pupils over a long period
of years without feeling any necessity to remedy this defect. I knew
a great deal of the machinery of the papal chancery in the thirteenth
and fourteenth centuries, and of the writings of the canonists; but
I knew nothing of the Piasts, the Przemyslids and the Ruriks—and
felt no imperative need to know anything—unless their activities
happened to impinge on German history. I had some notion of the
place of the emperor Charles IV in history, but knew little more
than the names of his contemporaries, Louis the Great of Hungary
and Casimir the Great of Poland. I had read all the surviving letters
of St. Boniface, the apostle of the Germans, but nothing of St.
Cyril and St. Methodius, the apostles of the Slavs.

These autobiographical details I introduce, for what they are
worth, by way of illustration. I do not suppose that my predica-
ment was unique; but it was no less disturbing—indeed, it was
even more disturbing—for that reason. Every historian is more
acutely aware of his vast ignorance of the past than of his limited
knowledge in the special field he has made his own : the important
point is rather the nature, the extent, and the significance of the
gaps. Rightly or wrongly, I began to suspect that the view of
history in which I had been brought up, and which I had accepted
almost as a matter of course, might represent a good deal less than
the truth; that it was a partial view, reflecting the outlook of a
particular phase or period of time, and perhaps of a particular
circumscribed area, the validity of which subsequent events had
made doubtful. I wondered whether it really gave us a view of the
past which did justice to the various forces at play; and I wondered
also what was its relevance to the world in which we live. I began
to look more critically at theories which I had formerly accepted
without undue questioning; I began a slow process of reorientation.

Some of the fruits of that process of reorientation are gathered
together in this volume. They spread, in substance, over ten years,
and the process of rethinking which, in however limited a way, they
represent, is at its beginning, rather than at its end. Consequently,
although every word has been revised, and many of the essays
remodelled, I do not wish to claim that they reflect a consistent

theory. It is impossible suddenly to produce the 'formula for a new historiography ',[1] like a conjuror producing a rabbit out of his hat ; and we shall be wise to examine the credentials of anyone who claims to have done so. Any reader who desires to pick holes, will certainly be able to discover inconsistencies of interpretation among the essays which follow. And, in fact, they come in the form of essays for this reason : not simply, that is to say, because they reflect particular occasions which have presented themselves to reconsider particular points, but because I believe the essay to be the most appropriate medium for what they are—tentative gropings towards what I believe to be a necessary reinterpretation.

As Sir Maurice Powicke once observed, ' problems cannot all be solved, for, as they are solved, new aspects are continually revealed : the historian opens the way, he does not close it.'[2] It is in this spirit that, over the past decade, I have tried to advance from one debate to the next, without reaching (or hoping to reach) finality. But although I do not claim consistency, I think it is fair to say that the contents of the present volume have a certain coherence, simply because they spring, one and all, from the basic preoccupations which have occupied my mind since 1945. What was necessary, it seemed to me, was ' not so much new knowledge as a new vision playing on old facts, and a realization of the inadequacy of old formulations in a new situation.'[3] What I have tried to do is, first, to discover the preconditions of, and then to apply in concrete cases, that new vision ; and it goes without saying that I have drawn liberally on the work of others—particularly, I should like to add, of fellow-historians in Germany. It is, of course, true that this is not the only possible approach to the problems with which the historian finds himself confronted to-day. The crisis—or what has been called the ' poverty '[4]—of historicism might profitably be considered in a more theoretical way than I have chosen : for example, by examining systematically the criticism inaugurated, in his usual trenchant manner, by Nietzsche in 1874,[5] analysed with

---

[1] Below, p. 183.   [2] Powicke, op. cit., 104.
[3] Below, p. 136.
[4] Cf. K. Popper, ' The Poverty of Historicism ', *Economica* (New Series) XI (1944).
[5] F. Nietzsche, *Vom Nutzen und Nachtheil der Historie für das Leben*. This is the second of the *Unzeitgemässe Betrachtungen* (1873–4), and appears in vol. II of Nietzsche's *Werke* (ed. 1906) ; it was translated as *The Use and Abuse of History*, in *Thoughts out of Season*, Part II, in the authorized English translation of the *Complete Works* (1909).

fine discrimination by Ernst Troeltsch,[1] and enunciated on many
different occasions by Paul Valéry.[2] In this way we might, perhaps,
obtain a clearer perception of the limitations governing the assumptions historians commonly make. But for the present, it seems to me,
more is to be gained by dealing in a more concrete way with substantive points of interpretation; and for this purpose I have
selected for discussion certain key problems or aspects of European
history, because it seems to me that European history still touches
us most nearly. Though many will disagree with the particular
reassessments I have made, few, I think, will disagree that reassessment is necessary and overdue. On the one side, we must
find a way of escape, as Sir Maurice Powicke has urged, from the
dangers that beset the new historical learning.[3] On the other,
' every age needs its own view of history; and to-day we need a
new view of the European past, adapted to the new perspectives
in which the old Europe stands in a new age of global politics and
global civilisation.'[4]

                    *   *   *

A few basic considerations underlie what I have to say in the
essays which follow, and since they depart in many respects from the
common attitude and assumptions of most historians to-day, and
are implicit rather than explicit in the treatment of the questions
under discussion, it is perhaps desirable that I should make my
position clear by stating them here and now.

   (1) In the first place, it seems to me that we live in an age of
change, in a sense different from that in which every age may be
described as an age of change, and that there is therefore likely to
be particular gain for us in studying and endeavouring to compre-
hend the other great ages of change in the history of our civilisation,
the turning-points and periods of spiritual turmoil when Europe
passed through a major crisis. For this reason I have devoted
particular attention to the ' seminal ages ', the period of late Antiquity, the crisis at the turn of the eleventh and twelfth centuries, the
problem of the age of the Reformation, and the impact of the French

---

[1] *Der Historismus und seine Probleme* (*Gesammelte Schriften*, vol. III, 1922); cf. also K.
Heussi, *Die Krisis des Historismus* (1932).
[2] Cf. particularly *Regards sur le monde actuel* (1931), 14 sq., 63 sqq.; *Mauvaises Pensées
et autres* (1942), 97 sqq., and the different volumes of the *Variétés* (1924 sqq.).
[3] Powicke, op. cit., 192.
[4] Below, p. 220.

Revolution ; and I have tried ultimately to consider how far our own age marks a similar climacteric.[1]

In this choice of subject-matter I am conscious that I am parting company from most of my fellow-historians. Most historians—so it would seem—believe that more is achieved by ' detailed microscopic investigation on the quiet and apparently less eventful periods that lie between the cataclysmic events ', than by concentration upon periods of crisis and spiritual turmoil.[2] I have already indicated why I cannot accept this view, and the assumption of steady development which underlies it. ' The historian who treated the Norman conquest of England as a mere incident in a continuous development would be as guilty of false emphasis as one who contended that it changed everything.'[3] In my view we should postulate our history ' neither upon trough nor upon wave.'[4] But that is no reason for refusing to recognize the waves as waves, for thinking and acting—as I confess many historians seem to me to do—as though they were only an accumulation of little drops of water. I believe that ' it is by returning again and again to the great central problems that history has renewed itself ',[5] and that the tendency, now inbred in historians, to treat all phases of the past and all historical facts (as a cynic once observed) as though they were born free and equal, stands in the way of this renewal. If we say that some phases of the past are more important than others *for us*, we do not, after all, mean to imply that all are not (or may not be) equally important (or unimportant) in the sight of God : we simply mean that there are certain affinities or similarities in circumstance, or in the questions with which men were coping, that make (or are, we think, likely to make) their study particularly rewarding to us. That may, or may not, be a scientific attitude ; but it seems to me that it reflects the way we actually do proceed. All history, however apparently disinterested, springs from some present need and reflects ' an individual deep-seated questioning '.[6]

(2) Secondly, I have concerned myself in particular with the sweeping generalizations which meet us at every turn in the study

[1] Below, pp. 36, 59–60, 78 sqq., 159–63, 203–20.
[2] Cf. Powicke, op. cit., 242.
[3] H. J. Randall, *The Creative Centuries*, xix.
[4] Cf. below, p. 181. [5] Below, p. 159.
[6] Cf. V. H. Galbraith, ' Historical Research and the Preservation of the Past,' *History* XXII (1938), 312.

of European history, the broad interpretations of which so much that we commonly regard as European history is composed. How often, among a series of ' facts ', do we find inserted, like a bad penny, a statement which upon further examination turns out not to be a ' fact ' at all, but ' a bland assertion which is neither self-evident nor irrefutable ' ! [1] It is still far too little appreciated that the history we read, though based on facts, is, strictly speaking, not factual at all, but a series of accepted judgements ; [2] and it is these generalized judgements, precisely because they are so plausible and so easily assimilated, that form the minds and colour the outlook of those who cannot know the fragility of the framework upon which they rest. Hence it has seemed to me imperative, at this critical juncture in the history of European civilisation, to re-examine afresh such concepts as ' the European inheritance ', ' the values of European civilisation ', ' the idea of European coherence ', or, more simply, the limits and divisions of European history. [3] Such criticism, unless I am seriously mistaken, is unavoidable, because until these basic concepts—so important in the articulation of the larger structure into which the historian's more specialized work has sooner or later to be fitted—have been tested and either affirmed or rejected, they will stand in the way of that new vision of European history, which is so vitally necessary to-day. Precisely because, if true, they would be of the utmost importance in determining our whole view of the course and character of European civilisation, such generalizations cannot be treated as dogmas ; ' they must be tested, and then tested again, in the light of widening knowledge and by the application of sharpened critical instruments '. [4]

Here again I am aware that I am parting company from the majority of English historians, who argue that such wider questions fall outside their field of study, and that their business is confined to establishing the facts. ' Interpretation,' it is argued, ' has to wait on scholarship.' [5] In fact, as we all know, it does not wait, but is already there, a powerful influence over the minds of those who have no equipment for testing the grounds upon which it is based. Moreover, the professional historian himself cannot advance one step without the type of generalization of which I have been speak-

---

[1] Cf. below, p. 159.   [2] Cf. Powicke, op. cit., 231.
[3] Cf. below, pp. 31 sqq., 46 sqq., 55 sqq., 127 sqq., 157 sqq., 165 sqq.
[4] Cf. below, p. 128.
[5] Powicke, op. cit., 230.

ing; the process of verifying or establishing one single historical 'fact' is so elaborate that no historian can base more than the smallest part of his work on factual knowledge. Hence the historian who refuses to face up to generalizations does not abolish them, or exclude them from the field of history; he simply leaves ' the amateurs and the propagandists in possession of the field '.[1] ' If the accurate, judicious and highly-trained fail to draw the lessons of history, the unscrupulous and unqualified will do it for them '.[2]

(3) For this reason I have tried not to shirk the thorny question of ' meaning' in history. As in the course of the last half-century historians have retreated step by step from the position staked out by their predecessors in the nineteenth century, the search for meaning in history has come to a standstill. Lord Acton's passionate belief that ' knowledge of the past ' is ' an instrument of action ', ' eminently practical ',[3] has been abandoned; the old view that history has a practical ' use ' has been surrendered, if not actually demolished; and instead historians have emphasized the *Einmaligkeit* of history, the uniqueness of every event, the unsurveyable potentialities of every situation, the impossibility of deriving ' lessons ' or guidance from the past. They have, perhaps, conceded that the individual, surveying the efforts of other individuals to cope with events, may from his contemplation derive ' wisdom ' in his own coping; but in the main they have argued (or assumed) that such ' meaning' as history may possess, is contained and confined in the exploitation of the particular. Perhaps the most significant thing about this attitude is the reaction it has provoked. As professional history became more and more engrossed in the particular, and more and more convinced that its only valid concern was the past ' for its own sake ', writers such as Spengler and Toynbee set out to discover, behind the transient incidents and the brute particularity of the event or moment, the drift (if drift there were), the motive forces and ultimately the pattern of civilisation. They have received short shrift from the historical pundits. But, if we are honest with ourselves, we should at least concede that they were seeking to perform a serious function which other historians were increasingly

[1] Cf. below, p. 42.
[2] C. V. Wedgwood, *Velvet Studies* (1946), 156; cf. below p. 222.
[3] ' The knowledge of the past, the record of truths revealed by experience, is eminently practical, as an instrument of action and a power that goes to the making of the future; ' *Lectures on Modern History* (1906), 2.

neglecting. They were striving to rescue history from that devoted worship and admiring contemplation of its own navel which has made many otherwise not unsympathetic observers ask whether the measurable results justified the immeasurable expenditure of effort. But, more important still, they evinced a salutary awareness of the existence of a public ' eager to know what it is all about ',[1] and a determination not to shirk the obligations and responsibilities which this fact implied.

It is easy to dismiss this search for meaning behind events as a ' naive craving for unity and symmetry at the expense of experience '.[2] But, before we do so, there are other considerations to be borne in mind. In the first place, as Sir Maurice Powicke once pointed out, ' the craving for an interpretation of history is so deep-rooted that unless we have a constructive outlook over the past, we are drawn either to mysticism or to cynicism.'[3] Secondly, however severely we may judge the particular reconstructions of a Spengler or a Toynbee, they remain significant as the first positive reaction in the writing of history against the excesses of historicism. At least they indicate a way out of an *impasse*, the reality of which most responsible historians recognize ;[4] and it might seem more profitable to explore the possibilities (and limitations) of this outlet, than, like the proverbial dog in the Ark, to plug it up with our muzzles, for fear lest truth and insight may seep in. There is no *a priori* reason, granted the necessary accuracy, why new insight and new illumination may not be won by viewing and studying our civilisation in the light of and by comparison with the known history of other civilisations ; and it would be folly to reject out of hand this road to understanding. That does not, of course, imply that we must accept either Toynbee's or Spengler's particular arguments and conclusions ;[5] but it is important to discover whether the comparative history of civilisations—which is certainly a field of enquiry worth investigation—can be placed on sounder methodo-

---

[1] Powicke, op. cit., 230 ; I have used Professor Powicke's phrase as the title of the last item in this volume ; cf. below, p. 221.

[2] Berlin, op. cit., 5.   [3] Powicke, op. cit., 174 ; cf. below, p. 222.

[4] Powicke, op. cit., 192, 230, etc.

[5] I myself would endorse practically everything that has been written in criticism of Toynbee's methods by Geyl, Hampl, Masur, and others. Cf. P. Geyl, *From Ranke to Toynbee* (1952), and *Debates with Historians* (1955) ; F. Hampl, ' Grundsätzliches zum Werke Arnold J. Toynbees', *Hist. Zeitschrift* CLXXIII (1952) ; G. Masur, 'Arnold Toynbees Philosophie der Geschichte,' *ibid.* CLXXIV (1952).

logical foundations than Toynbee, with the characteristic impatience of a visionary for detail, has provided.[1] Hence I find it hard to participate in the attitude of deprecation with which historians have greeted such work. It presents, at least, ' a serious challenge to traditional ways of thinking ' ;[2] and in what follows I have not hesitated to adopt a positive, but critical, rather than a negative attitude towards their interpretation and the attitude towards the past which it embodies.[3]

(4) The comparative study of civilisations, commonly associated with the work of Spengler and Toynbee, is significant, even for those of us who are unable to endorse their findings, because it is evidence of a serious attempt to revive, on new foundations, the old conception of universal or world-history. It is, of course, only one method among many, and if only because of its inherent difficulties —because, as many would assert, the plan is too grandiose, the span of vision too immense, for accurate assessment—not necessarily the most effective. Others, no less trenchant in their criticism of the assumptions which have become the unquestioned foundations of western historiography, have worked within a narrower but more manageable field. They have confined themselves in the main to Europe—that is to say, to the history of our own civilisation ; they have criticized the postulates upon which European history has been written ; they have tried ' to hammer out a new view of the course of modern history, to replace the world-picture which the war has torn to shreds '.[4] It is not necessary to list their names ; for they appear below, wherever I have occasion to refer to their findings and to their critique. But I will not hide my view that, at the present stage at least, theirs is the most profitable line to pursue. They have profited from a wider experience—much of it bitter and little of it pleasant—to view the past anew ; and the result is a vision of the course of European history more in accordance with the needs of a changing world.

It is frequently said to-day that there is no longer any possibility of world-history.[5] But the result is not that we have no world-history, but that we are left with an obsolete—or at least an obsolescent—conception of universal history, which stems in the main

---

[1] Cf. below, p. 233.
[2] Cf. below, p. 48.
[3] Cf. below, pp. 49, 52, 177, 201, 235–6.
[4] Below, p. 135.
[5] Cf. Powicke, op. cit., 202.

C

from the work of the German historian, Leopold von Ranke, remarkable in its own day, but now a century and more old.[1] Since then we have seen remarkable advances in French history and English history, in German and Italian and Spanish and Russian history ; we have seen a realization that European history is not merely the history of the greater powers, and therewith a closer attention to the history of the smaller countries, Holland, Belgium, Switzerland, Poland, Scandinavia, whose contribution to European civilisation was often quite disproportionate to their size and power;[2] we have seen the emergence of American history, which in Ranke's day scarcely existed. But with what justification could it be maintained that all these separate histories, each going its own way, but each purporting to be one related strand in the story of civilisation as a whole, has resulted in a general reappraisal of the structure of universal, or even of European, history ? We are, I think, the losers ; and the extent of our loss has become particularly apparent at a time when the national states, which loomed so large in the past, are disintegrating before our eyes. If history cannot find a bigger subject-matter, a wider outlook, more consonant with the conditions of the world in which we live, it is unlikely to evoke much response ; ' even the conception of political liberty in a democratic community can no longer satisfy us, if we do not merge it in a wider outlook.'[3]

Moreover, universal history, as Acton insisted,[4] is more than the sum of its parts ; it cannot be divided and sub-divided without being denaturalized, much as water, separated into its chemical components, ceases to be water and becomes oxygen and hydrogen. And yet, in a constantly narrowing world, the whole concerns us as much as the parts. Hence, as I believe, the time has come for a return to universal history, which has so long been out of vogue. No one will underestimate the difficulties ; but no one should underestimate the need. The majority of historians to-day, in England

[1] Cf. below, p. 169.
[2] Cf. the passage from the Dutch historian, Huizinga, cited below, p. 215.
[3] Powicke, op. cit., 177.
[4] ' By universal history,' Acton wrote, ' I understand that which is distinct from the combined history of all countries, which is not a rope of sand, but a continuous development, and is not a burden on the memory but an illumination of the soul. It moves in a succession to which the nations are subsidiary. Their story will be told, not for their own sake, but in reference and subordination to a higher series, according to the time and the degree in which they contribute to the common fortunes of mankind ' (*Lectures on Modern History*, 317).

at least, are suspicious of universal, or general, history. Our knowledge, they argue, can never extend so far ; it is impossible to attain
the necessary degree of accuracy, and if we attempt to write history
on this scale, we shall only mislead. But, it may be replied, do we
not also mislead if we fail to write history on this scale, fail to corre-
late, refuse to see the wood for the trees ? No doubt, we do not
study the past for any relevance it may have to the present ; but
that is no reason why we should neglect to make plain—acknowledg-
ing always the limits within which we work—the bearing of specialized research and the impact of historical investigation on current
conceptions. That this need is particularly urgent at the present
time, when so many of our old assumptions have ceased to carry
conviction, scarcely requires demonstration ; and it is, I believe,
only by a history that is universal—a history that looks beyond
Europe and the west to humanity in all lands and ages—that anything of the sort can be achieved.

In one of his latest pronouncements at the close of his life,
Friedrich Meinecke urged that ' we should not cease to think in
terms of world-history even in the night of world-history.'[1] Within
limits of which I am only too conscious, the essays which follow
attempt to put into practice Meinecke's precept. Even where they
are concerned with specific topics—the fall of Constantinople,[2] the
assessment of the work and place in history of the emperor Frederick
Barbarossa,[3] the history of Russia[4]—they endeavour to treat those
topics not for themselves, but for the light they throw on the
history of European civilisation. And in considering, more generally, the character and particular phases of European civilisation, I
have been concerned, above all else, to guard against the view that
it can be studied—as far too often it has been studied—in isolation,
except at the risk of getting our perspectives wrong and stultifying
all the ' lessons ' which—rightly or wrongly—are commonly
derived from the story.[5] But what we call universal history is (or
should be) universal in time, as well as in space. That does not, of
course, provide any excuse for ignoring chronology or drawing
false analogies ; but it does mean that—even when our purpose is
to understand the modern world—we shall pay as great attention

---

[1] *German History. Some New German Views*, 156.   [2] Below, pp. 131 sqq.
[3] Below, pp. 73 sqq.   [4] Below, pp. 185 sqq.
[5] Cf. below, pp. 49, 58, 64, 136 sqq., 140 sq., 145, 155, 174 sqq., 181 sqq., 208,
216 sqq.

(though not greater), in the history of Russia, for example, to the period between the eleventh and the sixteenth as to that between the seventeenth and the twentieth centuries.[1] It means that we shall resist the facile assumption that the things nearest to us in time are therefore nearest to us in spirit, as though the scum and froth on the surface of history count for more than its deep underlying currents. And it means that we shall not treat the earlier periods (as is so often done) as ' background ', hastily sketched in, but as an integral part of the story. Hence in the pages that follow I have been particularly concerned to demonstrate the relevance of themes and periods which may, at first glance, seem remote from our present preoccupations. Just as we cannot leave Russian history to the experts in Slavonic studies, or Spanish history to the experts in Hispanic studies, so we cannot leave mediaeval history as a closed preserve to the mediaevalist. That is no reflection on the specialized contribution they can and should make ; but the crying need to-day is not for specialization, which means fragmentation, but for integration, and this requires not simply specialized knowledge, but the general historian's understanding of the course of European —and, indeed, of extra-European—history, through which alone the contributions of the specialist can be brought into perspective. The historian who sets out to look at history in this way will not expect and will not claim that all his perspectives are correct ; but he may fairly claim that the attempt to discover such perspectives is not only an inescapable part of the historian's work, but also a necessary contribution to the needs of a changing world.

*　　　*　　　*

I have used more than once in the course of these remarks the criterion of ' relevance ', and in conclusion I should like—without attempting to exhaust the subject and its problems—to say a few words about this topic, because it is still another matter, and one of major importance, where re-examination of the common assumptions of historians seems to be overdue, if history is to play a significant part in the contemporary world.

The non-historian criticizes history to-day above all else on the ground that it has no apparent relevance to the problems which confront him in a changing world. The reasons are not difficult to

[1] Cf. below, pp. 136, 187.

find. It is not merely that the subject-matter of history is vastly more complicated than it was in Acton's time, and that it is therefore far more difficult to extract convincing 'lessons' or 'verdicts' from its study; more important is the change that has come about in the historian's basic attitudes. With something like pride historians to-day are apt to proclaim that the past exists for itself, and not for any 'relevance' it may have to the present. An approach which seeks to measure the past by the standard of its relevance to the present, can—so it is argued—only lead to pitfalls and false perspectives. We must study the past 'for itself' and judge past ages—if we judge them at all—by their own standards and not by ours; we must give importance to what was important then, and not single out, in earlier centuries, only those phases and incidents which seem of importance to us. History is not (as Bury once pungently remarked) 'the dossier of an incompetent Providence'; nor does it exist to provide us with 'a series of patterns we can immediately transpose into the context of contemporary politics'.[1] If we 'arrange the past neatly as a process in which the most significant things are those which are most easily appropriated by the present',[2] it will not be long before we commit the unpardonable sin of teaching and writing only that bastard variety of history 'which is appropriate to our organisation', 'congenial to the intellectual climate of our part of the world', and 'most adapted to the preservation of the existing régime.'[3]

There is so much in this argument that is salutary and true that it has rarely been criticized; but we are still entitled to ask where it leads us. What, in the first place, of the implication which it evidently carries, that the modern historian has discovered the secret of objectivity, and must not contaminate it by meddling with extraneous questions of 'relevance'? When, for example, the charge is levelled against Bishop Stubbs that his conception of the mediaeval English constitution was vitiated by ideas of 'parliamentary limited monarchy as understood from the nineteenth century', we are left with the impression that this was a peculiar nineteenth-century weakness which we to-day have outgrown. 'Our curiosity,' we are told,[4] 'is better directed to-day'. If this

[1] Cf. below, p. 184.
[2] F. M. Powicke, *The Christian Life in the Middle Ages* (1935), v.
[3] H. Butterfield, *The Englishman and his History* (1945), 1.
[4] Cf. Galbraith, *History* XXII (1938), 312.

comment were intended only to mean that our curiosity is directed
to those problems or aspects of the past which loom largest in our
consciousness, while the questions which Stubbs asked were not
those which interested a subsequent generation, it might be unob-
jectionable. But that is evidently not the case. On the contrary, it
is meant to imply that we—unlike our predecessors—study ' the
things that were important *then* ' rather than ' the things that are
important *now* '.[1] About this attitude there are two things to be
said. First, we do not know, and can never know, what things were
considered important in the past ;[2] but if we followed the indications of those who troubled to write down what they thought was
important, in ninth-century Gaul, for example, or in thirteenth-
century England, what would claim first place in our history (as
anyone who will spend an hour with a chronicler of the period may
convince himself) would be a dreary recital of miracles, tempests,
comets, pestilences, calamities, and other ' wonderful things '. Our
history is concerned—and (I may add) in my view rightly concerned
—not with what was important, but with what *we think* was (or
ought to have been) important. In the second place, the difference
in this respect between the modern and the older historian is not so
great as is sometimes supposed. T. F. Tout criticized Stubbs and
denounced ' the natural absorption in the present ' which ' has led
us to study the past with minds too much set on present presup-
positions ; '[3] but we may be sure—whether Tout himself realized it
or not—that the switch of interest from ' constitutional ' to ' administrative ' history, of which Tout's own work is the most distinguished example, was a reflection of a change in the direction of
modern government, and in men's attitude towards the functions
of government, the impact of which we may perhaps conveniently
date from the Liberal administration of 1906–14. Hence the reasons
which led Tout to undertake ' the study of the machinery and daily
routine of mediaeval executive government ', may have been less

---

[1] Galbraith, loc. cit.

[2] I do not wish to pursue the argument into detail at this juncture, but evidently
we might also ask the question : by whom ? The standards (let us say) of Charles II
and of George Fox would be utterly different ; and no one would be so foolish as to
suppose that the lowest common denominator between them (supposing there were
such a thing) would give us a serviceable criterion of importance. In the end, in brief,
it is we who make the judgement.

[3] Tout, *Chapters in the Administrative History of Mediaeval England* I (1920), 2.

objective than he supposed.[1] This observation is not intended to
imply a criticism of Tout's work ; but it illustrates the reasons
why we may have doubts about the ' vaunted objectivity ',[2] which
the claim to study the past ' for itself ' or ' for its own sake ' seems
to imply. ' Between reality and significance,' it has been well said,
' enters the individual mind ';[3] and for this reason, as I have already
observed, all historical work must be coloured by the historian's
own experience. Relevance, swept out of the door, is apt to fly
back through the window ; and we shall do well to examine closely
and suspiciously the credentials of any historian claiming to speak
only with the voice of the past.

   ' We investigate the past,' Tout wrote,[4] ' not to deduce practical
political lessons, but to find out what really happened.' But the
rejoinder : what then? is not altogether unfair. J. B. Bury, who
yielded to none in his insistence on scientific impartiality in the
study of the past, was not slow to warn that such an attitude,
though valid so far as it goes, is not in itself enough. ' I cannot
imagine,' he said, ' the slightest theoretical importance in a collection
of facts or sequences of facts, unless we can hope to determine
their vital connexion with the whole system of reality.'[5] It is no
belittlement of the historian's fundamental impulse to find out
' what really happened ', to say that this is only a step towards
something more fundamental still ; and that—even if we postpone
it, saying that the time is not ripe, our knowledge not yet sufficiently
profound—is something that may appropriately be summed up
under the heading of ' relevance '. We seek, in the end, to know
' what really happened ' in order to assess its bearing and meaning
for us. For it is simply not true that the past (as is so often stated)
' exists for itself '. The past may once have existed for itself ; but to-
day it no longer exists at all—it is as ' dead as the men who made it.'[6]

---

   [1] The objects Tout had in mind were ' to supplement Stubbs' great work ', and to
correct ' the tradition which would make parliament the central point of English
mediaeval political institutions ' ; but we sense also the impact of contemporary ' pre-
suppositions ' when he writes (op. cit. I, 4–5) that ' even under modern conditions
administration is more important than legislation '—an idea which Stubbs, writing
almost half a century earlier, could scarcely have conceived.   [2] Cf. below, p. 157.
   [3] A. Meyendorff, ' Bias in Historical Writing,' History XI (1926), 198.
   [4] Op. cit. I, 7.   [5] Cf. below, p. 157.
   [6] Galbraith, op. cit., 312. Cf. Wedgwood, op. cit., 157 : 'the greater number of
historians failed entirely to understand what was expected of them. They . . . turned
deliberately from the present to the past. They began to consider with misguided
conscientiousness their duty to the dead. This was nonsense, for no one has a duty to
the dead except in relation to the living.'

If we busy ourselves with it, try to reconstruct it or re-think it
(as Collingwood said), or sink ourselves in it, if we seek a glimpse
(albeit fleeting and momentary) of past reality, it is for our own
purposes.. We may not be sure what those purposes are ; the
meaning of our studies may sometimes be a matter of faith, rather
than of demonstrable fact ; but unless we thought they had meaning,
they would not be worth undertaking, and that meaning is their
relevance for us.

It is possible to hold—and has more than once been held—that
even though all this be true, it is none of the historian's business.
His business (it is said) is to set down the facts as he sees them,
to depict ' what really happened ' ; if anyone wishes to go further
and interpret the story or indicate its relevance, it is none of his
concern. Regarding this attitude—all too reminiscent of the Levite
who passed by on the other side—two things may be said. The
first is that the historian, who is intimately acquainted with the
matter of history, is (or should be) the person best qualified to
assess its bearing. The second is that the refusal of the historian
to interpret his work does not prevent history from being interpreted ; it simply means that interpretation is deprived of qualified
criticism, and that the historian's case goes by default. Thus it
comes about, for example, that the most widely influential interpretations of the middle ages are not those of historians. Whoever
wishes to convince himself that the middle ages are ' relevant '
to-day, needs only consult the widely-read books of writers such as
Maritain or Berdyaev. But the ' Middle Ages ' which they depict in
glowing colours as a ' remote spiritual fatherland,' offering ' the
only escape from the mortal *ennui* of triumphant civilisation,' bear
little relation to the picture of mediaeval society revealed by historical research.[1] The quandary that arises for the historian is
obvious. If he simply averts his eyes, he can scarcely evade the
charge of accepting what he does not reject ; while if he tries to
set out the ' relevance ' of the middle ages, as it appears to a writer
with historical training, he runs the risk of appearing to surrender
the proud credential of scientific aloofness. In these circumstances
theoretical discussion about the possibility of relating the past to
the present is beside the point. Man is an historical animal, with a

---

[1] As I have suggested below, they are transformed into a stick with which to beat
the present ; cf. below, p. 55.

deep sense of his own past ; and if he cannot integrate the past by a history explicit and true, he will integrate it by a history implicit and false. The challenge is one which no historian with any conviction of the value of his work can ignore ; and the way to meet it is not to evade the issue of ' relevance ', but to accept the fact and work out its implications.

No one would deny that the search for ' relevance ' in history carries with it perils and pitfalls of its own ; but that is, after all, true of anything worth while. In the first place, we must be careful how we define relevance, and where we look for it. Secondly, we must not ask and expect too much of history ; it is not a key to life's mysteries, and there are many things which history alone cannot explain.[1] If we cling to the view, which the theory of historicism popularized and propagated, that ' it contains within itself the explanation of the development of man from his primitive state to the point which he has reached,'[2] we must not be surprised if history deceives and disappoints us. Furthermore, we must beware of the sort of selectivity which sees in the past only what it wants to see. As Unwin once pungently observed, ' if we steadily ignore much that seems to lead nowhere, and much that leads in the opposite direction, we soon perceive a chain of historic causation leading to one great result.'[3] There is no more certain road to misunderstanding of the past than the ' teleological ' view of history, the doctrine that historical developments are the result of an overriding purpose or design, and that what stands aside from this supposed purpose is accidental, irrelevant and negligible ; and having smuggled into history in this way a purpose or objective, it is fatally easy to extract it again from history as a ' lesson '.[4] Equally serious is the temptation to ignore whole sectors of the past, which were evidently intrinsically important—as for all practical purposes Byzantine history and the history of eastern Europe were for long ignored in the west—because their relevance is not immediately apparent. A history which concentrates on England and on the civilisation of western Europe may serve to harden our prejudices and fortify us in our belief in the superiority of our traditions and values ; but nothing is more calculated to get the portents wrong,

[1] Below, p. 184.
[2] J. B. Bury, *Selected Essays* (ed. H. V. Temperley, 1930), 27.
[3] G. Unwin, *Studies in Economic History* (ed. R. H. Tawney, 1927), 37.
[4] Cf. Butterfield, *History and Human Relations*, 165.

to mislead and misinform us about the forces actually operative in the world in which we live : a world of which—as Dr. Toynbee has repeatedly emphasized—the civilisations of China, India and Islam are just as much a part of the historical heritage as the civilisation of the west. Finally, it is not necessarily true that what is nearest to us in time is most relevant. As I have observed at another point in this book,[1] ' there is nothing very contemporary about Bülow or Tirpitz or Lloyd George or even Stanley Baldwin ' ; while, on the other hand, many of the themes which carry us back to the fourth and fifth centuries of the Christian era are more ' actual ', nearer to contemporary life, than (let us say) ' the unedifying annals of eighteenth-century diplomacy '.[2] People treat the very recent past as though it were the den from which the lion that is going to devour them is bound to spring ; but, nearly always, it jumps out unobserved behind their backs. They would usually be better equipped, as Herbert Butterfield once observed,[3] to meet the developments of their own day, if ' they had studied in ancient history the deeper processes that political bodies have been observed to undergo over long periods.' The same might be said of mediaeval history. What —with doubtful accuracy[4]—is called ' mediaeval history ' is, in substance, the study of the solid foundations upon which European civilisation, as it exists to-day in east and west, has been built ;[5] it is the matrix in which the underlying traditions and inherent values of modern civilisation were moulded ; and those of us who study the middle ages study them ' not as mediaeval history, but as modern history, very modern history—in the sense that all history which means anything is contemporary history.'[6]

The past impinges at every turn on the present ; and the question of its relevance, the task of ensuring that the relationship of past and present shall be a right relationship, is therefore a practical question, which may well contribute to the shaping of the future. That does not mean that we should make ourselves slaves of the past, forgetful that every day something happens which no man ever foresaw and probably no man ever wanted. Historical knowledge can blind as well as illuminate ; and it is at least as important

---

[1] Below, p. 206.   [2] Cf. below, p. 42.
[3] Op. cit., 179 ; cf. also below, p. 217.
[4] Cf. below, pp. 56 sqq.
[5] It should scarcely be necessary to add that it holds a similar place in Islamic civili-sation.   [6] Cf. below, p. 63.

to be aware of what does not survive as to perceive what lives on.[1] The assessment of relevance has become more difficult ; the ' old smooth generalizations ' no longer fit ; and it has become evident that the wider our view over the past, and the better we are able to scan the horizons, the less likely are we to be deceived by what we know.[2] As I have tried to indicate, it is only a history that is universal in spirit—a history that looks beyond Europe and the west to humanity in all lands and ages—that can serve our purposes. That statement, of course, is not meant to imply that more specialized historical investigation is redundant or of an inferior order : only that *alone* it is not enough, because it deals with less than ' the whole system of reality ' which, as Bury perceived, is and must remain history's supreme objective. If we are to know where we stand in a changing world, and if history can help us to know where we stand, we must look beyond this island, and beyond the lands associated with it ; we must look beyond the continent of which it is a part. History will not, as is sometimes feared, lose meaning that way, as though only the history of the homeland or (some modern historians seem even to suggest) of the parish-pump has relevance to our habits and daily lives and modes of thought. On the contrary, it will gain in relevance, because it will be nearer to the conditions of modern life, in which—in spite of political divisions—the whole world is one, and—whether we like it or not—the fortunes of every one of us are linked to the fortunes of all the others.

*   *   *

Many who are not historians feel dissatisfaction, and even disenchantment and disillusionment, when they survey the field of history to-day. It seems to have betrayed the high hopes that were placed in it ; it offers no sure guidance among the dilemmas of a changing world. What is its use for the practical man who is not an historian? What is its contribution to the understanding of the present?

In part the criticism implied in these questions is justified ; in part it is based upon mistaken notions of the scope of history, which historians of an earlier generation too often took it upon themselves to foster. The expectation that history would be able to provide clear-cut answers for the conduct of present and future

---

[1] Cf. below, p. 199.   [2] Cf. below, p. 182.

affairs, was false ; and to ask the historian to provide such answers is, often, to require him to betray his integrity. The historian has too long been encouraged to pursue abstruse research in the confident belief that ' a complete assemblage of the smallest facts of human history will tell in the end.'[1] To-day we have good reason to be less certain than men of Bury's generation of the truth of this assertion ; the accumulation of historical knowledge has not clarified, but has complicated and perplexed, and Tout's happy confidence that ' we are half-way towards solving a problem when we have traced it from stage to stage through the ages ',[2] turns out to be the great illusion of a whole generation.

On the other hand, the sense of frustration which so much historical work engenders, the sense that it is dealing with abstractions which never existed and, even if they had existed, would have no relevance to-day, is not simply the result of misunderstanding. Encouraged to follow the road of abstruse research in the expectation that it would lead to practical results—that, somehow or other, the assemblage of the smallest facts would ' tell in the end '—historians have continued to advance down that road, long after it became evident that it was leading into a wilderness. It is time that they called a halt, and sought a way out of the cul-de-sac. This is necessary for the sake of history itself ; but it is even more necessary for the sake of a generation which history, as at present conceived and practised, is leaving in the lurch. For, after all, the ultimate question is what the historian has to offer to his generation. Too often— many would say—he forgets that what most people ' want to know in history ' is (as J. R. Green once wrote) ' to know which are the big facts and which are the little ones.'[3] Too often his contribution amounts to little more than an exercise in the technique of historical method, and it is even argued that the value of his work is ' independent of the kind of historical material selected.'[4] This argument might be plausible, if his only purpose were to raise up another generation of trained historians (though it has still to be demonstrated that the historian is made, not born) ; but it ignores the fact that the bulk of those who listen to us, and read our writings, and work

[1] Cf. J. B. Bury, *Selected Essays*, 17.
[2] T. F. Tout, ' The Place of the Middle Ages in the Teaching of History,' *History* VIII (1923), 6.
[3] *Letters of John Richard Green* (ed. Leslie Stephen, 1901), 304.
[4] Cf. H. H. Bellot, *History* XXXI (1946), 63.

with us, come to us not as potential historians, but as potential citizens. The historian to-day is in danger of forgetting that his ' primary responsibility ' is ' the relation of his subject to the wider affairs of contemporary life,'[1] and that, although his ' immediate business ' may be to lead his audience ' into the past ', he ' cannot, and does not, and should not, escape from presenting to them, the citizens of the future, an outlook upon the present.'[2]

After a period of change with which few ages in our European past can compare—only, perhaps, the years of pope Hildebrand, the age of Luther, and the time of the French Revolution[3]—there is need not merely for a new history, but also for a new attitude to history and a reconsideration of all the assumptions we have made about history. In challenging some of the current assumptions I have been concerned not with criticism for its own sake, but with the possibility of restoring history to the position which—despite (or perhaps because of) the vast increase in historical output in the last fifty years—it has forfeited in the estimation of non-historians. It is still, I believe, true that the historical approach—though not the only approach—has much to offer which cannot be acquired in any other way, to all those who are faced by the task of working out a philosophy of living in an unstable world. But if it is to contribute towards an intelligent, well-informed and critical judgement of the problems of modern society, radical revision is necessary. In the first place, we must combat the fragmentation which has overtaken history, and accustom ourselves, once again, to look at the past as a whole ; for unless we have a positive ideal of universal history, our history will inevitably tend to be less than universal. Secondly, we must seek for history an end outside itself—as it had, for example, when it was viewed as a manifestation of the working of God's providence. That statement is not intended to imply a return to a theological view of history (which, whether desirable or not, I regard as impracticable to-day) ; but it does mean that its study should have a constructive purpose and a criterion of judgement, outside and beyond the historical process. Thirdly, we should not evade the test of relevance ; for although the past may have existed for itself, history—the attempt to discover, on the basis of

[1] N. Sykes, ' The Study of History,' *History* XIX (1934), 99.
[2] W. K. Hancock, ' Machiavelli in Modern Dress : an Enquiry into Historical Method ', *History* XX (1935), 109.
[3] Cf. below, p. 78.

fragmentary evidence, the significant things about the past—exists for us. And finally, and above all else, we must make a determined effort to revive the connexion between past and present, between history and life, which—owing to the mistaken ideals historians have pursued—is in evident danger of perishing. The twentieth century is still in search of a history liberated from the preconceptions of an age which has passed, and adequate to itself ;[1] but the foundations are there—if we will but use them—for a new structure of history, which will serve us, and serve us well, in a world which has radically changed and is still changing.

[1] I adapt here the formulation (' Twentieth-century thought in search of a historian ') used by Emery Neff for the concluding section of his interesting book, *The Poetry of History* (1947).

2. The Continuity of European Tradition

DURING the years since 1945 the clarification of the principles upon which civilisation rests has become one of the major preoccupations of thoughtful people.[1]

Scarcely a day goes by without our reading or hearing of ' our inherited cultural tradition ', the ' typical values of western civilisation ', ' the idea of European coherence '—or, more simply, ' our western tradition ', ' our western values ', ' our western culture '. No set of ideas has become more commonplace, none been more assiduously drummed into our ears, since the end of the war. In part, this new emphasis on the inherited traditions of our civilisation is a reflection of our awareness of crisis ; it shows a tardy realization on our part that the dangers confronting the contemporary world —in particular, the dangers springing from the terrifying control which humanity now exercises over the material forces of destruction—can only be averted if they are counterbalanced by a far more intensive knowledge than our generation seems yet to possess, of the enduring elements upon which the structure of civilisation rests. And that is all to the good. What is more dubious is the implication that the enduring values and traditions of civilisation are linked, in some unique way, with western Europe. That view not only underestimates the importance of the independent civilisations of the Orient, but it also introduces an ominous division in Europe between the countries of east and west, with Germany as a sort of ' no-man's land ' lying in between. For there is little room for doubt that the intention is to contrast ' western ' values with the outlook and traditions of eastern Europe, and in particular with the ideology of Soviet Russia. In the background lies the idea, deliberate or unconscious, of providing a broad ideological foundation for the ' western ' conception of democracy, in its conflict with that other conception of democracy which predominates wherever Soviet influence is strong.

[1] Adapted from an article first printed in *Humanitas* I (1947), No. 4 ; I have incorporated some passages from an article, ' Is there a Western Tradition ? ', which appeared in *The Listener* in August, 1947.

The theory of an 'inherited cultural tradition', common to western Europe, is a platitude which has been familiar to historians for generations. It was erected on the basis of the great liberal historical tradition of the nineteenth century—the tradition of Ranke and Giesebrecht, of Bryce and Acton—but it was only in the aftermath of the second world war that it passed into wider currency, and emerged, detached from its historical setting, as a dogma or creed or article of faith. This significant transformation—familiar throughout the history of ideas—is to be explained by the fact that what, in an earlier phase, was an intellectual conviction, devoid of political implications (hence the failure of generations of historians to impress on society the elements of truth and salvation it indisputably contains), has now become the vehicle of organised political forces, charged with political content; it has come into its own as an ideological smokescreen behind which the more militant upholders of 'western tradition' are preparing to manoeuvre into position the compelling artillery of the atomic bomb.

But the theory of the unity of 'western European culture' and of the continuity of European civilisation is in the last resort an interpretation of historical fact, which stands or falls with the history upon which it is based; and as such it falls within the proper sphere of historical criticism. It is noteworthy that it has emerged as a dogmatic assertion precisely at the moment when, notwithstanding the respect which all historians to-day feel for the extraordinary powers of synthesis of their nineteenth-century predecessors, the interpretation of history upon which it is based has been shattered by historical criticism and discarded by historical scholarship; and it is perhaps still more noteworthy that the weakening and undermining by professional historians of the historical premises underlying the theory has failed to detract from its effectiveness as a political dogma, or to break the spell which, constantly reiterated and rarely criticized, it patently exerts over public opinion.

That the theory of a common 'western tradition' should exercise a powerful influence over our minds is not difficult to understand. It is, after all, a stirring battle-cry in a distracted age, this appeal from the divisions of the present to the unity of 'western European culture' and the continuity of western European civilisation; it links us in a chain with the great men of the past and sustains us with their faith. It makes us partakers in the greatness of Rome and Athens, ' defendants ' (as Gilbert Murray recently said) ' of the Hellenic culture and Roman empire ', with ' a magnificent heritage to keep alive '. For what, in the last analysis, is the warp and woof of this ' western tradition '? Its constituent elements, we are told, are ' the values of the Hellenic and Christian civilisations in which our own has its roots '. What has ' served to establish as a reality in the human mind the idea of European coherence ', is, above all else, ' the ideas of the Roman empire, of the papacy and more distantly of Athens '.[1] ' Europe ', the argument runs, ' owes its political existence to the Roman empire and its spiritual unity to the Catholic church ', and for its ' intellectual culture ' it is indebted to a third factor—' the Classical tradition '. These ' are the true foundations of European unity '; but—the theory continues— ' they do not of themselves constitute Europe. They are the formative influences which have shaped the material of our civilisation, but the material itself is to be found elsewhere '—namely, in the barbarian invaders who, in the fourth or fifth centuries, migrated into Europe and settled on the soil of the Roman empire. It was they ' who provided the human material out of which Europe has been fashioned '; and this fashioning was the work of the middle ages. The fall of the Roman empire in the west left ' a chaotic mixture of barbarian and Roman elements, which as yet possessed no spiritual unity '; and it was only in the middle ages—first of all in the empire of Charlemagne—that Europe emerged as a coherent whole. ' Carolingian unity ', it is said, ' may be regarded without exaggeration as the foundation and starting-point of the whole development of western civilisation '.[2]

What is immediately clear, if we examine this view of history in detail, is the fact that it attributes the highest importance to the middle ages as a key link between classical and western culture. The Latin language itself appears as the ' ark which carried the seed of Hellenic culture through the deluge of barbarism '; but more important still is Christianity which, with an unerring instinct scarcely

---

[1] Cf. the essay on ' The Idea of Europe ' by Charles Morgan—perhaps the most influential of the popular exponents of the theory of ' coherence '—in *Reflections in a Mirror* (1944), 36.
[2] Cf. C. Dawson, *The Making of Europe* (1934), 48, 67, 286. It is perhaps right to add that, if I cite Mr. Dawson above all others for the views which (it seems to me) stand in need of criticism, it is because he is in my view the most able and persuasive of his school, for whose powers of interpretation I have the greatest admiration.

D

(some may think) to be explained without the inscrutable guidance
of Providence, seized—it is not explained how—' upon what was
vital in the Roman world ', thus allowing the Catholic church to
become at once ' the heir and representative of the old Roman
culture and the teacher and guide of the new barbarian peoples '.[1]
' It was civilisation struggling for survival '; and ' in the struggle
between a world which was civilised and latinised and barbarians
who were just then coming out of the darkness of their native
forests . . . civilisation '—which ' meant Latin and Rome '— ' was
bound to conquer '. Through the idea of ' a universal empire '
and ' parallel to a universal empire . . . a universal church, no less
dependent on Roman traditions ', through Roman law and above
all through the unifying and civilising bond of the Latin language,
' the forces of continuity ' prevailed and the foundations of the
' western tradition ' and of ' the edifice of European culture ' were
laid.[2]

There is no doubt that this story of the compounding of a new
civilisation from the classical heritage, the Latin language, and the
Christian religion is an impressive construction ; it raises the Middle
Ages to a new dignity, providing the highest justification for their
intensive study ; it attracts no less because of its inherent simplicity
than through the comforting sense of unbroken purpose which it
engenders. Yet for the historian who tries to stand apart from the
west and view the wide panorama of the past with impartiality—
and who would deny that such should be his endeavour?—what is
it but ' parochial ' history, throwing the past into the mould which
best flatters our predilections ' instead of liberating the mind from
provincialism by widening the intellectual horizon '?

Let us pass over, in the first place, the difficulty (of which every
schoolboy is aware) that the Roman empire, with its centre of
gravity in the Mediterranean—and increasingly, as time passed, in
the eastern basin of the Mediterranean—drew its sustenance from
eastern and non-European lands, and was therefore scarcely more
appropriate, as a model for an ' idea of European coherence ', than
is the British empire to-day. Let us pass over also the mistranslation
of the Latin word, *barbari*, which underlies this whole conception

[1] Cf. Dawson, op. cit., 46, 49 ; C. Foligno, *Latin Thought During the Middle Ages*
(1929), 33.
[2] Foligno, op. cit., 26, 95, 103 ; Dawson, op. cit., 49.

of European history; for *barbari* did not mean 'barbarians', and since the substantial works of Alfons Dopsch passed into common currency, every undergraduate (if not every schoolboy) knows that the accession to power of the 'barbarian' peoples was no catastrophe, and that the revolt against Roman political hegemony was not accompanied by a frontal attack on Roman civilisation.[1] More insidious (because less easily combatted) is the deprecatory, almost contemptuous attitude towards the Eastern empire, which this attitude implies, as though Roman 'traditions' of empire, instead of passing to the 'New Rome' on the Bosphorus, remained tied down for all time in the west. There is a famous dictum that 'all history is contemporary history', in the sense that our picture of the past reflects our own outlook on the world, our ideology and our predispositions; and for me, the interpretation of the past outlined above is a reflection of the liberal ideology which perished, as an effective force, in the war of 1914–18; it is a sort of comforting hang-over from the rather resplendent prosperity of the late nineteenth century.

It puts a premium, in the first place, on 'culture', as though culture were the essence instead of the last refinement of civilisation —the sugar-icing (as it were) on the top of the cake. It flatters, because it shows western Europe, through the intermediacy of the Catholic church, as the heir of Rome, forgetting that there was also an Eastern church with traditions equally strong, and that the direct heir of Rome was not the west but Byzantium, where Roman civilisation and the very structure of the Roman state continued— changing, of course, but in unbroken succession—down to the fall of Constantinople in 1453.[2] It is comforting, because it inculcates a sense of continuity, forgetting that continuity (as one acute historian has observed) 'is by no means the most conspicuous feature of history', and that 'the connexion of one civilisation with another is often obscure', 'a matter of faith rather than of sight'. It was one of the protagonists of the continuity of western European civilisation who incautiously admitted that, in order to appreciate the process by which in the Middle Ages western European civilisation was compounded, 'it is best to look at the process in its complex entirety rather than in its thousand details'[3]; and it is unquestion-

---

[1] Cf. A. Dopsch, *The Economic and Social Foundations of European Civilisation* (1937); p. 89 sqq. on the word *barbari*, p. 30 sqq. on the myth of the 'primeval forest'.
[2] Cf. below, p. 131.   [3] Foligno, op. cit., 44.

ably true that when we descend to detail, much that seemed obvious
(and even significant) becomes a matter for legitimate doubt and
questioning. In short, this whole conception—with its progressive,
liberal flavour—is open to criticism in detail; and it is arguable
that criticism in detail can shatter the whole structure, and force
us to seek a new interpretation.

Consider, in the first place, the idea of a ' classical tradition ',
which, handed down in unbroken succession from Rome, has (it is
said) ' been the constant foundation of western letters and western
thought '. At first glance such a statement sounds plausible. But
it is a commonplace that by the third century A.D., when ancient
civilisation was falling into decay, what is known as the ' classical
spirit ' was extinct in Rome, swamped by strong currents flowing in
from the Orient and from the Germanic world. It is a commonplace
that the admirable spirit of rational enquiry, so vigorous six centuries earlier, had given way to superstition and mystical cults ;
that creative literary activity had ceased ; and that even in architecture ' the Greek laws of proportion had lost their meaning '.[1]
When we are told that the evidence of the Christian arts can be
' relied upon to prove the continuity of tradition ',[2] it is well to
remember that such was not the conclusion of Max Dvořák, the
founder of the modern study of art history, who on the contrary
expressly defined their character as ' unclassical ' or even ' anti-
classical '.[3] Or consider, again, the theory that the Latin fathers
were ' the heirs of the western tradition ', and that the Latin
church, in the fifth century, became at once the repository of
the ' old Roman culture '. In fact, what is remarkable about the
church of that day is how little it rested on specifically Roman or
western European foundations. Far from ' seizing upon what was
vital in the Roman world ', we find the church—as represented (for
example) by Tertullian and Jerome, by St. Ambrose and St. Augustine—filled with antipathy to Roman traditions, which it regarded
as the work of anti-Christ. The places that really mattered in the
early Christian centuries were not in Europe at all, but were cities

[1] Cf. R. Laquer, H. Koch, W. Weber, *Probleme der Spätantike* (1930), 60 ; the passage
is cited by F. W. Walbank, *The Decline of the Roman Empire in the West* (1946), 66.
[2] Foligno, op. cit., 39.
[3] M. Dvořák, *Kunstgeschichte als Geistesgeschichte. Studien zur abendländischen Kunstent-
wicklung* (1924), 38 (' noch im Rahmen der Antike und doch ganz und gar unantik '),
40 (' nicht nur antiantik, sondern auch positiv stilbildend ').

like Alexandria and Carthage in Africa, or Nicaea and Cappadocia in Asia Minor ; and even as late as the seventh and eighth centuries half the popes in Rome were Greeks or Syrians by birth.[1] It is a commonplace that the language of the church, even in the west, was in the first place Greek, and that Christianity failed for the first two centuries of its history to produce a Latin literature.[2] But even in the following century—although intellectual leadership still remained with the Eastern churches—the first stirrings of Christian thought outside the Eastern churches took place not in western Europe but in North Africa. It has even been suggested that it was in Africa, and not in Rome, that the cardinal dogma of papal primacy was fabricated.[3]

Considerations such as these should warn us against exaggerating the Latin element in western Christianity. As the late Dr. Coulton once remarked, ' Cardinal Newman's vision of the mediaeval monk as a classical scholar is largely imaginary '. Nor is it easy, if we approach the question from the opposite angle, to visualize the precise process by which the Catholic church transmitted the classical traditions to the western peoples. Much has been made, in this respect, of the services of the Latin language both as a vehicle of tradition and as a bond of unity ; but Traube, whose authority remains unimpaired, speaks with greater caution, asserting in the first place that the maintenance of the Roman tongue has no intrinsic connexion with Catholicism, and passing on to the observation that any attempt to treat mediaeval Latin as a universal language must be taken with a pinch of salt.[4] When we find, for example, that in 1222, out of seventeen livings in the diocese of Salisbury, five were held by priests unable to construe even the opening words of the first prayer in the Canon of the Mass, we may well wonder how deep a tradition confined to the Latin language really penetrated.[5] Rightly Traube emphasizes the contrast between the possibilities of a rich and unitary culture, which Latin offered, and the historical reality ; underlines the atrocious barbarism of Latin usage even in the schools

---

[1] As Cardinal Tisserant has emphasized, ' The Holy See and the Byzantine Church and Empire ', *Review of Politics* IX (1947), 278.
[2] Cf. L. Traube, *Einleitung in die lateinische Philologie des Mittelalters* (*Vorlesungen und Abhandlungen* II, 1911), 42.
[3] Cf. E. Caspar, *Primatus Petri* (1927), 24, 72.
[4] Traube, op. cit., 35, 39. Dr. Coulton has recently added many more pinches of salt, and built up at all events a formidable molehill ; cf. *Europe's Apprenticeship* (1940).
[5] Cf. Coulton, *Studies in Medieval Thought* (1940), 78.

at the Carolingian court; points out that the existence of a manu-
script is no proof that it was read; and that not even mention or
imitation of classical work is evidence that it was understood.[1] This
is true of Charles the Great himself, whose love of Augustine is
not necessarily a proof of appreciation of Augustinian thought; it
is true even of Alcuin, whose typically mediaeval exegesis of Plato
the latter would scarcely have understood. Where there is continuity, in short, it is formal in character, not a persistence of classical
modes of thought, but a repetition of classical phrases, selected,
isolated and re-interpreted, to which a new meaning has been attributed; and many arguments can be adduced to support the view
that this process of adaptation was less the maintenance of tradition
than the creation of something new.[2] That is true of Aristotelian
philosophy, which on its rediscovery in the west was crudely
misinterpreted and refashioned through misinterpretation, and it is
true of the inheritance of Roman law. Few who have had the opportunity to study in detail the civil law of the middle ages would
hesitate to endorse Hermann Kantorowicz's dictum, that ' it was
only the form which was provided by the Roman law, while the
substance . . . was rooted in the contemporary social structure '.[3]

Fundamentally more important than any of this, however, is the
question of the validity of the conception of ' mediaeval unity '—
that ' feeling of the unity of western civilisation ' which (it is said)
' we inherit from the middle ages '. That unity, if it existed at all,
was either spiritual (and as such represented by the church), or it
was material (and as such represented by a supra-national empire);
but from either point of view it is a conception hard to reconcile
with the known facts.

Much of the apparent unity of thought is due primarily to the
fact that Catholicism extirpated its opponents and burnt the literature
in which they expressed their ideals; it is due also to the fact that
the clergy had for many centuries a monopoly of writing, and that
the surviving evidence of a non-clerical ethos is sparse and usually
indirect. But it is clear enough to-day that anti-Catholic thought was
extraordinarily vigorous and its diffusion extraordinarily widespread;

---

[1] Traube, op. cit., 36, 52, 64, 72.
[2] Cf. also below p. 229.
[3] Cf. *Law Quarterly Review* LIII (1937), 278, on the jurisprudence of the twelfth
century, ' which applied the categories of the Roman law to the contemporary institutions of canonical, Germanic or feudal origin, for which they were not suited '.

and the existence of this hostile tradition—the tradition (it is often called) of ' Christian dualism '—is alone a challenge to the theory of spiritual unity. Nor is it clear that there was general acceptance, even within the organized church, of the idea of the ecclesiastical coherence of western Christendom under the direction of the pope. We know, for example, that an anonymous ecclesiastic, commonly associated with York, who was writing in the early years of the twelfth century, was vigorously rejecting the pope's primacy on doctrinal grounds, and protesting against Roman attempts to introduce uniformity ; we know of equally trenchant criticism in Italy around the year 1180 ; and we know that similar convictions were strongly held in the French church in the middle of the thirteenth century.[1] Can we, in face of such facts, really maintain that the unity for which the papacy stood was a characteristic feature even of the two centuries when the papacy was most influential, to say nothing of the centuries preceding and following, when the tendency to division into ' national ' or territorial churches is admitted on all sides to have been strong?

The other approach to this question is from the standpoint of the empire, for next to the papacy the empire is usually described as the symbol and embodiment of mediaeval unity. And yet from this point of view the most obvious feature of the Middle Ages is not unity but dichotomy. From the time of Charlemagne, there were always two empires, the western empire and the Byzantine empire ; and we shall never understand the development of mediaeval Europe if we ignore their interaction and concentrate exclusively on the west.[2]

In the second place, it is essential to bear in mind that the western empire itself was never the equivalent of western, or Latin, Christendom ; it excluded Britain, it excluded Scandinavia, and it excluded Spain. Furthermore, the ' Roman ' character of the mediaeval empire, which was a matter of faith to the generation of Bryce, is to-day in hot dispute, and as the pawns move forward to the attack, some of the major pieces are already in evident danger of

---

[1] The remarkable ' York tracts ' were, in fact, probably written at Rouen ; cf. G. H. Williams, *The Norman Anonymous* (1951). For the Italian criticism, cf. Ilarino da Milano, *L'eresia di Ugo Speroni* (1945). French opposition is excellently described by K. Schleyer, *Anfänge des Gallikanismus im 13. Jahrhundert* (1937).

[2] This aspect has been dealt with by W. Ohnsorge, *Das Zweikaiserproblem im früheren Mittelalter* (1947) ; cf. my review, *English Hist. Review* LXIV (1949), 96–98.

falling.[1] At most it was the Roman aristocracy which (for political reasons in no need of explanation) preserved some sense of Roman imperial traditions ; but their empty claims were met by Frederick I with the contempt they deserved, and it would be hard to prove that they reverberated beyond the confines of the city.[2] Even the papal theory of the empire, as it developed after the pontificate of Gregory the Great, showed little sympathy with the imperialism of antiquity,[3] and elsewhere—for example, at the Frankish court— there were palpable manifestations of hostility. Not only was the Frankish empire not a revival of the Roman empire ; it was not even conceived of as a new Roman empire.[4]

And what is true of the Frankish empire, can be demonstrated even more easily of its successors in the west.[5] It is easy to think of the mediaeval empire as a ' supra-national unity ', and it is perfectly true that many theories were devised to imbue it with an œcumenical character ; but in fact its sphere was limited (like that of modern empires) to the constituent lands within its boundaries. If we wish to discover the positive influence of Roman imperial traditions anywhere in the mediaeval world, then we should turn not to the west, but to Byzantium which—unlike the western empire —was both the linear descendant of Rome and (in Sir Maurice Powicke's words) for eight hundred years ' the chief Christian state in the world '. And this is a fact of the greatest historical significance ; for when Constantinople, the ' second Rome ', fell to the Turks in 1453, it was to Russia that the imperial and Christian tradition of Byzantium passed.[6] After 1453 Russia emerged as heir

---

[1] From the very considerable literature it is sufficient to cite K. Heldmann, *Das Kaisertum Karls des Grossen* (1928) ; E. Pfeil, *Die fränkische und deutsche Romidee des frühen Mittelalters* (1929) ; A. Brackmann, *Der römische Erneuerungsgedanke und seine Bedeutung für die Reichspolitik der deutschen Kaiserzeit (Sitz. Berichte d. preussischen Akademie)* (1932) ; E. E. Stengel, *Kaisertitel und Suveränitätsidee (Deutsches Archiv für Geschichte des Mittelalters* III, 1939) ; and C. Erdmann, *Forschungen zur politischen Ideenwelt des Frühmittelalters* (1951). All these, it seems to me, are examples of new interpretation which, whatever their faults (and in the case of Pfeil they are considerable), break into the established position.   [2] Cf. G. Barraclough, *The Origins of Modern Germany* (1946), 170–171.

[3] Cf. Pfeil, op. cit., 47, 49 : ' Zwar gab es Kreise in Rom, die der antiken Grösse gedachten.... Wichtig für uns ist allein, dass solche antike Reminiszenzen in die grossen politischen Aktionen der Kirche nicht Eingang fanden.... In den vielen Briefen, die Päpste an die fränkischen Herrscher schrieben, und in denen die Stellung des heiligen Petrus proklamiert wurde, ist nicht einmal die Rede vom antiken Rom und seinen Ansprüchen, deren Erbe man etwa sein wollte.'

[4] Pfeil, op. cit., 102 : '. . . Aber das sind doch alles nur sehr vage Anklänge ; ein neues römisches Reich sah man im fränkischen nicht.'

[5] Cf. below, pp. 105–30, where the question is discussed in more detail.

[6] Cf. below p. 134.

to the Byzantine inheritance. The Russian ruler was hailed as the 'new Constantine', legitimate successor to the 'Roman emperor and czar who ruled the whole world', and Moscow established the proud claim to be the 'third Rome'. 'Two Romes have fallen', proclaimed the monk, Philotheus of Pskov, 'but the third is standing; and there shall be no fourth'.[1] In this way the imperial mission of Rome was transmitted through the Orthodox church from Byzantium to Holy Russia.

We have here, I think, the best indication of any that the west has no monopoly of the Roman or of the Christian tradition. There is, in fact, no sense in which it can be claimed that the Carolingian empire was the successor of the Roman empire in the west, in which it cannot be claimed that Russia was the successor of the Roman empire in the east; and it would be hard to think of any way in which the Christian religion has served as a spiritual bond between the western peoples, in which it has not equally effectively served as a bond of union among the peoples of eastern Europe. The fundamental traditions in both cases are the same; and we should bear this fact in mind before we use historical arguments in support of the present tendency to oppose the 'western European traditions' of 'Latin Christendom' to the 'eastern European traditions' of the Slav world. I am well aware that in the hands of St. Ambrose, St. Leo and St. Augustine western Christianity took shape as something different from the orthodox faith of the east; but when it is asserted that this difference, consisting in the 'assimilation' or adoption of 'Roman culture', marked a decisive break, I find it difficult—considering the unity maintained for centuries thereafter between the Greek and Latin churches, and the degree to which the Western church was permeated with Greek thought— to avoid scepticism. Anything such as this should, it seems to me, be resisted—no matter from which side it comes—as an unwarrantable attempt 'to divest the notion of civilisation of its universal content'.

*　　　*　　　*

I have thought it necessary to offer some criticism of a current theory which is at once so plausible and so congenial to our present

[1] On all this the best and fullest discussion is in H. Schaeder, *Moskau das Dritte Rom. Studien zur Geschichte der politischen Theorien in der Slavischen Welt* (1929). But the immediate political consequences of the theories should not be exaggerated; cf. below. p. 197, n.2.

frame of mind that it is in danger of passing unchallenged ; but I would not have my criticism misunderstood. I am not so foolish as to suppose that it is my vocation to demolish in a few sentences a powerful synthesis which has engrossed and often enchanted the best brains of many generations ; still less do I suppose that a problem of this magnitude can be solved with a simple affirmation or negation. I am only concerned lest—as that penetrating English scholar, J. Horace Round, once hinted with reference to a different but intrinsically similar question[1]—we should confuse words and things. The problem of continuity or discontinuity in history is, as Traube observed,[2] one of the most important in our whole civilisation, and it would be folly to ignore that such a theme, even if it carries us back to the fourth and fifth centuries of the Christian era, is more ' actual ', nearer to contemporary life, than (let us say) the history of sanitation and street-lighting in Bolton or the unedifying annals of eighteenth-century diplomacy. But for that very reason it must be insisted—unless we accept the nominalist heresy that victorious regimes make their own history—that the truth of such theories as I have attempted to criticize cannot be established by the staccato (and scarcely disinterested) reiteration of political propaganda. On the contrary, their elucidation requires the devoted labour of acute and accurate scholarship ; and it is no credit to modern historical scholarship that it tends to take refuge from the enduring but controversial themes of history in abstruse research, leaving ' the amateurs and the propagandists in possession of the field '.[3]

To-day, as in the past, it remains one of the great tasks of historical scholarship—in which the mediaeval historian is called upon to play a leading role—to investigate the persistence of classical traditions and their share in the formation of modern civilisation. But such results as are won will only carry a valid message if we remain aware of their limiting conditions. The connexion with classical antiquity is there, obvious and undeniable ; for the garment of Clio (as we all know) is a seamless web, and there was no break or sudden reorientation of men's lives in 476. What is at issue is,

---

[1] Cf. J. H. Round, *Feudal England* (1895), 98.
[2] Op. cit., 64.
[3] Cf. A. S. Turberville, ' History Objective and Subjective ', *History* XVII (1933), 297 ; and cf. Miss Veronica Wedgwood's even more trenchant remarks, *Velvet Studies* (1946), 156.

therefore, not the existence of continuity of some sort, but rather its character ; and it is here, as it seems to me, that the attempt to establish anything in the way of a direct connexion between ' western European ' and classical civilisation is both unhistorical and dangerous. It carries within it the risk of creating an artificially closed system, derived from the myth of a common mediaeval civilisation ' when all civilised men spoke the same tongue, thought the same thoughts, and agreed in a common faith and in common ideals '. In fact there was no time when all civilised men spoke the same tongue, or thought the same thoughts, or agreed in a common faith and ideals. Hence we shall rightly remain sceptical when we are told[1] that ' the ultimate foundation of our culture is not the national state but the European unity '. As Dr. Coulton showed us, this transcendental unity, even when supported—as, for example, during the Albigensian crusades—by the harsh regimentation of military power, was never real or strong enough to override more fundamental differences, and such demonstrations of European disunity should not be lightly disregarded.[2] It is for that reason that I am sceptical whether history, if we really analyse its processes in detail, provides a valid argument for the existence of a ' common Latin culture ' or of a ' common western European tradition ', creating bonds (or potential bonds) of unity between England and France (for example) or France and Spain, different in their nature from the bonds (or potential bonds) existing between England or France and Russia, which also through Byzantium is heir to the classical tradition. No doubt the circumstances in the instances mentioned are very different, and distance or proximity alone have counted for much ; but, as Dr. Coulton has said, it is upon common interests, personal contacts, and ' the slow attrition of facts ' that the bonds between peoples are based, not upon transcendental unities which are not facts but hypotheses or ideals.

It will, therefore, be clear (I hope) that I am concerned not to deny the reality of the classical tradition and of its formative influence in western European history, but rather to keep it within measurable bounds, lest it should swell into a monstrous, cloudy phantom, obscuring not only our view of history as a whole, in

[1] Cf. Dawson, op. cit., xxii.
[2] G. G. Coulton, ' Nationalism in the Middle Ages ', *Cambridge Hist. Journal* V (1935), 154.

which western Europe is but a fraction, but also our approach to
the problems of the present. It is when we have established the
formal continuity of tradition from classical antiquity through the
middle ages to our own times that our real task begins ; and it is
at this stage, I think, that the current view of western European
civilisation unduly simplifies the issues. Such a view is, of course,
not altogether incorrect ; but (to adopt one of Hans Hirsch's telling
phrases) it fails to satisfy in so far as it presents only the external
aspects of the problem. The process of history is not merely a
compounding of pre-existing ' factors ' ; rather I believe, with Max
Dvořák, that we must consider historical change not as the tracing
of a single, unbroken line of development, but as an organic process
establishing at every stage new conditions of individual creative
activity and releasing at all stages new branches from which new
developments unfold.[1]

Viewed from this angle the problem of continuity and tradition
will seem infinitely more complex and yet infinitely more lifelike,
for it will not be subordinated to a single overriding pattern. I
am convinced, for example, that even within the mediaeval western
church, at the height of its development in the thirteenth century,
there was wide diversity, that the unifying force of Roman canon
law and of the doctrine of *plenitudo potestatis* was only one factor in
the situation, and that the terms *ecclesia Anglicana, ecclesia Gallicana,*
were not merely geographical expressions, devoid of substantive
content.[2] And so I am led to question the historical justification for
the assumption of the existence of a specifically western European
civilisation, differentiating or even separating western Europe as an
historic unity from the Slavonic east.[3] Rather history points, if it
points at all, in the opposite direction, revealing to the searcher not
impatient of detail or craving for a unitary scheme, how different
peoples in different regions at different stages took different elements in different proportions, and created therefrom the hetero-
geneous cultures—only painfully reduced to any semblance of unity
or uniformity or even harmony—which are the reality behind the
abstraction generically termed ' mediaeval and modern civilisation '.

---

[1] Cf. *Kunstgeschichte als Geistesgeschichte,* ix–x : historical development is not ' eine
kontinuierliche Linie ', but rather ' ein stets neue Voraussetzungen des individuellen
Schaffens und stets neue Entwicklungsreihen hervorstossender Prozess '. Cf. also the
passage, pp. 45–48.   [2] Cf. *English Historical Review* LIII (1938), 532.
[3] The problems involved are discussed more fully below, pp. 49 sqq.

The conception of European unity certainly is a high ideal, worthy of effort and sacrifice ; but it draws its strength from our hopes for the future and not from our interpretation of the past. If it is to become a reality, it will be through our determination to grapple realistically with the hard facts of the present, as we find them, and not through the revival of the illusory unity of an imaginary golden age ; and not least among the dangers, as I see them, of the cult of a common western European civilisation, which is so rife to-day, is the fact that, far from promoting European unity, it is visibly in danger of becoming an ideological obstacle to the attainment of that measure of unity which a practical, non-ideological approach to contemporary problems still has to offer.

3. Is there a European Civilisation?

PEOPLE to-day talk with a good deal of assurance about the civilisation in which we live, about its unique qualities and characteristics, the things it stands for and the things it is opposed to.[1] Very often they speak of a ' western ' civilisation or a ' west-European ' civilisation as something different from, if not superior to, other civilisations. They rarely stop to ask themselves what exactly are the features which mark out our civilisation either from non-civilised, barbarian societies or from other civilisations. And yet none of these things is really obvious and self-explanatory, once you start to look at the problem with the detachment and objectivity you would give to an experiment (for example) in the chemistry laboratory. One of the main things we have learnt from the fascinating studies of primitive peoples by modern anthropologists is to realize that the boundary-line between civilised and barbarian peoples is anything but easy to trace. We know now that there is a lot of the barbarian in everyone of us, and a great deal of natural civilisation in the savage. And the same sort of consideration applies when we begin to compare our civilisation with other civilisations. The more we know about other peoples, both to-day in other parts of the world, and in the past in older civilisations, the harder it is to pick out one thing, or one set of things, and assert beyond all possibility of dispute that this is something unique, which European civilisation alone has developed.

The story of civilisation, as it was told only thirty or forty years ago, used to seem quite simple and straightforward. It is set out, perhaps most clearly of all, in H. G. Wells's famous *Outline of History* but you will find it also, with quite a different emphasis but much the same shape, in Fisher's *History of Europe*. It is a story of continuous development from the early civilisations of the Euphrates and the Nile, through Greece and Rome and mediaeval Christendom, to the Industrial civilisation which, after the exploration of the

---

[1] Adapted from a talk for Sixth Forms, introducing a series : ' European Civilisation and its Values ', on the B.B.C. Schools' Programme (November 3rd, 1950).

New World, has expanded until it embraces the whole globe. The implication, or the underlying assumption, which permeates this interpretation, is that our society is the culmination of five or six thousand years of history, a consummation to which every era of the past has made its contribution—Athens the idea of Liberty, Rome the conception of civilised order, the Middle Ages the ideal of European unity, and so on.[1]

As a theory of historical development this interpretation is evidently flattering for us ; but how (we must ask) does it stand up to criticism? There are, I think, three main points of attack. First, it is said (and I think rightly said) that in order to get this picture of one steady line of development, whole civilisations which (so to say) did not ' lead anywhere '—which did not, in other words, contribute in any direct and self-evident way to the formation of the modern world—are left out of account : China, for example, or (nearer home) the Byzantine empire. Secondly, it is attacked precisely because of the implication I have already mentioned—the implication that our present civilisation is the culmination, if not the objective, of all previous history—when (for all we know) it may in a couple of thousand years appear as a mere speck in the story of mankind. It is attacked, in other words, because it is a very self-centred view of history. And finally it is not easy to accept the assumption of progress from one civilisation to another which is vital to this view of the course of civilisation. No one doubts that history shows ups and downs, periods of real decline ; it has its Dark Ages. But to emphasize these breaks, we are told, is to make the mistake of only taking a short view. On a long view no Dark Age ever quite submerges the achievements of the preceding civilisation, no generation starts off afresh from the foundations ; we are caught up in the march of evolution and carried forward in spite of ourselves.[2]

But this view, as I have indicated, has been challenged. It was challenged, in particular, by the remarkable German writer, Oswald Spengler, and Spengler's challenge was taken up and developed at great length and with an immense panoply of learning in Arnold Toynbee's famous *Study of History*. Inevitably both writers have

[1] I have in mind, in making this point, C. Delisle Burns' little and once famous book *Political Ideals* (4th ed., 1921), which seems to me to epitomize this point of view, and as a much used text-book was important in propagating it.

[2] For a further discussion of this argument, cf. below, pp. 225 sqq.

incurred a lot of criticism; but it is important to recognize that
they do both present a serious challenge to traditional ways of
thinking. Contrasted with the older historians, they see civilisation
not as the story of a continuous development, but as the story of
distinct societies or civilisations, linked together, but each with its
own separate identity, and each passing through a period of rise
and fall.

Spengler formulated his views because he thought he perceived
a clear parallel between modern European history and that of ancient
Rome—he thought he saw the same turning of the tide, not a steady
rise but the beginning of decline. Professor Toynbee thinks he can
distinguish twenty-six distinct civilisations, in which mankind has
risen above the level of primitive societies only to fall back again.
And Spengler has tried to show that each civilisation has its own
underlying ' idea ' or theme—rather like the theme of a fugue, which
may be played with many variations, even inverted, but still gives
coherence and character to the whole. In no two civilisations (he
argued), have men's minds moved in quite the same directions, or
sought quite the same solution to perpetually recurring problems.
Compare, for example, the Egyptian pyramid-temples, the Doric
temples of ancient Greece, the Gothic cathedrals of mediaeval
Europe. In each case there is the striving to create the fittest place
for religious worship—but how different the conceptions of fitness!
For, if space, ' infinite space ', is the ideal of the Gothic builder, that
of the Greek is concrete perfection, balance and symmetry on a
deliberately limited scale, while the keynote for the Egyptians was
' inexorable necessity '. Hence, in Spengler's view, it is not only a
total misconception to expect the Greeks to take the same line as
us in things of the spirit, but also their answers and solutions, conceived in a different spirit, have no validity for our world. What
Aristotle writes of the *polis*, for example, is not transferable to the
modern ' state '. Above all else, the expansiveness of modern civilisation was of no interest to the Greeks ; they did not want to dominate the skies, reach out to the stars, expand to the four corners of
the globe. ' Infinite space ' is the underlying idea of our civilisation,
but not of theirs.

What, then is the nature of this civilisation of ours, to which
Spengler attributes the underlying idea of ' infinite space '? Is it
a ' European ' civilisation? It is important and significant that

neither Spengler nor Toynbee will accept this identification. Both reject the idea, so frequent in common parlance, of a distinct ' French' or a distinct ' Italian ' or ' German civilisation ', because (they say) in none of these cases can you lay your hands on anything sufficiently distinctive to stand independently on its own feet. ' French civilisation ' and ' Italian civilisation ' are parts of a whole ; they are not themselves separate units. On the other hand, they will not agree that the whole of which they are a part, is Europe. Both Spengler and Toynbee speak of ' western ' civilisation, but neither will admit that there is, or ever has been, one civilisation common to the whole of Europe.

We must, I think, admit for a start that there is no particular reason why one particular geographical area called Europe should house one civilisation, and only one, within its rather arbitrary boundaries. Greek civilisation is an example of a civilisation which had its seat within Europe, and yet was not European in the sense of extending over the whole of Europe. On the other hand, Roman civilisation was far more a Mediterranean than a European civilisation ; Asia Minor, Egypt and North Africa played a more important role in it than did continental Europe, and it cut right across geographical divisions and absorbed as much from the east as it did from the west. Nor is it clear that the same does not apply to our own civilisation to-day ; many of the forces and impulses which have been fruitful in European history, including Christianity, have come from outside Europe, usually from Asia. Indeed, we should beware of the idea of a self-contained unit, if only because as a historical fact there are no barriers, no ' iron curtain ', separating Europe and Asia and Africa.

But if that is the case when we consider Europe as a whole, it must be evident that it applies still more to western Europe. It is easy to speak of ' western civilisation ', but it is extremely difficult to draw its boundaries, to maintain that this belongs to the west and that this does not. Or rather, one should perhaps say that it is extremely difficult to do so, except on a basis of prejudice. At various times and in various circumstances the boundaries of ' western civilisation ' have been placed on the Rhine, on the Elbe, on the Oder, on the Vistula, and even (when the bulk of the Spanish peninsula was in Moslem hands) on the Pyrenees. The Polish historian, Oskar Halecki, has demonstrated with admirable conclusiveness how prejudiced and untenable such arguments are.[1] In any case it is obvious that we cannot get much further with ideas as fluctuating as these.

When people talk of European civilisation, however, or of western civilisation, they are not usually thinking of the civilisation within a particular geographical area, but rather of the area where a particular civilisation grew up. About that, in the case of our own civilisation, there is in general terms no particular mystery. Our civilisation evidently grew up, on ground prepared by Rome, through a fusion of three elements : the surviving Roman population and its civilisation, the new peoples who flowed into Europe from the east, and the inspiration of the Christian faith.

So much, it may be said, is plain sailing—but not much else. In the first place, it is quite clear that all these elements might be present, and yet no new civilisation would result. It is obvious, I think, that the new peoples themselves had to be at a certain precise level of culture—difficult, no doubt, to define, but neither more nor less—for their contact with Rome and Christianity to provide just that stimulus which resulted in the formation of a new civilisation. The great German historian, Ranke, thought that the essential fact was the fusion of races, the Roman and Germanic, to form what he called the ' Romano-Germanic ' stock ; but there are many insuperable objections, which it would take us too far to examine in detail, to that or to any other racial argument.

Three considerations alone are perhaps worth picking out for emphasis. The first is this : that Ranke probably was right in think-ing that the mixture of peoples is important, but that mixture varies immensely throughout the length and breadth of Europe, and it is only necessary to consider the case of Scandinavia, where there was obviously no infusion of Roman elements, to perceive that capacity to share in European civilisation is not really affected by race. The second is what may be called the time-factor : namely, that different peoples came into the ' common pool ' at different times. Here again the case of the Scandinavians, who are generally admitted to be among the most ' civilised ' of European peoples to-day, is a

---

[1] ' Those who call European civilisation Western ', he says, ' are inclined to decide in advance one of the most difficult and controversial questions of European history '. ' " Western " is a purely relative designation which explains nothing—what we call the Near East is western for the Far East, which in turn lies west of America ' ; *The Limits and Divisions of European History* (1950), 11.

sufficient indication that a ' late start ' does not necessarily make any odds. I say ' necessarily ' because it seems to me very possible that there comes a point at which a civilisation is so highly developed that it cannot be exported successfully. That was not so, in my view, in the case of Germany or Scandinavia, or even in the case of Russia, which only entered into the main stream of European history at the turn of the fifteenth and sixteenth centuries. But it is perhaps worth considering—though the point is evidently highly debatable and dangerous—whether it may not perhaps be one reason why, to many people in Europe, American civilisation, although like our own in many external features, seems to lack something of the essential spirit (or, it might be better to say, the instinctive sense) of European civilisation? That does not, of course, imply inferiority —it may even, as many Americans think, imply superiority—and in any case it is not a point upon which there will be any general agreement ; but probably everyone can think for himself of countries to which it does apply—perhaps a case is modern Turkey, which only tried to ' join in ' during the present century.

The third point about which I wish to say a few words—one of the most difficult of all—is eastern Europe and in particular Russia.[1] Here again you have the legacy of Roman civilisation and Christianity, both fusing with a new people. This time, it is true, it is the same story with a difference. The Roman legacy, this time, is transmitted through Byzantium ; the Christianity which takes root in Russia is ' orthodox ' Christianity, not (as in the case of the western peoples) Arian or Catholic ; and the peoples themselves belong to the Slavonic, not to the Germanic or Latin groups. Also, because of the Mongol invasions, which spared western Europe but desolated eastern Europe, the development of Russian civilisation was delayed some centuries and its direction in some ways changed.

That these are considerable differences, no one would deny. Even so, I wonder whether they amount, in sum, to a difference of quality, equivalent to a difference in the whole character of civilisation in eastern Europe? Bearing in mind the vast differences from area to area in the west, between Scandinavia and Sicily (for example) and Saxony, I cannot but think that we should do well to hesitate before making dogmatic conclusions. In my view, the safest con-

[1] For further discussion of the relations of Russia and Europe, cf. below pp. 185 sqq

clusion is that there is one civilisation throughout Europe. It is
not identical everywhere, for none of the ' ingredients ' (as we may
call them) are everywhere identical. Perhaps also it is not everywhere at the same stage ; at any rate, it is worth considering whether
those countries which matured early may not have declined early,
or again whether some which matured late may not (like Germany)
have forced the pace, rather like a hot-house plant, and wilted
prematurely. Those are possibilities which would require further
thought and analysis. All I wish to do is to emphasize the extreme
difficulty of thinking of our civilisation in any other terms than that
of one civilisation common to Europe as a whole. No doubt there
are a hundred gradations and variations, sometimes even within the
boundaries of one country, such as Germany, and even, no doubt,
within England itself ; but I cannot myself think of it except as one
civilisation, which I should call European.

The final question is whether this European civilisation of ours
has developed any distinctive characteristics of its own, which mark
it off from other civilisations in other parts of the world--from
China, for example, or India—or from other civilisations in other
periods of history—for example, Greece and Rome. It is easy to
see that this point is closely related to Spengler's idea of every civilisation having its own characteristic outlook and modes of expression. In general terms I cannot help thinking that there is
something in it. But when you come down to any particular point,
there is no doubt that very serious difficulties arise. First of all,
most of us know very little about any of Toynbee's twenty-six
civilisations, except our own, and so it is really very difficult to say
with any degree of assurance that any particular characteristic is a
unique feature of European civilisation. Secondly, many things
which seem characteristic of our civilisation to-day are probably
characteristic not of our civilisation as such, but simply of a particular phase in the development of all civilisations. For example,
people talk of respect for the individual and the desire to provide
a minimum standard of well-being and liberty as typical of European
civilisation. But there are many periods in European history when
these things are more noticeable by their absence than by their
presence ; they are typical only of the phase through which our
civilisation is at present passing, and much the same tendencies
may be found at a parallel period in the history of the ancient world.

And when people talk of the successful achievement of unity in diversity, or a peaceful solution to the question of the relations of capital and labour as characteristic of Europe, the short answer, I imagine, is that it is still too early in the history of our civilisation to know whether these are real achievements or merely a passing phase.

What is obvious, on the other hand, is that our civilisation has seen a stupendous technical progress in all directions, quite without parallel in the past. No one would doubt that, at present, that is the most characteristic distinguishing feature of European civilisation, and if you were to ask an Indian or a Chinese, he would almost certainly pick it out immediately as characteristically European. But equally certainly he would add that we do not seem to be masters of our technical equipment, and he might also express grave doubts how far our technical progress had on balance really benefited mankind—particularly the peoples in Asia or Africa, on whom we had imposed it. And there, without doubt, is the real problem. Bernard Shaw long ago pointed out that civilisation is not simply a matter of the steam-engine and the electric telegraph—or (we might now add) of the jet-aeroplane and the hydrogen-bomb. What really matters is something far less tangible. It is the moral values a civilisation expresses—if, indeed, it expresses any moral values at all—and its capacity for moral leadership. How does European civilisation stand in this respect? Have we the moral qualities essential for the proper use of our immense technical knowledge? This is the standard by which, in the end, our civilisation will be judged, and it will matter less what it is than how it acquits itself.

4. *Medium Aevum : Some Reflections on Mediaeval History and on the term 'The Middle Ages'*[1]

ABOUT three hundred years ago a very indifferent German scholar, Keller or Cellarius, made a discovery (or coined a phrase) which has made history. The phrase he coined, the discovery he made, was the Middle Ages—a distinct (if also a dismal and desolate) period of historical time separating the civilisation of ancient Rome from the new civilised Europe which began with the Renaissance. Earlier scholars had had an inkling of the idea ; but it was Cellarius who fitted it, like a straight-jacket, over all future historical thought, and so established the familiar division of European history—which was all the history that seemed to matter—into three fixed periods : ancient, mediaeval and modern. For Cellarius (and for many others then and later) the second of these periods was simply a long halting-place, an interlude between the fall of the Roman empire in the west in 476 and the sack of Constantinople in 1453, a time of deterioration when, instead of progress, there was decline, instead of civilisation, barbarism, instead of enlightenment, ignorance and bigotry.

The idea, so simple and convenient, took hold. The word 'mediaeval' soon became a term of abuse, used (like 'Gothic') to describe anything crude, harsh, or stupid, and it was applied as often as not to things which the Middle Ages had never known. And then, suddenly, the wheel began to turn. It was the Romantics, early in the nineteenth century, who first began to see that there was more in the Middle Ages than ignorance and barbarism, whose romantic yearnings found an echo in the Gothic cathedrals, the epic poems and the illuminated manuscripts of mediaeval times. And when their efforts were seconded by the patient research of scholars, who explored the subtleties of scholastic thought or revealed the deep insight of the mystics, of St. Bernard and St. Francis, of

---

[1] Adapted from a talk on the *Third Programme*, broadcast on November 1st, 1952.

Joachim of Fiore and Catherine of Siena, the Middle Ages came into their own.

The word ' mediaeval' had been a term of abuse ; now the Middle Ages became a stick to beat the present. Writers such as Berdyaev and Maritain confidently asserted that the thirteenth century represented ' the highest point reached in the development of European culture ', and that everything that happened since the Reformation was a falling away from mediaeval standards.[1] And much the same point of view found its way into the writings of influential sociologists, such as Mumford, who contrasted the spontaneous vitality of mediaeval man, and his spirituality, with the weary emptiness and artificiality of material civilisation to-day.[2] To those who held, with Burckhardt, to the belief ' that the Renaissance discovered man and the individual ', the chastening reply was given that all the Renaissance discovered was ' the old Adam ', and that ' it is more correct to say that man's inner being was discovered in the Middle Ages, when he was engaged in spiritual work and stood in the centre of Christian faith and Creation '.[3]

In this way the Middle Ages, once regarded as a long twilight between two civilisations, are now seen rather as a bright, hopeful, sunny morning, carrying the promise of a millenium which (through our stupidity) we have failed to realize, and the last four hundred years are simply ' lost ground ' which we have to ' recover ' if we are again to acquire a sense of purpose and vocation. But whether we follow the older or the newer interpretation, the division of time established by Cellarius stands intact ; the Middle Ages are still treated as an historical reality. We may regard them, as Dr. Coulton once wrote,[4] as the story of ' a vast catastrophe, involving the whole of Europe, and of gradual convalescence from that almost mortal sickness ', or we may regard their history as the tale of an achievement we have let slip : in either case this thousand years stands before us as an entity, a self-contained unit as distinct from classical antiquity as it is from modern times ; and people speak and write of ' mediaeval civilisation ' as a civilisation complete in itself and distinct from other civilisations.

And yet a fundamental problem still remains : the whole question

---

[1] N. Berdyaev, *The Meaning of History* (1936), 128, 141 ; J. Maritain, *Scholasticism and Politics* (1940), 240.

[2] Cf. L. Mumford, *The Condition of Man* (1944).

[3] Berdyaev, op. cit., 131.   [4] *Studies in Medieval Thought* (1940), 10.

of what we mean by 'the Middle Ages', and how true it is to consider
these centuries as a self-contained period of time. Few historians,
it would seem, are prepared to bother unduly about it ; they agree
that the term ' Middle Ages ' may be ' artificial ' and ' arbitrary ',
but they cling to it as a ' convenient usage '.[1] It is, they seem to
imply, as good a division as any other and they accept it for what
it is worth. And it is, of course, perfectly true that it is necessary
to break up the ceaseless procession of time into periods and divisions, and to group and classify the events of the past, if we are to
have any hope of making them intelligible. All knowledge, all
science, depends upon classification for ordering the phenomena
with which it deals ; and from this point of view at any rate, history
is a science. The past in its entirety is so vast and complex that we
can make nothing of it unless we order and classify and break it up
into periods. But there are two essential limitations. First of all,
we must never forget that all our divisions are artificial, never final,
always subject to revision. When we talk of turning-points, we must
remember that history is continuous ; when we talk of ages of
transition, we must remember that all ages are ages of transition.
Secondly, whatever classifications we may adopt, or periods we may
create for our own convenience, they should correspond as nearly
as possible with the facts as we know them ; otherwise, far from
helping us to understand the past, like milestones guiding us through
a wilderness, they will (more likely) be a hindrance or obstacle in
our path, confusing us and obscuring our view.

And this, I believe, is what has happened with the concept, the
Middle Ages. It is, after all, only a concept, a convenient mental
category, not a reality. There never was a ' Middle Ages ' ; as a
matter of fact, people in what we call the Middle Ages usually
thought of themselves—when they thought about it at all—as
standing at the end of time, in an age of senility, when the world
was old. But once we have this idea of the Middle Ages in our head,
we become its prisoner. We write our history to accord with it,
leaving out (for we cannot write history at all without leaving out)
what seems untypical of the Middle Ages ; we even create an abstraction, ' mediaeval Man ', and talk of his ideas and outlook, as
though a man in the tenth and a man in (say) the thirteenth century
must have the same ideas and outlook. We talk of ' mediaeval

[1] Cf. C. W. Previté-Orton, *The Shorter Cambridge Medieval History* II (1952), 1112–3.

philosophy or 'mediaeval theology', forgetting how violently it swung between the two poles of St. Augustine and St. Thomas, so that even the great Thomist synthesis, which many people think of to-day as the essence of mediaeval thought, is only a flash in the pan, representative not of the Middle Ages but of one fleeting moment, and no sooner formulated than discarded.[1] And finally, having this period firmly embedded in our minds, we try to give it a unity ; we seek its origins, we watch it grow (almost like a human being), we weave it into a pattern, we even provide it with an innate idea, a spirit, which (we seem to think) it was striving to realize. . . .

And yet there were no Middle Ages. They were simply the idea of a mediocre German scholar three centuries ago, who had far scantier historical data to work with than very ordinary people have to-day. What is surprising is how Cellarius' division of time has stuck, so that it is still, in the twentieth century, the framework (if not the straight-jacket) of historical writing. And yet the history of the thousand years between 476 and 1453 is not really a unity, capable of being told as one story ; and I am not sure that the attempt to treat it as a unity may not be a serious hindrance to our understanding of the past. Cellarius' categories were fairly plausible in his own day, but time has knocked the bottom out of them. First of all, archaeologists and pre-historians, pushing back our horizons by centuries, have exploded the idea of ancient history as a unity reflected in the civilisation of Greece and Rome. Secondly, the mere passage of time has reduced the concept of modern history to a myth. After all, what is by now three hundred or four hundred years old is only 'modern' by courtesy, and it is hard to discover any valid reason why a watershed should divide what happened in 1450, as 'mediaeval', from what happened in 1550, as 'modern'. Indeed, so obvious has this become that of recent years another category has been added : namely 'contemporary history', meaning apparently anything that has happened since 1870. But 'contemporary' also is a vague and fluctuating category, for what is contemporary now will not be contemporary in fifty years, and then we shall have to start again. To draw a line between 'modern' and

---

[1] 'Le caractère propre du XIVe siècle', writes Gilson (*La philosophie au moyen âge*, 1930, 243) thinking of Occam, 'c'est d'avoir désespéré de l'œuvre tentée par le XIIIe '. And from another point of view A. J. Carlyle (*A History of Mediaeval Political Theory*, VI, 505) observes that 'the post-Aristotelian tradition was too firmly rooted to be shaken even by St. Thomas' great authority '.

'contemporary' is at best a sort of first-aid measure, a patching of Cellarius' tattered garment, a last attempt to shear up the tottering structure of his building. What is wanted is something different : not patching, not first-aid work, but a clear-headed attempt to re-draw the map of the past with new perspectives.

Such a redefinition of boundaries is overdue; and it will, I believe, make short shrift of the Middle Ages as we conceive them now. After all, the very term means no more than an indefinite intermediate time; it is totally negative, not a real category, but a lumping together of ten centuries in a sort of limbo. How in-adequate it is has already been shown by the fact that it was soon found necessary to subdivide the Middle Ages themselves into three distinct periods : first, the Dark Ages; secondly, the Middle Ages proper, or the 'high' Middle Ages, as continental scholars term them; and finally the later Middle Ages. But this sub-division does not really help either—or rather, it only helps to show how artificial the idea of the Middle Ages as a unity, really is. The great Belgian historian, Pirenne, argued forcefully, and not without justification, that the Dark Ages belong in reality not to mediaeval history but to the last phase of the Mediterranean civilisation of Antiquity. And the real question about the so-called later Middle Ages, from about 1300, is whether they should be grouped with the Middle Ages at all.

A new chronology, conceived in line with the lengthened and widened perspectives we possess to-day, will (I think) give a totally different picture. First of all, we shall not concentrate so exclusively upon Europe, but rather give due weight to the impact, as a real division in time, of the great civilisation of Islam. For in the centuries we call mediaeval, Islamic civilisation was much richer than that of the west; Baghdad loomed larger in the ninth century than Constantinople, and far larger than Rome; and even a couple of centuries later the centre and seat of civilisation in the west was Cordova in Moslem Spain, not Paris. How different our history would be, how much more real and interesting, if historians would accept these simple facts and plan and proportion their work accordingly! As Pirenne suggested—and despite all subsequent criticism I think the main point remains true—it is the rise of Islamic civilisation that gives us a valid dividing line, marking the end of classical antiquity.

At the other end it is imperative for us to consider whether the Reformation and the Renaissance really constituted a decisive break between the mediaeval and modern periods, or whether, as Troeltsch so brilliantly argued, the ' modern ' outlook was not formed until the time of the Enlightenment.

So controversial and hotly disputed a question cannot, obviously, be settled here and now.[1] No doubt, the customary emphasis on the Renaissance is derived chiefly from the Swiss historian, Burckhardt, whose *Civilisation of the Renaissance in Italy* was first published almost a century ago, in 1860. This famous book certainly embodied the concept of a genius ; but it was a one-sided concept. Since Burckhardt's day our whole view of the Renaissance has undergone transformation.[2] We see now how deeply it was rooted in the mediaeval world, how many points of contact the average humanist had with his mediaeval heritage. We know to-day that the revival of interest in classical antiquity, and the new impulses derived from that interest, had a long history ; it was not a case of a sudden break, but rather of a chain of ' renaissances ' leading back step by step into the twelfth century.

Some historians, notably the American scholar, Charles Homer Haskins, have sought to trace back the new interest in man and nature, in humanity and the world around us, to Frederick II and his Sicilian court, where Islamic and Byzantine influences met.[3] How far this particular view is justified, is not the point ;[4] the important thing, in the present context, is to perceive the new lines of thought. Scholars such as Dr. Lynn Thorndike have traced the continuity of scientific studies through the Middle Ages right down to Copernicus, and more recently Professor Butterfield has argued that the real turning-point in the history of science came not with the Renaissance but with the ' scientific revolution ' at the close of the seventeenth century.[5] On the other hand, a number of other

---

[1] Troeltsch's views were criticized at some length by G. von Below, *Die Ursachen der Reformation* (1917), 8 sqq. (where most of the controversial literature is cited), 163 sqq.

[2] The fourth volume (1943) of the *Journal of the History of Ideas* is devoted to a discussion of the many problems involved ; cf. also *Il Rinascimento. Significato e limiti* (1953), and W. K. Ferguson, *The Renaissance in Historical Thought* (1948).

[3] C. H. Haskins, *Studies in the History of Mediaeval Science* (1924).

[4] I should myself place greater emphasis upon the humanism of the twelfth century ; cf. below, p. 81.

[5] Lynn Thorndike, *Science and Thought in the Fifteenth Century* (1929) ; H. Butterfield, *The Origins of Modern Science* (1949).

historians—most notable among them the Dutchman, Jan Huizinga[1]
—investigated the roots of the Renaissance away from Italy, and
came to results very different from Burckhardt's. They found that
the Renaissance north of the Alps, the ' Christian Renaissance of
the North ', as it is sometimes called, grew out of, rather than grew
in opposition to, traditional ideas, and that it grew also from different
roots, among which classical study was not conspicuous.

The other side of this process of reassessment was taken over
by scholars who studied the later periods, the sixteenth and seventeenth centuries. They, also, reacted against Burckhardt's tendency
to create an ideal type—' Renaissance man ', as he is sometimes called
—and make him typical or representative of a whole epoch. And,
on the other side, they discovered that the old died much harder
than had been thought. Professor Tillyard, for example, showed
how much that was specifically ' mediaeval ' continued to exist
in the outlook of the Elizabethan Englishman,[2] so that the sudden
break we are still apt to introduce with 1485 and the ' Tudor
monarchy ' appears on a nearer view to be a deception. And A. J.
Carlyle showed how the essentials of mediaeval political thinking
were garnered and handed on through the sixteenth century by
Richard Hooker, whose affinities are with Thomas Aquinas rather
than with Thomas Hobbes.[3] Down to the middle of the seventeenth
century religion remained the dominant theme, and theology the
dominant mode of thought. Even Hobbes himself, whose *Leviathan*
is often regarded as the starting-point of the modern theory of the
state, devoted nearly half of his famous book to ecclesiastical questions. As Professor Sabine comments, ' in this respect English
thought must have moved rapidly between 1650 and the end of
the seventeenth century '; for ' when Locke wrote, forty years
later ' than Hobbes ,' he assumed a separation of political and religious questions such as Hobbes never imagined '.[4]

Down to 1660, in other words, or at any rate to the Peace of
Westphalia, in 1648, the old—or, as some would say, the ' mediaeval '
—confusion or inter-connexion of religion and politics, was still a

---

[1] J. Huizinga, *The Waning of the Middle Ages. A study of the forms of life, thought and
art in France and the Netherlands in the 14th and 15th centuries* (1924).
[2] E. M. W. Tillyard, *The Elizabethan World-Picture* (1943).
[3] Cf. R. W. and A. J. Carlyle, *A History of Mediaeval Political Theory in the West* VI
(1936) ; cf. also A. P. d'Entrèves, *The Medieval Contribution to Political Thought* (1939).
[4] G. H. Sabine, *A History of Political Theory* (1st ed., 1938), 474.

reality. Only thereafter, with the onset of the Enlightenment, is there a reorientation. And for this reason historians to-day are tending more and more to set the start of ' modern ' history around 1660–1680, rather than (as the old scheme required) in 1494 or 1485. The great break in outlook, the change in intellectual climate, which Paul Hazard termed ' la crise de la conscience européenne ',[1] came, not with Renaissance or Reformation, but with the Enlightenment which set the course for the developments of the nineteenth and twentieth centuries.

* * *

Taken together, these shifts of emphasis and changes of view amount to a very substantial revision of judgement, requiring a new synthesis and a new chronology. First of all, we have to rid ourselves of our too exclusively European point of view ; it is (for example) useless and misleading from the point of view of Chinese history to classify as ' mediaeval ' centuries which, for the Chinese people, were not mediaeval at all. It is, indeed, a major question whether we can devise any scheme of chronology which is applicable to every country or to every people at once. Even within Europe it is perfectly clear that the tempo of development was different in east and west, that the Russians (for instance) and the French were not always at the same stage of development at the same time, and for that very reason it is, in fact, customary among historians to continue the Russian ' middle ages ' down into the seventeenth century. But from our point of view, in western Europe, one thing may be asserted with some confidence : and that is that all our history, from the decline of Rome, should be regarded as ' modern ', in the sense that it is the history of our modern civilisation and so directly relevant to our understanding of modern civilisation. If we take this civilisation as our starting-point, then I suggest that a rational chronology will establish four main periods : first, the pre-history of the European peoples, when they were only on the fringe of historical knowledge and written records, extending to 800 or perhaps 900 A.D.; then the period of the formation of the European societies, falling between 900 and 1300 ; then, if you like, the ' middle ages ' of Europe, which (I think) cover the whole span from 1300 to 1789 ; and finally our modern history, still very young if

<hr>

[1] P. Hazard, *La crise de la conscience européenne*, 1680–1715 (1935) ; an English version appeared in 1953 under the title : *The European Mind* (1680–1715).

we range it against that of Greece and Rome, beginning with the
French Revolution and extending ahead of us for who knows how
many centuries to come. . . .

None of these considerations is new ; but it is fair to say that
they have still not penetrated from the professional historian's
study to the history which is purveyed to the man in the street. All
historians to-day are familiar with, and prepared to dispute learnedly
about, the writings of Pirenne, and the new perspectives they opened
up ; but their solution is usually to work them deftly into the existing
framework, not to scrap the traditional framework and erect a new
one better fitted to house the results which Pirenne and others of
his contemporaries won.   One may admire the neatness of the
achievement ; but one may also confess that there does not seem to
be much prospect of progress along such lines. Every generation
must interpret its past, write its own history in the light of its
experience ; and precisely because the centuries we call mediaeval
have become so much more relevant in recent years, because experience has taught us the limitations and precariousness of what,
only a generation back, seemed to be the triumphant progress of
nineteenth-century civilisation, and forced us to look further back
in our past for enduring values and the solid foundations of our
culture, something more is needed. For one thing, political history
still receives undue emphasis, although, so far as the middle ages
are concerned, their political history, remote and fossilized, is for
most of us the least significant of their achievements. And secondly,
with the new balance in Europe between east and west, we require
a new conception of European history which embraces equally the
eastern and the western halves ; the origins of the eastern European
peoples, the basic facts in their development, the source and character of their ideas—all embedded in what we call the Middle Ages—
are essential knowledge to-day.

But, above all else, it seems to me, we need a new conception
of these centuries which will bring home to us their relevance.
Those of us who study them, study them not because they are
mediaeval, but because we believe that knowledge of immediate
causes and contemporary events may blind, and not illuminate,
unless it is counterbalanced by a deeper understanding of the
continuity of history, its enduring factors and its underlying currents.
From this point of view the very concept ' The Middle Ages ' is

objectionable, because it cuts them off as remote and distinct, a separate period which has little bearing on our lives and fortunes to-day. Yet this was the time when the foundations of modern Europe were being laid, when the different states with their characteristic institutions and their distinct attitudes to the problems of political society were in process of formation ; it was the time also when some of our stubbornest beliefs and prejudices took root, as well as ideals we would fight and die for. If we understood it better, not as mediaeval history, but as modern history, very modern history—in the sense that all history which means anything is contemporary history—we might understand ourselves better, and our problems and potentialities.

5. Mediaeval Kingship

IN England, as elsewhere in Europe, kingship is a legacy of the Middle Ages.[1] Many of the elements of which it is formed go back further and have their own history, which carries us far away from mediaeval Europe to the oriental world; but it was the Middle Ages that gathered them up, selecting this strand and that, and wove them into a new pattern. One thread leads back by way of the Old Testament to the Hebrew concept of kingship; another thread leads via Rome to the great Sassanid dynasty of Persia, the influence of which also extended eastwards through Asia. But each epoch has cast its own imprint on monarchy; and although the office of king reaches ' back into the great civilizations of the past for its symbols and part of its inspiration ', kingship as we know it was ' moulded by the genius of mediaeval Europe into sharp contrast with the oriental monarchies from which many of the insignia were derived '.[2]

Nevertheless, kingship in mediaeval Europe conformed to no single pattern. In a society, unlike ours, built up in a hierarchy of separate orders, each estate had its own ideal of kingship; what for one was right and proper in a king, to another might seem the negation of kingly qualities. Existing statues and portraits, for us the most vivid representation of the mediaeval king, were designed practically all for religious purposes; and their abstract, idealized symbolism, so characteristic of artistic style until the fourteenth century, reflected the churchman's ideal of the devoted religious monarch. We must beware of treating them, or the mannerisms of fifteenth-century portraiture, as a norm. The clergy, in their copious ' Mirrors of Princes ', set out the moral qualities indispensable in a ruler; the schoolmen in the rising universities wrote at length of ' The Princely Regiment ', the duties of kings, the place of monarchy in the divine order, the obligations of subjects. But their precepts and admonitions were far removed from the ideals of the great

---

[1] Adapted from a talk broadcast in the *Third Programme* on March 22nd, 1953.
[2] B. Wilkinson, *The Coronation in History* (1953), 22.

noblemen, the feudal baronage on whose support and co-operation every king depended in peace and in war.

For churchmen the king was first and foremost God's vice-regent on earth, the exponent of divine law, responsible to God for his every act, defending religion and propagating the faith against heathen and heretic alike ; but the feudal nobility demanded other qualities of their rulers. A king, in their eyes, should be spirited and warlike, a man of fine physique, as fitting to outdistance his companions in the chase as to lead in battle ; he should be liberal and open-handed but firm, as ready to take as to give, to enforce his own rights without prejudicing theirs ; for in their view only a king who maintained them in their rights deserved their loyalty. Their type is the famous William Marshal, who faithfully served the young king Henry against his father Henry II, Henry II against Richard Coeur de Lion, Richard against John Lackland, and John against the revolted barons, not because these kings were God's representatives upon earth, but because, each severally, they had received his homage. It was a feudal conception of kingship, based upon the sanctity and reciprocal obligations of the feudal oath.

But others in the Marshal's day already took a different view. Of the common people, as usual in mediaeval times, we know little or nothing. For the poor, who would suffer in any case, a good king was a king who would make the rich and high-born suffer equally with the lowly, who like St. Louis of France did not hesitate to punish the baron who hanged at the nearest tree three miserable poachers taken in his woods. Impartial justice, and the power to enforce justice impartially, was for them the essence of kingship. But the courtiers, the justices, the trained administrators who carried out the king's business, had other ideals still. If the feudal nobility admired a prodigal king, their admiration was reserved for the ruler who filled his coffers with gold to finance efficient govern-ment ; who avoided war and sought to gain his ends by treaties and alliances, regarding peace as the greatest benefit a king could confer ; they preferred a monarch dressed in simple clothes, who worked hard, to a king decked in the ecclesiastical pageantry of coronation vestments.

Not the least fascination of mediaeval kingship is to watch the interaction between these different strands, the interplay of concep-tions of monarchy each of which reflected the ethos of a different

F

social class. For kingship was not static in the middle ages ; it evolved and changed with the society in which it was placed. As the rough feudalism of Norman days gave way to a more diversified social structure, as the Norman keep was displaced by the country mansion, and a gentry allied with a wealthy merchant class added weight to the middle ranks of society, new qualities were called for in monarchy. But we must not exaggerate the speed of change. The qualities of thrift, unceasing vigilance, and personal attention to the detail of government, which Peter of Blois and Walter Map admired in Henry II, scarcely won general acceptance as attributes of monarchy before Tudor times, when they emerged as royal virtues in the pages of Bacon's life of Henry VII. Down to the end of the fifteenth century the religious and the aristocratic conceptions of kingship prevailed. The severe feudal ideals of William Marshal scarcely outlasted his life ; they were dead, with the society which nourished them, by the time of Edward I. But the new feudalism of the fourteenth and fifteenth centuries, the brittle gilded chivalry expressed in the *sirventes* of the troubadours and popularized by Edward III and the Black Prince, preserved the more superficial ideals of the knightly king without the deep ethic of feudal loyalty. Piety and prowess, pomp and procession, remained the standard of measurement down to Bosworth Field and beyond. Even Richard III, for Shakespeare a monster in human form, was for contemporaries in 1483 an upright and pious prince, courageous and generous.[1]

These ideals, so different from our own, have almost of necessity resulted in remarkable reversals of judgement. Few of the kings whom we account great, were great or popular in the eyes of contemporaries ; and the few who were, were admired for reasons which are not ours. The modern historian sees in the wars and foreign adventures of Edward III, and in his easy yielding to the aristocracy at home, the fatal turning-point which led to the lawlessness of the fifteenth century. Yet to contemporaries he approached as near as any to the ideal of kingship ; while Richard II, who perceived the need for peace and retrenchment, forfeited thereby both popularity and esteem. Henry II, in our eyes the greatest of the Plantagenets, was little to the liking either of the clergy, who complained less of his notorious vices than of his want of deference to the church, or of the nobility, who could not reconcile his preference for diplo-

[1] Cf. A. R. Myers, *England in the Late Middle Ages* (1952), 183.

macy to war, and his prohibition of tournaments, with the qualities they looked for in a king. Even St. Louis of France was bitterly assailed by his barons because, true to his Christian principles, he made peace with Henry III of England when he might have exploited Henry's difficulties at home to drive the English out of France.

Because few kings combined in their persons all the qualities attributed to kingship, men turned from the imperfect reality to legend and myth, seeking in the historical figures of the past an ideal which escaped them in the present. Legend and myth are the stuff out of which mediaeval kingship was compounded ; and none were more important than the legends which gathered around the person of Charlemagne. Charlemagne became the model for mediaeval kings ; so great was the impression left by his victories that his very name ' Karl ' (*Król*) was used among the Slavs as an ordinary designation for king and ruler. He is the most popular hero of the *chansons de geste* ; and even in lands which had never known his sway, such as Ireland and Scandinavia, poets sang his praise in their native tongues. To trace descent from Charles became the highest legitimation of a royal dynasty. Philip Augustus of France, whose mother claimed Carolingian blood in her veins, was saluted with the title ' Karolide ' ; and the chronicler of St. Denis noted with pride and satisfaction that, on Philip's accession, ' the lineage of the great Charlemagne, emperor and king of France, which had failed for seven generations, was restored '.[1]

It was not the real Charles, hard living and hard drinking, the Charles whose court shocked the clerical reformers of his day, who lived on in legend and in poetry. The famous *Song of Roland*, which magnifies into a central theme his minor campaign against the Moors of Spain, and turns Charles incongruously into a crusader defending Christendom against Islam, shows how far from reality the legend had moved. But aspects of the real Charles were caught up and perpetuated. In particular the Christian king, the stern judge and lawgiver whom his bishops likened to David and Melchisedek, is the Charles of history ; and this is the most important aspect in the end. If kingship in the middle ages is a religious office, it is not because of abstract theories deriving all dominion from God, but because of the example and precedent given by Charles. The religious king, the Christian king, the Lord's anointed, is the king who

[1] R. Fawtier, *Les Capétiens et la France* (1942), 57, 77, 84.

rules in Charles's image. When in the twelfth century the great
Barbarossa set out to restore the power of the Empire, it was characteristic that he had Charles canonized in order to sanctify the tradition
in which he meant to rule.[1]

There is no doubt that religion, by which was meant the Christian
religion, was considered a necessary quality in a mediaeval king.
Saladin, crusaders said, would have been an ideal ruler—if only he
had been a Christian.[2] But it is another question whether the binding
force of religion was the distinctive mark of mediaeval kingship,
differentiating it (as some have thought) from the Roman imperialism
which preceded and the Renaissance monarchies which followed.
It would be hard to think of any mediaeval ruler who made religion
the basis of his policy in the way that Roman emperors such as
Theodosius or Justinian had done. The religious element in kingship
is as old as kingship itself ; what is significant is not that this element
continued to prevail during the middle ages, but the particular form
the middle ages gave to it.

With examples such as Henry III and Henry VI of England in
our minds, we are apt to think of devout and religious kings as
weak, priest-ridden and subservient. Such judgements miscast the
part played by religion in mediaeval kingship. Henry III was not,
as historians used to paint him, a creature of the papacy, for ever
at the pope's beck and call ;[3] and the effect of religion was not
normally to weaken the king's hands, by subjecting his deeds to
priestly scrutiny, but rather to strengthen them, by giving his actions
divine sanction. Here again Charles the Great pointed the way,
when he roundly told the pope that it was his (the monarch's)
business to guide, defend and rule the church, the pope's to pray
with hands raised to God for Charles's success.[4] Charles summoned
synods and sat at their head, dictated doctrine, rebuked the pope.
He was ' king and priest ', ' ruler of the people of God ', ' propagator
of the faith ', ' father of the church ', Christ's vicar on earth ; and

---

[1] Cf. R. Folz, *Le Souvenir et la Légende de Charlemagne dans l'empire germanique médiéval*
(1950), 186 sqq. ; cf. below, p. 88.

[2] Cf. D. C. Munro, ' The Western Attitude towards Islam ', *Speculum* VI (1931),
334–5, 338–9 ; for the western attitude to Saladin, G. Paris, ' La Légende de Saladin,'
Journal des Savants (1893), is basic.

[3] As has rightly been emphasized by F. M. Powicke, *King Henry III and the Lord
Edward* I (1947), 72–73, 351.

[4] The remarkable letter in which Charles announced these principles has been
translated (in part) by L. Halphen, *Charlemagne et l'Empire carolingien* (1947), 122.

above all else he was the Lord's anointed, whom God alone, who had set him up, could cast down. No wonder that princes in future generations looked back to him as their model! No wonder that they sought a religious foundation for their authority, which would raise it above human criticism!

'The breath of worldly men cannot depose
The deputy elected by the Lord.'

So monarchy rose on foundations provided by religion. The rite of unction was the highest legitimation of the monarch, but not the only one. The miraculous power of healing, exercised by the kings of England and France, was another revelation of the working of God's grace. The French kings, not satisfied with ordinary chrism, even contrived to have special oil for their anointing brought down from heaven by a dove.[1] It was seen to be a good thing to have a saint in the family; and just as Barbarossa secured the canonisation of Charlemagne, so Henry II of England persuaded the pope to canonize Edward the Confessor, and Philip the Fair of France obtained the canonisation of his grandfather, St. Louis. To us these devices seem trivial; but they were the visual ceremonies and symbols which impressed the religious virtues of monarchy and its exalted status on the minds of subjects.

And yet these attributes did not lead, as the divine attributes of the Roman emperors led, to autocracy. The middle ages knew no theory of divine right. In part this was due to the fact that the king, precisely because of the religious sanctions which fortified his position, was forced to recognize that he held his kingdom in trust from God, and was bound by God's moral law. But partly also it was due to the fact that the foundation of kingship was not solely religious. Religion might consecrate and exalt the monarch, but it did not create his rights. If the king had obligations to God, he had obligations also to his subjects; and these obligations were expressed in the coronation oath which every king swore at his accession. For the king, although he was God's representative, was also elected by his people. Primogeniture, hereditary right, the succession of son to father, only slowly became the rule, as religion conveyed a special

[1] On these (and other similar) devices cf. P. E. Schramm, *Der König von Frankreich. Das Wesen der Monarchie vom 9. zum 16. Jahrhundert* (1939), and M. Bloch, *Les rois thaumaturges. Étude sur le caractère surnaturel attribué à la puissance royale, particulièrement en France et en Angleterre* (1924).

status on the legitimate dynasty; in England it was not established
before the thirteenth century. Before that the king's position was
much less secure; and disputed elections made for limited powers.
If there were no other way to secure the crown, few princes hesitated
to make promises and solemn engagements to those who elected
them, and these pacts acted as a restraint and as a justification for
resistance to arbitrary rule.

The history of monarchy in the different countries of Europe
depends very directly upon the fluctuating balance between the
promises contained in the king's coronation oath and the principle
of hereditary rule. The creation of a balanced constitution was not
easy to achieve. Most European states failed to achieve it, and more
than once England looked as though it might fail also. The balance
between the rights of government and the rights of the community,
which underlies the English political order, was perhaps due, more
than we are apt to think, to circumstances and to good fortune,
rather than to any inherent political sense; elsewhere things worked
out differently. In Germany the result was the formulation of
elaborate ' electoral capitulations ', which tied the emperor's hands;
and German disunity was the consequence of this emasculation of
the kingship. In Aragon a famous tag laid down that subjects would
only obey the king so long as he performed his obligations, ' and if
not, not '.[1] In France, Louis XIV's ' l'état, c'est moi ', proclaimed
the triumph of the opposite extreme; but its outcome was the
revolution which swept away a monarchy that recognized no limits
on its absolute power. England alone found something like a
satisfactory balance. Richard II, who declared the laws to be in his
bosom, was deposed and murdered; but the monarchy was left
untouched. So long as the king was prepared to respect ' the good
customs and usages made and observed in time past ' (as Richard's
successor, Henry IV, promised to respect them), no constitutional
check was placed on royal powers. The result was to make possible
the growth of a ' constitutional monarchy ' adaptable as no other to
changing times and circumstances.

Our kingship is in a very direct sense a thing of the middle ages.
It is worlds apart from Egyptian or Byzantine absolute rule. A few

[1] For a comprehensive picture on a European scale, see F. Kern, *Kingship and Law
in the Middle Ages* (1939), where the famous Aragonese legal formula : ' y si no, no ',
is cited, p. 115.

of the external trappings, like the orb and sceptre, originate from ancient Rome ; but little of the essence reaches back beyond Charlemagne. There is nothing in it of the Roman idea of a transference of power, total and irrevocable, from people to ruler ; and the Roman theory of the prince who stands above and outside the law is alien to our tradition. Our debt to the middle ages in this respect is great. The dim but melodramatic history of the primitive rulers of the western peoples, Amals, Lethings, Asdings, Gepids, Balthas, Oiscings, Mervings, strange names who flit in rapid succession across the pages of the past, poisoned by their wives, murdered by their lovers, massacred by ambitious relatives, upstarts exercising a tyranny tempered only by assassination, show with startling clarity that no firm tradition of kingship was handed down from ancient Rome.[1] Kingship was not indigenous to the western peoples ; many, as they come into the light of history, have no kings ; many only acquired them as they battled for a place in the lands over which Rome had ruled. ' War begat the king ' ; but the king, a transitory figure, the mere leader of a war-band, was one thing, kingship another. The consolidation of monarchy was a long process, but an essential one, if society were ever to secure stability and peace within itself. It was this stability which the middle ages gave, by fortifying kingship with religious sanctions, by assimilating it to the standards of Old Testament monarchy, by distinguishing between legitimate dominion, blessed by God, and brute force and tyranny.

Nor was there any sudden breach in mediaeval tradition, as is still so often implied, with the accession of the Tudors. Henry VIII, asserting that his kingdom was an empire, was only echoing Philip IV of France ; even his proclamation of royal supremacy was less a radical break with the mediaeval past than the culmination of a royal tradition of dominion over church and state reaching back as far as Charlemagne. People speak of the ' New Monarchy ' of Tudor times ; but it was not the monarchy that was new, so much as the milieu in which it worked. Theories of the ' Renaissance prince ', derived from Machiavelli, made little headway in Tudor England. Richard Hooker, the greatest exponent of Tudor monarchy in the days of Queen Elizabeth I, only elaborated a view of kingship which

[1] Cf. P. Grierson, ' Election and Inheritance in Germanic Kingship ', *Cambridge Hist. Journal* VII (1941), 1–22.

the middle ages had created ; his work is the best evidence of the continuity of mediaeval values through the great upheavals which we call the Renaissance and the Reformation. When under Elizabeth the English monarchy advanced to new heights, it was on the firm foundation of kingship which the middle ages had laid.

6. *Frederick Barbarossa and the Twelfth Century*

EIGHT hundred years ago,[1] on June 18th, 1155, Frederick the Swabian, ruler of Germany since 1152, was crowned Emperor by the Englishman, pope Hadrian IV. He is, in all probability, the most disputed figure in German history prior to his eighteenth-century namesake, Frederick the Great of Prussia, if not the most controversial of all German rulers and statesmen down to Bismarck in the nineteenth century. The brilliance of his long reign, from 1152 to 1190, his remarkable capacity in his conflicts with the papacy and with the Italian communes for recovering from setbacks and retrieving apparent disaster, the proud claims of the imperial manifestos issued in his name, and not least of all his tragic death as a crusader on the borders of far-away Cilicia, all appealed to the imagination not of historians alone but of generations of Germans ; and when, in the nineteenth century, the romantic yearnings of German nationalism turned back for inspiration to the middle ages and to the achievements of the mediaeval German emperors, it was the reign of Frederick Barbarossa—to use the nickname the Italians gave him on account of his burnished red-gold beard—that seemed to represent the culmination of German prestige and standing in Europe.

Far more than his half-Sicilian grandson, Frederick II, whose character and activities reflected a Mediterranean rather than a German outlook and interests, Barbarossa incorporated the ideal of a German ruler. Frederick II's Sicilian court was a focus attracting cultural and intellectual currents from the Orient and Islam, from Greece and Spain, as well as Italy ; Frederick Barbarossa's court was the home and centre of the new German poetry, the romances of courtly love and the epics of knightly virtue, beginning about 1150 with *King Rother* and with Conrad of Regensburg's rendering of the *Song of Roland*. Poets and Minnesänger, such as

---

[1] A commemorative lecture delivered before the Cambridge University History Society on January 21, 1955.

Frederick of Hausen and Henry of Morungen, who had grown up
at Barbarossa's court, accompanied the emperor on his Italian
expeditions ; they belonged to the 'Hohenstaufen circle', and
seemed to reflect, like the Archpoet and the imperial chaplain, Godfrey of Viterbo, the ethos of Frederick's entourage and the chivalrous
qualities of which he himself was the personification. Throughout
the poem, a commentator has said of Conrad's *Roland*, 'one could
replace Charlemagne's name by Frederick's and no essential contradiction would result'. Frederick's great court at Mainz in 1184,
attended by more than seventy princes from all the lands between
Illyria and Spain—an assembly, the chronicler wrote, so notable
and distinguished that no other could compare with it—and the
festivities at Milan two years later, when his son, Henry, married
Constance of Sicily and was raised to the rank of 'Caesar', stood
out, for those looking back from the divisions and weaknesses of
subsequent centuries, as high-water marks not only in Frederick's
reign, but also in Germany's past.

But this picture of achievement and progress and the flowering
of German culture has not gone unchallenged, and the more closely
we look at Frederick's reign and work, the more we become aware
of inner contradictions.

First of all, Frederick's Italian policy, as Georg von Below
trenchantly demonstrated in 1927, was of doubtful benefit to
Germany.[1] The vast effort to restore imperial rule in Italy, which
had gradually come to a standstill during the fifty years preceding
Frederick's accession, was—von Below argued—a diversion of
German energies away from their natural orbit, just at the moment
when eastern colonization was opening new possibilities north of
the Alps ; it forced Barbarossa, also, to dubious compromises with
the German princes, which strengthened their position in relation
to the crown, and so hindered a healthy development of German
government, in line with that which was taking place simultaneously
in France and England. Moreover, if Barbarossa's achievement
was so remarkable, why did it fail to leave a more substantial legacy?
Only eight years after the emperor's death in 1190, Germany was
involved in a major crisis and a civil war from which it never fully
recovered. Was this, as so many German historians have argued,

---

[1] G. von Below, *Die italienische Kaiserpolitik des deutschen Mittelalters mit besonderem
Hinblick auf die Politik Friedrich Barbarossas* (1927).

simply the result of an unholy fate, which robbed Germany of its ruler, Henry VI, at the early age of thirty-two, or was it not rather a sign of hidden defects in Barbarossa's work? England in the same period stood the strain of Richard I's absence and Henry III's minority; and it is not unwarranted to suppose that a strong political structure in Germany might have done likewise. If accidents like the death of Henry VI were really decisive, the reason must be sought in some weakness or deficiency in the constitutional situation, and so historians were led to examine more closely the structure and machinery of German government under Frederick Barbarossa.

But here again interpretation and assessment have been widely divergent. Karl Hampe, who was famed for his careful and balanced judgement, considered Frederick's policy neither ' creative ' nor constructive; it was not, he held, Frederick's policy, either its direction or its results, but ' his strong, heroic personality, the perfect expression of German knighthood in the first bloom of its youth ', that accounted for his high place in German memories.[1] Subsequent German historians, on the other hand, impressed by the new tendencies of Hohenstaufen territorial policy in the twelfth century, by the ' centralization of administration ' and the systematic use of a new class of *ministeriales* as ' dependent officials ', saw in Frederick Barbarossa an innovator of the calibre of Henry II of England, during whose reign both the constitutional structure of Germany and the very conception of the nature of government were totally transformed. One recent writer, in fact, has gone so far as to ascribe to Frederick the introduction of ' state planning '. Barbarossa and his son, he says,[2] had ' a clearly conceived system ' ; they developed communications, founded towns and cities, pursued an ' economic and commercial policy ', all with the object of converting the king's scattered demesnes and manors, and the multifarious, disparate rights and holdings inherited from times long past, into a highly integrated ' modern ' state, on the basis of which they intended to overpower and obliterate the principalities and give Germany, in place of its traditional regionalism, a unified, progressive government.

Against this picture, however, which evidently postulates

---

[1] K. Hampe, *Deutsche Kaisergeschichte in der Zeit der Salier und Staufer* (10th ed., edited by F. Baethgen, 1949), 142.
[2] K. Bosl, *Die Reichsministerialität der Salier und Staufer* I (1950), 20 sqq.

creative statesmanship of a high order, we must set the judgement of
the American historian, J. W. Thompson, according to whom
Frederick neither understood nor sympathized with 'the new
political philosophy, the new economic conditions', or 'the new
social transformations which Europe was undergoing' in his day.
' In spite of '—or (perhaps we should say) because of—' his brilliant
talents ', Frederick was, in Thompson's view, ' a dangerous anachronism ' ;[1] and this is an assessment in which, in one degree or
another, many historians outside Germany have concurred. German
society in the twelfth century, French historians such as Marc
Bloch have maintained, was ' archaic ', not progressive ; and
Frederick himself was ' a backward-looking statesman determined
to restore the past '.[2]

Much the same conclusion was reached from another angle of
approach by the Austrian, Fritz Heer, in the most stimulating and
at the same time the most controversial reinterpretation of the
twelfth century which has appeared since the war.[3] Far from
Frederick being the ' prototype ' of the new courtly society, Heer
maintains, the first and essential precondition of the flowering of
German civilisation at the close of the twelfth century was the
collapse of Frederick's world. In architecture and plastic art the
age of Frederick was ' a time of lassitude ', in poetry it was marked
by bluntness, uncouthness, tastelessness, and lack of style, and
nothing was more remote from the feeling for nature and humanity
which enters German poetry at the turn of the twelfth and thirteenth
centuries with Wolfram of Eschenbach, Gottfried of Strassburg
and Walther von der Vogelweide. Deceit, harshness, cruelty—not
the chivalrous virtues of self-discipline and the golden mean (*mâze*),
of generosity (*milte*) and courtesy (*hoevescheit*)—were Frederick's
characteristics ; he was untouched by the spiritual and cultural
ferment of his century. His rule in Italy was a regime of fear and
terror, the whole theory of Hohenstaufen imperialism was ' the
greatest reaction, in the political and ideological sphere, which we
know of in the history of the Christian west ', and the lack of any
new constructive idea, which is so strikingly apparent in German
architecture at the time, was symptomatic of the inner weaknesses

---

[1] J. W. Thompson, *Feudal Germany* (1928), 275.
[2] *The Shorter Cambridge Medieval History* I (1952), 562; cf. M. Bloch, *La Société
féodale* II (1940), 222 sqq.
[3] F. Heer, *Aufgang Europas* (1949) ; *Die Tragödie des heiligen Reiches* (1 52).

and uncertainty and the backwardness of Germany during Frederick's epoch. Because Frederick was the prisoner of an outmoded way of life and an out-of-date philosophy, his whole scheme of government was ' reactionary and anachronous '.

These judgements, conflicting and often flatly contradictory, reflect something of the problems which any attempt to assess Frederick's work, and his place in German and European history, must take into account. Some of the difficulty arises from the fact that his personality remains enigmatic. We do not know, for example—although attempts have been made to distinguish in the official correspondence between Frederick's own style and that of his chancellor—how far the policy of his early years reflected his own conceptions, how far it was the work of the imperious, gifted Rainald of Dassel, who held the chancellorship from 1156 to his death in 1167. But we must bear in mind the inevitable changes of attitude and temperament which experience forces on any ruler or stateman, particularly if he reigns for thirty-eight years, and resist the temptation to construct a single, consistent line of policy, and still more a coherent system. Many discrepancies and not a few errors in judgement may be attributed to neglect of this elementary precaution. More serious, however, is the tendency to adopt modern standards of measurement. Ever since the middle of the nineteenth century, when Germany was divided between the *kleindeutsch* and the *grossdeutsch* parties, historians have read into Frederick's actions the problems of their own day. For nineteenth-century Austrians, such as Ficker, his imperial policy was beneficial both to Germany and to Italy ; for Prussians, such as Sybel, it was an ill-rewarded sacrifice of Germany's national interests to the supra-national ideals of a Christian commonwealth. But after 1871 and still more in the nineties, when Germany embarked on its new ' world policy ', Prussian historians endorsed Frederick's imperialism as a useful background for Hohenzollern pretensions ; while at a later stage, during the Third Reich, it came into its own as a precedent for German political direction and hegemony in central Europe. To-day—as might be expected—Germans see in it a worthy precursor of the ideal of ' western union ' ;[1] while Heer's views are bitterly assailed as a reflection of the defeatist mood of 1945. In addition, the Italian Risorgimento contributed its own

[1] *Historische Zeitschrift* CLXXVIII (1954), 491.

interpretation, in which the events of the reign, particularly the conflict with the Lombard communes, were judged from the point of view of Italian nationalism.

In all these ways modern preoccupations have distorted historical perspectives ; and it is obvious that if we wish to escape these distortions, the first thing we have to do is to place Frederick's policy and actions, their possibilities and limitations, against the background of his own time and circumstances. Only thus can we hope to build adequate safeguards against tendentious intepretation.

*   *   *

Looking back from the vantage-point of the present, we can see, and historians are becoming increasingly aware, that the twelfth century was one of the great constructive ages in European history. Its importance in the development of Europe can only be understood by taking a wide view.

Three times in a development spanning more than a thousand years western Europe has passed through a major crisis ; three times it has undergone a revolutionary upheaval, which not only shattered the existing political order, but also transformed men's outlook upon the world, their attitude to God, to nature, and to their fellows ; and three times it has emerged strengthened, rather than weakened, and with new aspirations and new energies to devote to new tasks. The first crisis followed the accession of pope Gregory VII in 1073, and lasted fifty years, perhaps three-quarters of a century. It was a time of ferment with which in magnitude only two other ages in European history can compare : the one is the period which began in 1517, when Luther nailed his Ninety-Five Theses to the church-door in Wittenberg, and which lasted to 1555 ; the other comprises the revolutionary decades which followed the summoning of the States-General by Louis XVI in 1788, and lasted until 1815. To conservatives and traditionalists the upheavals which followed these three events seemed to mark the dissolution of all social bonds and to portend the imminent collapse of European civilisation. But, as so often, the pessimism of contemporaries was unjustified. The attack on the old order, the weakening of established controls and inhibitions, and the piercing of the age-old crust of habit and tradition, created a situation in which forces and impulses hitherto latent or suppressed, found new scope ; the hammer-blows of revolutionary events, following hard one upon another, opened men's eyes, increased their experience, and widened their horizons ; and the result was the rise of social forms and of a level of civilisation immeasurably richer and freer and fuller than had gone before, though also far more complex and difficult to manipulate. The liberating force of the Reformation, the new outlets it created for human activity in every sphere, are common-places of history ; just as it is a platitude to say that the nineteenth century is the child of the French Revolution, not merely in the sense that every fruitful idea of the period after 1815 was born either of opposition or adherence to the revolutionary tenets, but also, more pregnantly, because it mobilized new forces which the *ancien régime* failed to use, and threw them with immense vigour into the task of building a new world. The place of the twelfth century in an earlier but no less significant and formative phase of European development, is strikingly similar ; and that is why it has always received the close attention of those historians whose vision of history has been guided first and foremost by the desire to penetrate below the surface to the forces, and events and personali-ties, which have shaped the course and determined the character of European civilisation. As a ' seminal age '—as one of the three great turning-points when European society swung upwards on to a new plane—the twelfth century has a relevance and actuality to-day, which few other periods of European history share in equal measure.

A few indications must suffice of the nature of the crisis in which the new cosmogony of the twelfth century was born. First of all, it was a crisis in the relations of church and state. The church, in the name of ecclesiastical liberty, demanded and secured a strict separation and delimitation between spiritual and temporal. The state was ' secularized ', excluded (on principle at least) from inter-ference in the spiritual sphere. Thereby the position of the monarchy in society was radically altered. The king was shorn of his priestly character and qualities, and of the rights over the church that went with them, and became a ' secular ruler '. He was forced back, as never before, upon the secular foundations of government ; and everywhere the king, ' secularized ' or ' desacralized ' in this way, began to expand his secular prerogatives.

But if the two powers were separate, it followed that the state was supreme in its own sphere ; it was an end in itself, rather than an instrument for furthering the realization of the City of God on earth. This was a revolutionary change in the basic assumptions of political thought, from which thinkers such as John of Salisbury soon drew practical consequences ; it justified rulers in building up the legal and material basis of their supremacy. No longer able to rely on the bishops and clergy, they began to develop new organs of administration. And the conception of the nature of the state changed correspondingly : hitherto an association of personal groups, held together by bonds of personal loyalty, it now became a territorial unit—a metamorphosis which the change in the English king's title, from *rex Anglorum* to *rex Angliae*, aptly symbolizes. Furthermore, this change favoured greater homogeneity of government ; and although the nobility successfully resisted depression of its privileged status, everywhere by the thirteenth century social stratification had been simplified, the infinite gradations of earlier societies reduced to manageable proportions, more amenable to the control and exploitation of an increasingly uniform organization of government.

The second great consequence of the Investiture Contest—as it is traditionally but inadequately called—was therefore a social revolution ; and if one aspect of this was the depression and obliteration of old social groups, of far greater importance was the rise to pre-eminence of a new class : the knighthood. This is the first great shift in class-structure in European history, and it is characteristic that every time European civilisation has made a great leap forward into the dark and unknown—as it did in the twelfth century, and again after the Reformation and after the French Revolution— it has been carried forward by a new class which had assured its position in the preceding turmoil. The great constructive vigour of the twelfth century was contributed by the knight-class—a small stratum of society by modern standards, but infinitely wider than any which had borne the burden of government in Europe before[1] —and it was through enlisting the knighthood in its services that the monarchy in the twelfth century strode ahead.

But the ferment after 1075 cut into the texture of European civilisation more deeply than merely at its political edge. The church, which had claimed independence in order to deepen its

---

[1] 'Many times ten thousand,' says Michael Seidlmayer of the German *Rittertum* of the period ; *Weltbild und Kultur Deutschlands im Mittelalter* (1954), 44.

spirituality, discovered new religious values, which quickly permeated thought and sentiment. The very conception of God was
subtly transformed : not the divine majesty, august and awe-
inspiring, but the passion and suffering of Christ on earth, the
human in the divine, became the dominant note. The cult of the
Virgin Mary worked similarly, introducing a new tenderness which
powerfully affected the ethic of chivalry. With St. Bernard, who is
as representative of the end of the period of change as Gregory
VII is of its thunderous beginning, mysticism came into its own.
Spiritual turmoil, the search for a mystical union with God, the
drama of suffering and redemption, individualized religious experience, and made it accessible to the unlettered multitude.

On the other hand, the polemics and propaganda of the revolutionary period sharpened intellectual weapons ; in the ferment of
the Investiture Contest the new science of dialectic scholasticism,
with its close analysis of words and concepts, was born. And just
as the new sensibility quickened lay society, and quickly found its
way into poetry and literature, so also the new intellectual discipline
was something the laity could use, for example in the analysis and
logical grounding of royal rights. Precisely because the church had
insisted on a sharp division between clergy and laity, and placed
the latter in an inferior position, lay culture, as it arose, followed a
course of its own, distinct from and sometimes hostile to that of the
church. The development of lay society had gone forward too
quickly for men—and women—to accept the passive, inferior role
which clerical assumptions assigned to them. Not a few, seeking an
active Christian way of life, from which the hierarchic church seemed
to exclude the laity, strayed into heresy ; but the majority concentrated
upon the creation of a new secular culture, in which they could
better enjoy the good things of the world about them. Thus, side
by side with the asceticism of the Cistercians and the heresies which
are so characteristic of the twelfth century, there arises—for the
first time in western Europe—a distinctively lay civilisation which
affirms and embraces with *élan* the world of here and now—that
same world which had so long been condemned and derided as a
transitory, worthless vale of tears.

Thus the years between 1075 and St. Bernard's death in 1153
saw the irruption of new ideas and perceptions, new disciplines
and new attitudes to the world, which found their anchorage in the

G

'national' monarchies—the term is anachronistic, but it is hard to
think of a better—which were everywhere in process of consolidation. For the final result of the Investiture Contest was a revolutionary change in the political structure of Europe. In the long
struggle with the imperial power, popes such as Gregory VII and
Urban II had turned for support to the states on the periphery of
the Empire, had formed links with the Norman conquerors of
England and Sicily, and with the Christian rulers of Spain, who were
engaged in reconquering the peninsula from the Moors ; they had
taken refuge in France, and developed relations with Denmark in
the north and Hungary and Croatia in the east, and even with far-off
Russia. The result was to activate the new monarchies, to make
them conscious of their independence, but above all it changed
the balance of power in Europe. Where, in the tenth and eleventh
centuries, the great imperial *bloc* in central Europe, which had
recovered earliest from the anarchy of the ninth century, dominated
the scene, in the twelfth century Europe became a 'many-voiced
choir of relatively free personalities'. The First Crusade, in 1095,
demonstrated the unity of Europe in the face of Islam and the
East ; but it was a unity in plurality, based on the interplay of
diverse cultures. The vernacular literatures of the twelfth century
attest at the same time both the effervescence of lay civilisation and
the progress of national differentiation ; and it has been said of the
period, without undue exaggeration, that its most lasting contribution lies in the fact that, in place of the monolithic society of the
middle ages, a weary derivation from late antiquity, it brought
about the birth of the rich, diversified European society in which
our own civilisation is embedded. If for eight hundred years Europe
has been the chief centre of political experiment, economic expansion
and intellectual discovery, it first gained this position as a result of
the revolution we have tried briefly to survey.

The course of events brought the new currents, which had been
moving below the surface, into the open. So long as the forces
which had brought about the revolution—above all, the reformed
papacy—retained the initiative and enforced a self-confident leadership, the counter-currents which the impetus of reform had stirred
and stimulated, were held in check ; hence the extraordinary
complexity of the early twelfth century. The characteristic of
this period is not the prevalence of clear-cut lines of development

but the lack of prevalent tendencies. But after the settlement of
the political conflict between empire and papacy in 1122 by the
Concordat of Worms, itself a weary compromise, the vigour,
idealism, and deep conviction which had carried forward the reforming movement, began to decline. The papacy, having made itself a
political force and an instrument of power, became the prisoner of
its own success; the pope was ever more deeply involved in legal,
worldly, administrative transactions, and the papal throne was
coveted for the power it gave. The first threat of schism came in
1124, on the death of Calixtus II, who had negotiated the Concordat
of Worms; it turned into reality on the death of his successor,
Honorius II, in 1130. Unlike the preceding schism, which had
been brought about by the conflict with the emperor, Henry IV,
the schism between 1130 and 1138 was essentially an internal
affair, a canker in the heart of the church, which painfully demonstrated the collapse of the old unity of purpose. It was no acciden-
that it was followed, almost immediately, by the revolt of the
Commune of Rome, where the effects of the growing papal immert
sion in worldly affairs were most directly felt, and by the attack of
Arnold of Brescia on the wealth of the pope and clergy, and the
demand for a return to apostolic poverty.

Already here the inner contradictions which marred the reform
movement and brought it to a halt, are fully evident. But the final
check was the failure of the Second Crusade. If the First Crusade
had revealed the papacy at the height of its power, with the knighthood of Europe grouped together under its banner, the Second
Crusade, in which all the antagonisms of the new European powers
flared up with disastrous results, was an open demonstration of its
powerlessness and inability to impose a pattern on Europe. When
St. Bernard, the inspiration behind the Crusade, died in 1153—
shaken, disappointed, and self-critical at the outcome—it was the
end of an epoch; his *De consideratione*, with its heart-felt cry for a
total revision of the pope's attitude to his new-won powers, was
a last despairing attempt to reverse the downward trend; but
already before his death Bernard—the enigma in whose soul had
so faithfully reflected the discrepancies and contradictions of the
preceding age—had ceased to represent the mood and temper of
the times. The failure of the church to live up to its ideals had

galvanized into life a reaction which, already before 1153, was gathering force.

*   *   *

It is against this background that we must seek to place Frederick Barbarossa, and to assess his work. He profited from, and rose on the crest of, the reaction which became a positive, directive force after the failure of the Second Crusade in 1149.

But this reaction was general throughout Europe. It expressed in its simplest form the widespread desire of all classes for order, stability, and stronger government after the turmoil of the two preceding generations, and everywhere it played into the hands of monarchs to whom the previous conflicts had given a new consciousness of their rights and prerogatives. In Sicily, where contact with the Mediterranean civilisations of Islam and Byzantium was an early stimulus, Roger II (1105–1154) had already made rapid progress. Under Henry II (1154–1189), England followed the same course. In France, though here achievement was less spectacular, Louis VI (1108–1137) and Louis VII (1137–1180) were laying the foundations for the achievements of Philip Augustus (1180–1223), while, by a process still obscure, their country was gaining an undisputed intellectual pre-eminence in the west. Even the Roman Empire of Byzantium in the east, which had seemed near to collapse after the defeat of Manzikert in 1071, had made a brilliant recovery ; under the emperor Manuel Comnenos (1143–1180), it was again pursuing an active policy not only in central Europe, but also in Italy, where Manuel sought to recover both the former Byzantine territories and (following precedents of his father and grandfather, in 1112 and 1139–41) the old, undivided imperial title, as it had existed before 800.

We must bear these facts in mind when we seek to understand Frederick's position. That he should, after he succeeded to the German throne in 1152, have been influenced by the new currents, which were carrying forward the monarchy everywhere—and, in particular, by the example of the new imperialism of Constantinople —is not surprising ; and much which seems to single him out, if Germany is considered in isolation, is in fact part of a common advance, observable throughout Europe. What is important, in assessing his place in history, is not to establish that Germany, under his rule, participated in the general recovery, but rather to pick out those factors in the situation he inherited, which made his task different from that confronting contemporaries, such as Henry II of England. In this way we can get some idea of the limitations within which he worked, and a clue to the reasons why, in spite of brilliant successes and apparently solid achievements, the foundations he left for the future were so much less stable than those bequeathed by his contemporary, Louis VII of France, to his Capetian successors.

The first and obvious fact, from this point of view, is that the upheavals of the Investiture Contest hit Germany and Italy far more seriously, and for longer duration, than other countries, and the task of rebuilding was therefore more complicated. Just when in France some semblance of order was arising out of the feudal anarchy, Germany was plunged into disorder, while in Italy the civil wars and the collapse for half a century of royal government gave the rising communes of Lombardy, already flourishing from the expansion of Mediterranean trade and avid for autonomy, the opportunity for self-assertion. In Germany, to a degree far greater than in the England of Stephen's reign, the weakening of the monarchy resulted in the strengthening of an aristocracy, which had always tended to emphasize its independence and its ' inborn rights ' ; while the material basis of royal power, the king's lands and estates and even his judicial rights, shrank to such a degree that already the monarchy had lost its foothold in the whole of northern Germany.

And yet this same monarchy carried, as a legacy from the emperors of the tenth and eleventh centuries, a burden of tradition which no other country in western Europe had to bear. This is the second differentiating feature in the situation which Frederick Barbarossa found confronting him. The imperial connexion and the imperial tradition were there, unalterable facts which could not simply be written off as anachronisms ; for if, in fact, the connexion between Germany and Italy had become brittle and tenuous under Barbarossa's two immediate predecessors, Lothar II (1125–1138) and Conrad III (1138–1152), this was due to abnormal circumstances and implied no renunciation of imperial rights or claims.

But this inheritance from Carolingian and Ottonian times was not merely an additional political complication of the first magnitude, which the economic and political rise of the Italian communes made more problematical than ever before. It was also the source of an old-fashioned ideology, binding Germany to a past which had irretrievably disappeared in the upheavals of the Investiture Contest. 'Because its whole development had been intimately bound up with the traditional concept of a universal Christian empire, Germany in its endeavour to retain its imperial pre-eminence, clung instinctively and far more tenaciously than any other European people to the old world-order and the old norms, with which the imperial idea was inseparably connected.'[1] Thus 'it was thrust on to the defensive', stood in the leeway of the new developments, and opened itself hesitantly and suspiciously to the manifold impulses coming from the west. Frederick himself, who had been born with no expectation of succession to the throne, and received only the simple upbringing of a Swabian nobleman, had his roots in the old world. In spite of his later recourse to the sharp weapon of Roman law, there was nothing about him of that caustic realism —hard, biting and 'modern', yet teeming with acute intellectual curiosity—which is so characteristic of the court of Henry II of England. It was the vision of his uncle, bishop Otto of Freising, which moulded and formed his mind : the vision—Frankish, Ottonian, pre-Gregorian—of a united Christian commonwealth, governed harmoniously by empire and papacy in co-operation, the very antithesis of the separation of church and state to which, after the upheavals between 1075 and 1122, Europe was irretrievably committed.

Because his mind was nurtured in this conservative environment, the empire in its accepted significance, the imperial ideas and traditions which had survived from the eleventh century, were the dominant motives in Frederick's outlook as a man, and in his policy as a ruler. To judge from his own utterances and from the proclamations and statements put out on his behalf, they were more important to him fundamentally than his position as a German king; and the tendency in recent historical investigation to transfer emphasis from his imperial policy, from the dramatic story of his conflict with the Italian cities and pope Alexander III, to the more prosaic analysis of his German administration—though it has admittedly corrected earlier exaggerations—has perhaps done poor service, in so far as it has obscured, if not reversed, his own scale of

[1] Seidlmayer, op. cit., 35.

values. His central thought was that which he announced to pope Eugenius III at the beginning of his reign : the restoration and revival of the empire, and the re-establishment of its ' former emin- ence ', and since this was his own assessment, it is here, and not in his German policy, that we must take our starting-point.

But if, for Frederick, the empire was no merely temporal institu- tion, but one of the twin pillars upon which the Christian world rested, that does not mean—as so often has been maintained—that he was inspired simply by an unpractical vision of reviving the empire of Henry III or Otto I or Charles the Great. Frederick's imperialism was rather a singular combination of old and new, which never fused into a harmonious whole. New, in the first place, were the grounds of his conflict with pope Alexander III. Unlike the conflict between Henry IV and Gregory VII, it was concerned not with fundamental issues in the relations of church and state, but with concrete territorial questions, spheres of interest, the extent and limits of Frederick's dominion in Italy.[1] Secondly, it seems beyond doubt that Frederick, from the very beginning, had his eye on the wealth of Italy. His imperialism, in other words, was tainted by economic motives, crude but characteristic of the new era ; the sense of religious duty, which had inspired Henry III's actions, was now diluted and adulterated by concrete secular interests, and Frederick did not hesitate, when it suited him, to base his claims on the brute fact of conquest.[2] We do not need to doubt that the conception of the empire as a divinely-ordained institution, serving universal rather than particular ends, was a reality in his mind ; and yet his imperial policy, as it was put into effect in Italy by German *ministeriales*, was so entangled in German interests that the Italians—who (apart from Milan) had for a brief moment welcomed his intervention—soon resisted it as a hateful, foreign, military occupation. But, above all else, the very circumstances which made a revival of the empire a matter of practical politics, were a result of the new conditions of the twelfth century. It was the new international situation in the Mediterranean world, the conflict of interests between Roger II of Sicily, the emperor Manuel Com- nenos, and pope Eugenius III, that created the opportunity and occasion for Frederick's intervention in Italy. He exploited the new possibilities, and in part at least his imperialism was a defensive

[1] Cf. Hampe, op. cit., 170.   [2] Cf. the passage cited below, p. 121.

reaction against the pretensions of the emperor Manuel. On the other hand, the rights and claims inherited from his German pre-decessors, the imperial tradition of Ottonian and Carolingian times, were no less fundamental. They provided the justification for his intervention—not merely to defend his rights to the Italian and imperial crowns, but also to assert his position as the legitimate protector of the Roman church—and Frederick could not jettison the older conception of empire, universal and Christian, which had haunted his predecessors, without cutting away the ground from under his own feet.

Frederick's imperial policy was thus, as a French historian has written,[1] ' two-faced ' ; it ' oscillated between two poles ', and sought to put through old claims with new weapons. The use of new notions of sovereignty, derived from Roman law, emphasized the secular foundations and character of the empire ; it was evidently an attempt, probably influenced by Byzantine example, to adapt imperial theory to new conditions. The canonisation of Charle-magne, on the other hand, which Barbarossa secured from the anti-pope, Paschal III, in 1165, appeared to denote a revival of the theocratic conceptions of earlier times. But such conceptions were an anachronism in the twelfth century. When, in 1160, Frederick attempted, as Henry III and others had done, to impose a pope of his own choice on the church, the revulsion was general. When, in 1162, Rainald of Dassel used Roman legal notions to claim the *dominium mundi* for Frederick and to depress the sovereigns of Europe to the status of provincial rulers or *reguli*, he produced a storm of protest. Who, wrote John of Salisbury, has made the Germans judges over the nations?

It is important to remember that for the bulk of his reign Fred-erick had the opinion of Europe against him, and that his imperial policy, far from restoring the status and authority of the empire in Europe, provoked hostility to it as an institution, and to the Germans as its possessors, such as had not hitherto existed. Only after his defeats at the hands of the Lombards had forced him to jettison the imperialism of his early years, and to compromise with pope Alex-ander III, did Frederick's reputation recover. The extraordinary success of his policy after the peace of Venice in 1177, and still more after the peace of Constance in 1183, has magnetized historians.

---

[1] R. Folz, *L'idée d'empire en occident du Ve au XIVe siècle* (1953), 117.

In Italy he had saved more than ever could have been expected of the material bases of imperial power; in Europe he had at long length secured a primacy, which found expression in his undisputed leadership of the Third Crusade. But these successes should not hide the profound transformation which had occurred. The settlement of 1183 was a compromise, in which Frederick's own deepest convictions were sacrificed. After 1183 the empire, which in Frederick's earlier vision had been imbued with the aura of divine dispensation, became, so far as Italy was concerned, the framework for a partnership of vested interests, the perquisites of which were shared between Milan and its associates—Frederick's old adversaries and new allies—German knights and administrators, Italian notables driven into Frederick's camp by fear of the communes, and the emperor himself. The unctuous verses and fulsome panegyrics of Godfrey of Viterbo or Gunther of Pairis, might gloss over, but for us they cannot conceal the fact that the ' system of Constance ', on which the imperial position now rested, was a highly artificial structure, full of inner contradictions, with few if any of the elements of stability.[1] As a concatenation of profitable rights, the empire was far more effective in 1190 than it had been in 1152 ; but as an attempt to realize Frederick's own imperial conceptions and beliefs, it had failed. The future lay with other forces, temporarily constrained within its framework but only awaiting the opportunity to break loose.

*   *   *

So long as there was any prospect of his imperial policy succeeding, Frederick relegated Germany to the second place—not, like his grandson, Frederick II, in the sense of sacrificing Germany to Italy, but rather because, with his high conception of his imperial mission, he rated his universal above his German responsibilities. It is, of course, true that his first concern at the beginning of his reign was to appease the aristocratic and dynastic feuds which had torn Germany under his predecessor, Conrad III ; the settlement with the powerful duke of Saxony, Henry the Lion, the conferment upon him of the duchy of Bavaria, and the creation of the duchy of Austria, in 1156, were necessary preconditions, without which an active imperial policy in Burgundy and Italy was out of the question

[1] Cf. H. Mitteis, *Der Staat des hohen Mittelalters* (2nd ed., 1944), 313.

But direct measures to strengthen royal government in Germany only came later, and seem to have been the consequence of Italian developments. Only after the formation of the Lombard League in 1167 had demonstrated that he could no longer rely for his resources upon Lombardy, did Frederick show a positive interest in building up and consolidating his German lands ; just as, later, the peace of Venice was the preliminary to his settlement of accounts with Henry the Lion, and the territorial reorganisation of 1180.

It is, of course, true that the strengthening of the German princes in the half-century preceding his election forced Frederick to be circumspect ; any hasty measure or incautious assertion of royal power might easily have brought about a recrudescence of anarchy. But it is clear also that he was prepared, because of the central importance he gave to the empire, to buy the support of the German princes for his activities in Italy by ' extravagant concessions '.[1] It has sometimes been implied, if not asserted, that behind this policy was a deep-laid plan to secure the resources of Lombardy in order to fortify the king's position in Germany and eventually to strike at the princes' power. But such arguments are not very plausible. The old thesis of a hidden conflict from the beginning of the reign between Frederick and Henry the Lion is no longer accepted by historians ; on the contrary, it is clear that Frederick was prepared to co-operate loyally with Henry and the other princes, and that the conflict with the Saxon duke was not of the emperor's seeking. We must remember that Frederick himself, by birth and upbringing, came from the ranks of the princely aristocracy, and shared their outlook ; he had no special preparation for the kingship, and, unlike Henry IV, felt no inherent contradiction between royal aims and princely interests. In his imperial capacity he may have seen himself imbued, in the spirit of Roman law, with the splendour of imperial majesty ; but there is no evidence that Roman conceptions played any part in Germany. As emperor he may have believed himself to possess the singular authority of God's chosen representative in the Christian commonwealth ; but as German ruler he was a feudal monarch exercising feudal suzerainty in a state which was a federation of feudal principalities, or—in an even more personal sense—an association of feudal princes, marked

[1] Many examples are collected by H. W. C. Davies, *English Historical Review* XXIV (1909), 770.

out by birth for dominion. Here again we can perceive an unresolved duality, or dichotomy, as characteristic of the man as of the Germany over which he ruled.

Such a conception of his position as German ruler was not, of course, irreconcilable with the strengthening of the prerogatives which accrued to the king, as the head of the feudal hierarchy, in a feudal society. It was, in fact, in this way and on this foundation that both Henry II of England and Philip Augustus of France consolidated their position, and the whole tendency of the age, after the loosening of bonds at the time of the Investiture Contest, was towards a closer articulation of feudal society and a new emphasis on the centripetal forces in feudal government. It is unwarranted to suppose that Frederick was a blind reactionary, unaffected by these tendencies. But it is equally unwarranted to suppose that he was in the van of the new movement, striving by careful systematic planning to weld Germany into a unitary state; and much recent interpretation, particularly by German historians, seems to exaggerate both the ' modernity ' of his outlook and the measure of his achievement.

It is true that the territorial power of the dynasty in south-west Germany was strengthened, the royal estates consolidated and built up by purchase and exchange; it is true that he employed the new knightly class of royal *ministeriales* as administrators on a scale without parallel in the past; and it is true also that every opportunity was used to extend the area of direct royal government in a wide belt running eastwards from Alsace and the upper Rhine through Franconia to the borders of Bohemia. It is easy, looking back, to see in all this a deliberate plan; but it is, of course, a fact that royal rights and possessions had suffered cruelly in the preceding anarchy, and that reorganisation was as obvious a remedy as it was an imperative need. Ever since the beginning of the century the German princes, profiting from the weakening of the monarchy in the Investiture Contest, had been building up their lordships, rounding off their territories, overcoming aristocratic opposition, and laying the foundation for the principalities of later times. That Frederick should tread the same path is not surprising, but is no proof of exceptional statesmanship or far-sighted vision. German historians have frequently asserted that he was ahead of the princes in the development of a new territorial administration, and that he provided a precedent and a model which they eagerly followed. It seems to me, on the contrary, that he does no more than keep in step ; and, as already indicated, reorganisation in Germany was less an end pursued for its own sake, because Frederick recognized its primary importance, than a result of checks in Italy. So far as the introduction of new principles and methods of government goes, it is difficult to find anything to differentiate Frederick from Henry the Lion, or from lesser potentates such as the dukes of Zähringen.

It is, indeed, precisely at this point that Frederick's limitations— the limitations both of his own statesmanship and of the material with which he had to work—become evident. German society was still ponderous, archaic, unmanageable, by comparison with the west or with Italy. Reconstruction, articulation, the implementation of new principles of political organization, were brought to a halt by an inert body of conservative prejudice, which absorbed their impact like a cushion. Feudalism, in England and France a powerful instrument of social and political cohesion, failed in Germany to produce the same effects ; all those elements of feudal practice, such as the feudal relief, which gave the monarchy a lever through which to exercise control, atrophied instead of developing.[1] Just when the English king was weaning the knighthood from a narrowly feudal conception of their place in society, the German *ministeriales*, advancing in rank and wealth and standing by their services to the crown in Germany and Italy, became a feudal class, aristocratic in outlook and aligned with aristocratic interests. To speak of the Hohenstaufen *ministeriales* as ' officials ', as is so often done, is a deceptive misuse of terms. Above all else, Frederick failed to develop central institutions to hold them in check. The strict accountability of the English sheriff at the exchequer in Westminster, the control exercised over the *baillis* of Philip Augustus by the *curia regis* in Paris, are without parallel in Frederick Barbarossa's Germany ; it is the most striking deficiency in his government, which shows more than anything else how far it was from being ' modern ' in conception.

In this connexion nothing is more symptomatic, in an age when money (rather than ' landed ' wealth) was becoming the sinew of government, than the lack of a specialized financial department.

---

[1] Cf. H. Mitteis, *Lehnrecht und Staatsgewalt* (1933), 672.

This deficiency reflects, without doubt, German economic back-wardness—the fact that it was still essentially a rural society, in which the towns only began to count in the period immediately following Barbarossa's death.[1] But it also reflects the lack of an administrative centre, in which the organs of central government might be located. At a time when Paris and London and Palermo were rapidly developing into capitals, when even Henry the Lion had an administrative centre for his Saxon state in Brunswick, Germany had neither a central administration nor a capital city. The reason, without doubt lay in the duality of Germany and the empire. Where, if the Empire were to have a capital, was it to be? Rome was excluded; for there the pope was supreme, and any attempt to set up imperial government in Rome was bound to provoke antagonism. But Rome, in any case, was eccentric as a capital for Frederick's dominions as a whole. Milan might have suited better, but the resistance of the Lombards prevented that. But fundamentally the issue went deeper, for a capital outside Germany would have been resented by the Germans, while a German capital was an affront to Italian sentiment and scarcely reconcilable with the theory of empire, as Frederick conceived it. Here again, in fact, we see an unresolved and insoluble dichotomy, which is like a canker at the heart of Frederick's work. When we are told that he built a structure capable of lasting and that only a series of misfortunes and accidents prevented success, we must bear in mind the inner contradictions which are visible from whatever angle we approach Frederick's work.

*   *   *

A final verdict will, I think, take into account the fact that Frederick responded to the new impulses of his time, and, particu-larly in the detail of his German government, his territorial policy and the use he made of the ministerial class, went along in step with them. He was no backward-looking visionary, attempting to restore the past, and even his imperialism was adapted to the circumstances of his time. But he was also not in advance of his age, and recent attempts to depict him as a great constructive statesman, with novel plans for a total transformation of German society, do not ring true. Rather, he reacts to events by a series of expedients, which reveal—as his experience grows—considerable

[1] Cf. G. Kirchner, *Deutsches Archiv* X (1954), 473.

tactical and diplomatic skill, but still mark a departure from, if not an adulteration of, his own inherent beliefs.

By 1183 the imperialism with which he began his reign had been emptied of spiritual content, and for that reason—not simply because of blows inflicted by enemies without—the empire crumbled. His rule in Germany has nothing to mark it out from that of the rising principalities, and there is little evidence that he thought to introduce new principles or to govern otherwise than in association and co-operation with the princes. His conception of government was aristocratic, and it is doubtful whether he entertained any notion of displacing the older form of government, held together by personal loyalties and the bond of man to man, by a territorial state, divided into uniform territorial districts and administered by bureaucratic methods.[1] Such ideas may well have been in the mind of Frederick II, who was familiar with that type of government in Sicily ; but it would be anachronistic to attribute them to the earlier Hohenstaufen.

The famous events of 1180, when Henry the Lion was deprived of his duchies of Saxony and Bavaria, provide perhaps the best indication of Frederick's attitude and limitations at the height of his power. As is well known, both duchies were divided, and thus weakened ; but the emperor himself retained none of the escheated lands in his own direct control. Was the reason, as has sometimes been argued,[2] simply that he was prevented from bringing them under the direct administration of the crown by an inflexible principle of German feudal law—the so-called *Leihezwang*—by which the king was compelled to grant out escheated fiefs after a year and a day? In reality, it seems more likely that he granted them out again because he lacked the means to administer them as part of the royal demesne. But, in either case, the backwardness of German government, by comparison with France—where Philip Augustus in 1204 had no difficulty in sequestrating Normandy and adding it to the royal demesnes—is very striking. And yet more fundamental is the doubt whether Frederick would have wished to sequestrate Saxony and Bavaria, if he could have done so. From the beginning of his reign he had relied on the princes to bring the unruly nobility, who had risen so high in the preceding anarchy, under control ; and it seems most probable that, in his view, the

---

[1] Cf. H. Heimpel, *Kaiser Friedrich Barbarossa und die Wende der Staufischen Zeit* (1942).
[2] Cf. Mitteis, *Staat des hohen Mittelalters*, 299.

government of the great duchies by the princes was natural and
proper, and that he had no intention of breaking with the guiding
principles of aristocratic society.

Frederick, as I see him, was essentially a man of conservative
and traditional temperament, who accepted implicitly the environment into which he was born. That it was impossible, after the
upheavals of the preceding generations, to go on in the old way was
not his fault, but he did his best to uphold what he regarded, simply
and unquestioningly, as God's dispensation. In detail he was
prepared to innovate; but his ideals and objectives were in a tradition
which events were overtaking, and though it is evident, as time
passes, that he is trying to respond and to adapt his policy to new
conditions, he never fully succeeded in bridging the gap. Hence we
are brought back to the fundamental dichotomy, the inner contradictions, on which I have insisted more than once. These contradictions, striking an echo in German society, complicated the transition from the old to the new. Put in the simplest of terms, the
failure—if failure it was—lay in the fact, that, having too much to
hold on to, the Germans slowly lost what they had; ' it was those
who had least who were able to move most freely to the new world
which was coming into existence '.[1] But it is permissible to question whether the word ' failure ' is really applicable to Frederick's
work. Even those who, looking backwards, know the outcome,
must take into account the many new developments after
Frederick's death, and it is impossible to demonstrate that the
undoubted weaknesses in the imperial structure, which Frederick
left untouched, could not have been resolved, if his son and
grandson had acted differently.

Frederick's achievement was, in fact, anything but inconsiderable. It can be measured by the difference between the pessimism
of Otto of Freising's world-chronicle, written in the uncertainty
and gloom of Conrad III's reign, and the proud confidence of his
Gesta Friderici. An age of tears, wrote Otto, had been succeeded
by an age of laughter; after a dark, rainy night, Frederick had
brought Germany a fresh, clear morning. But what he achieved
was due more to the strength of conservative tradition in Germany,
to the impetus of his own personality, and to the reaction which had
set in about the time of his accession, than to Frederick's power to

[1] R. W. Southern, *The Making of the Middle Ages* (1953), 20.

shape and create. So long as that reaction continued, it carried him along ; but when after a generation it began to slacken, and the older generation which had clung to traditional values passed away, the limitations of his work were not slow in making themselves evident.

All in all, the reign of Frederick Barbarossa marks the end of the old rather than the beginning of the new. His government depended too much on the personal energy of himself and his assistants, too little on the impersonal machinery of government, surer and less erratic, which elsewhere was coming into existence through specialization and differentiation in the royal household and the *curia regis*. The imperial structure which he sought to rebuild was too rigid to contain all the forces coming to life in the twelfth century ; and his attempts to find a place for them disrupted the old without satisfying the new, or bringing about a real revival. Germany was already differentiated from the west and Italy ; just as, in the nineteenth century, its response to the challenge of the French Revolution was different from that of England and France, so in the twelfth century, after the upheavals of the Investiture Contest, Germany went a way of its own. The interest of Frederick Barbarossa's reign is to see how and why this differentiation took place ; its lasting significance for Europe needs neither emphasis nor explanation.

7. The International Order and the Middle Ages

IT is a common assumption that the middle ages were the time of a 'universal community', and as such they have often been contrasted with the period of warring national states that was to follow.[1] Historians and others speak of 'mediaeval unity', and compare it with modern disunity, with the international anarchy unleashed by the rise of nationalism. It seems (so many think) that a stable international order, and a civilisation united in spirit, were fractured at the time of the Reformation, and that ever since then mankind has been engaged, fruitlessly and unsuccessfully, on the task of fitting together the shattered fragments. And so there are many people to-day, when Europe is desperately searching for a statute, who look back to the middle ages as an example and an ideal. They achieved (they say) what we are dismally failing to achieve. Have they not, then, something of real value to teach?

Those who look back in this way, seeking guidance from the past, point to one main difference between the mediaeval and the modern order. To-day the international order is built on shifting sands; it rests upon the unstable balance of a fluctuating number of states and governments, unequal in power and resources but all equal in their claim to sovereign independence; indeed, one might go further and say that it does not exist at all in its own right, but is simply a ratio, or formula, a coefficient between the Powers, which are the only realities in the international situation. In the middle ages, on the other hand, international society was upheld by the twin pillars of Empire and Papacy. The overriding authority, universally respected, of Empire and Papacy endowed the international structure with a stability and purpose and direction lacking to-day; and it was only the quarrels of Empire and Papacy, culminating in the bitter conflict between pope Innocent IV and the emperor Frederick II, that undermined the authority of both, and left

[1] Reprinted, with amplifications and some notes, from *The Listener*, April 1949.

the way free for the rise of ' nation states ' which knew no master
and recognised no law save the law of the jungle.

The classical formulation of the theory of Empire and Papacy
reaches right back to the last decade of the fifth century, when pope
Gelasius I addressed to the emperor Anastasius a letter which, it
has often been said, sounded the keynote for the next thousand
years of history. ' This world,' Gelasius wrote, ' is ruled by two
things, the sacred authority of the priesthood and the kingly power ';[1]
and the famous pronouncements of later popes, of Gregory VII or
Innocent III, with their similes of the ' sun ' and the ' moon ', and
their analogies of the ' two swords ', were little more than amplifications of the basic Gelasian principle. But it is important to look
not merely at the theory, but also at the actual political situation
obtaining at the time when Gelasius wrote. It was easy (and indeed
flattering) for the pope to write to the emperor as though empire
and papacy were the only two powers that counted ; but what do
we see if we look at Europe and the Mediterranean world at that
date? First of all, Europe was full of kings who recognized neither
pope nor emperor. In Gaul the Franks under Clovis were still
heathen ; Italy was in the hands of the Goths under Theodoric the
Great, and the Goths, though scrupulously respectful of the pope's
position, were not Catholics ; fifty years earlier the independence of
Vandal Africa had been formally recognized ; and these new Germanic states were already joined together in a series of alliances
forming an intricate system of balance of power. In the east, moreover, there was a great Persian empire, the equal of the Roman
empire ; they were (a Persian ambassador once said) ' like two light-
houses illuminating the world '. Later on, when the great Moslem
power of Islam arose, towering over the east, the imperial government did not hesitate, when it served its purpose, to speak of Rome
and Islam—not of the Empire and the Papacy—as the ' two powers
of the whole universe ' which ' excel and shine like the two great
luminaries in the firmament '.[2] Such statements, in short, were
diplomatic phrases, *politesses*, not a reflection of reality ; but they

---

[1] ' Duo sunt quippe, imperator auguste, quibus principaliter hic mundus regitur :
auctoritas sacra Pontificum et regalis potestas.' The text of the letter is printed in the
Canon Law (*Decretum, Dist.* XCVI, *c.* 10). An admirable brief commentary on this
famous document and on its history in the middle ages is to be found in R. Hull,
Medieval Theories of the Papacy (1934), 13–28.

[2] Cf. A. Vasiliev, *History of the Byzantine Empire* (2nd ed., 1952), 306.

were, of course, phrases used with a purpose. Pope Gelasius himself had a serious and understandable purpose : to warn the emperor not to trespass on the church's spiritual authority, and to do this he asserted the independence of the two powers, spiritual and temporal. But he could not have taken up this attitude of independence, if he had not been able to rely upon the protection of the Gothic king in Italy.

From the beginning to the end of the middle ages, therefore, we must be careful never to abstract theories from the actual political situation to which they relate, or from the concrete political objectives they were intended to serve. They were rarely statements of accepted fact, but rather means to an end ; and if we separate them from their context and string them together to form one consistent theory of ' mediaeval unity ',[1] we shall fail to understand the mainsprings of mediaeval political action just as surely as if we supposed to-day that the principles of the United Nations charter were in themselves a sufficient key to the ramifications of contemporary international politics. Innocent III's famous ' deliberation ' on the Empire was not—as sometimes seems to be assumed—a dispassionate statement of accepted political theory, but an argument carefully chosen to weaken the hold of the German emperors over Italy. In the same way Dante's famous defence of the Empire a century later will appear—if we set it against the actual political background in which it was written—not as an expression of belief in universal monarchy, and of a conception of ' Europe as a unified Christian community ', but as a theoretical (or ideological) rallying-cry for those in Italy who, hoping for the establishment of an Italian national kingdom, were opposed to the papacy, and in particular to the political influence which, with papal support, France was exercising at that time throughout the Italian peninsula.[2] And when Dante's contemporary, Engelbert of Admont, stated bluntly that ' there is only one state of the whole Christian people and therefore necessarily only one head of this state ', he was not stating a fact—the facts at the beginning of the fourteenth century were quite the contrary

---

[1] This, as it seems to me, is what Gierke does in his famous essay (translated by F. W. Maitland), *Political Theories of the Middle Ages* (1900).

[2] This view of Dante's position was convincingly set out by F. Bock, ' Kaisertum, Kurie und Nationalstaat im Beginn des 14. Jahrhunderts ', *Römische Quartalschrift* XLIV (1936), 105–122, 169–220, particularly pp. 207–210. Cf. also the same author's book, *Reichsidee und Nationalstaaten* (1943).

—but setting out an argument against those, in France and in Italy, who were planning the dismemberment of the German empire as it then existed.

The statement that ' there is only one state of the whole Christian people and therefore only one head of this state ', was no more true of the middle ages than it is true to-day. The unity of Christendom, such as it was—this unity which itself was more a theory than a fact—was never expressed in political terms, never took the shape of a single political organization for the whole of Christendom, or even for the whole of western or Latin Christendom. That is not intended to imply that Engelbert's words (or those of Dante or pope Innocent) were empty phrases, lip service paid with the tongue in the cheek. People in the middle ages had a real longing, just as we have, for a unity reflected in an ordered relationship of political societies ; indeed, in a way this desire burnt in them more fiercely, because much of their thought was cast in a religious mould, and so they tended to think of international order, not in political terms, but as part of the Divine Order of the Universe, in which the Deity himself had related each part to the whole.

From the eighth to the thirteenth centuries there were few who doubted God's will that Christian men should, somehow and at some time, be bound together in a Christian ' empire '. But there was no agreement as to the character this unity should take. Charles the Great's ideas are strikingly different from pope Gregory VII's, pope Gregory's from those of the emperor Henry VI ; there were, in fact, Frankish, papal, Roman, Byzantine theories of the Empire, and each of these underwent change in the course of time. Furthermore, the very fact that mediaeval people treated political relations as part of the Divine Order meant that they rarely stopped to think seriously about the actual mechanism of international society ; they derived it instead by induction from first principles, and it all remained in a realm of theory, which sometimes is arid and sometimes is impressive, but which never descends from a moral to a practical plane.

The ideal, hoped for, dreamt of, was a union of all Christian folk, a Christian ' commonwealth '. The reality was the state we call the Holy Roman Empire.[1] It has often been argued that the one

[1] On the title ' Holy Roman Empire ', which is still often used with confusing inaccuracy, cf. below, p. 106.

was an approximation to, the earthly counterpart of, the other. Such possibilities may have stimulated the imaginations of a few great mediaeval thinkers, such as Alcuin ; but they never reflected the facts, and it would be rash to assume that they represented the attitude of statesmen. We know something of the mind and calculations of emperors such as Charlemagne, Otto the Great and Frederick Barbarossa, and we can say with a good deal of certainty that their ideas of their imperial position, and indeed of the meaning of *imperium*, were far more limited and concrete. World-dominion, a ' universal state ', did not enter into their calculations ; the ' empire ' for them was the complex of territory over which they actually ruled. Some of them, Charlemagne himself, and Otto I, made use of the Christian ' ideology ' (as we may call it) to subjugate and establish their hegemony over the heathen peoples on their borders ; but others did not hesitate to league with non-Christian peoples against Christians—with heathen Slavs, for example, against Christian Poles and Hungarians—when it suited their political purposes.[1] Moreover there was no attempt—unless the emperor Henry VI is thought to have been an exception[2]—to extend their sway over the whole of western Christendom. England first and foremost, and Catholic Spain and the northern countries, always remained outside the sphere of the Empire ; and after the break-up of the Carolingian state, France consistently rejected anything approaching imperial suzerainty.

Are we, then, to say that there was no difference, in regard to the problem of international order, between the middle ages and the modern world ? That is clearly not the case. First of all, there obviously was a sense, anchored in deep religious conviction, of overriding unity. This was, indeed, a partial unity, a unity of Christendom or even only of western Christendom, which excluded the two great civilisations of the mediaeval centuries, the Moslem civilisation of Islam and the Orthodox civilisation of Byzantium. Even so, the line of approach was fundamentally opposite to that of to-day : the starting-point was the ' whole ' (whatever was meant by the ' whole '), and no one thought of the international order as simply the sum-total of existing sovereign states.

One reason for this is obvious ; namely, that the very ideas

---

[1] Cf. F. Dvornik, *The Making of Central and Eastern Europe* (1949), cap V.
[2] That is not my own view ; cf. *The Origins of Modern Germany* (1946), 195 sqq.

which underlie our current conceptions of international order, the
idea of the state itself, of sovereignty, of nationality, were not in
existence from the beginning and evolved but slowly. The old
view that the very conception of nationalism was foreign to the
middle ages—one of the great legends from which the fabric of
history is woven—is, no doubt, an exaggeration ;[1] but it still remains
true that there only slowly came about that enslavement of the
consciousness of existing national differences to the narrow, self-
seeking political objectives of governments which is what makes
nationalism dangerous and obnoxious. This was because government itself in the early middle ages was weak and incapable of
consistently pursuing national aims. But as soon as Europe had
recovered from the anarchy which assailed it in the ninth century,
the elaboration of a system of sovereign states and the creation of
a European balance of power began. This development was checked,
to begin with, by the preponderance of German power, which
constituted a solid *bloc* in central Europe ; but it was not hindered
by inhibitions springing from a sense of overriding unity, and as
the power of the German emperors declined, an articulated system
of balancing forces immediately took shape. The first stimulus
seems to have come from pope Gregory VII, who encouraged the
strivings of countries such as Hungary, Poland, Bohemia, Croatia
and Denmark, in order to create around the frontiers of the German
empire a girdle of independent states which would look to him as
a counterpoise to imperial power. The alignment of forces in the
Investiture Contest called into existence the European balance of
power, as we know it ; the articulated, interlocking system which
has dominated international relations without intermission down
to to-day, was operative from the start of the twelfth century.[2]

And at the very same time philosophers and historians and propagandists began to build up the ideological foundations of the new
national states. The process starts in England and Normandy ; but
it soon became general. Innocent III at the beginning of the
thirteenth century did not hesitate to proclaim the independence of
the king of France, who ' recognizes no superior in temporal
affairs ' ; and an English canonist formulated a famous maxim, that

[1] Cf. G. G. Coulton's article, ' Nationalism in the Middle Ages ', *Cambridge Historical
Journal* V (1935), cited above p. 43, n.2.
[2] Cf. W. Kienast, *Die Anfänge des europäischen Staatensystems im späteren Mittelalter*
(1936 ; also in *Hist. Zeitschrift*, CLIII) ; see also above, p. 82.

every king exercises as complete authority in his dominions as the emperor in the empire. 'Although by the law of antiquity', he added, ' there should be a single emperor in the world '—that was the theory—in fact, a ' division into kingdoms ', ' approved by the pope ', had occurred, and that was the reality to be counted with. After another half-century had passed, we find St. Thomas not merely taking account of the fact, but asserting that kingdoms, independent states, are the best form of government. And a half-century later, in the reign of Philip the Fair of France, we emerge into the cold grey dawn of modern discontents, and find the principle and practice of ' reason of state ' staring us in the face in all its stark and ugly nakedness.[1]

International politics in the days of Philip the Fair and Edward I of England lack none of the excesses with which we are so familiar to-day: the ruthless sacrifice of small states, like Scotland or Flanders, to the interests of the great powers, the systematic misuse of plebiscites, lying propaganda and bribery and corruption employed as normal intruments of diplomacy, the terrible weapon of economic blockade bringing famine and disease to the innocent, and even the abduction and murder of leading political personalities.[2] When, in addition, we consider that this was a period of conflict between the conservative forces in Europe and a new, revolutionary ideology with its home in Paris ; when we consider that in the Mediterranean it saw the clash of two rival imperialisms, French and Spanish ; and when we appreciate that the division of Europe into two armed camps was accompanied (for example, in Flanders) by bitter class-warfare, and that in more than one country social divisions determined the political alignment of the ruling-classes—then, I believe, we shall be tempted to wonder whether, in spite of all outward differences and all technological advances, any period of history has more affinity with our own than the age of Philip the Fair.

* * *

It may seem as though these observations might better have been called ' the International *Dis*order and the Middle Ages '. For

---

[1] The texts referred to are assembled by W. Kienast, *Deutschland und Frankreich in der Kaiserzeit* (1943), 102–110,—the best brief account to date, where the very considerable literature on the subject is summarized and reviewed.

[2] There is a brilliant description in F. Kern, *Die Anfänge der französischen Ausdehnungspolitik* (1910), particularly in the analysis of ' the technique' of power-politics (cap. 3).

what, in summary, is the upshot of what I have tried to say? It is simply this : that the mediaeval attitude to the ' international order ' (as we choose to call it) *was* different from ours, precisely for so long as the mediaeval states were too weak internally to pursue national policies. But as soon as their internal consolidation took place, they set out, one and all, as fast as they could, along the path of ' reason of state ', national policy and sovereign independence, down which (like the Gadarene swine) they are still rushing to-day. Half of the historian's time is spent on clearing away the myths which encumber our knowledge of the past ; and one of these myths is the idea that, in this respect, men of the middle ages were different from us—except, no doubt, that the evil potentialities of international anarchy were more limited then than now. Does this lead, you may ask, simply to the trite conclusion that ' human nature never changes '? That, I think, is not the case ; the evidence of fundamental change revealed by history is far too striking for any historian to believe that.[1] But we do learn that nationalism is something far older and more fundamental than many have thought— it is not simply an aberration of the last four hundred years—and we do learn also that the middle ages had no effective alternative to offer in its place. The mediaeval empire, which we call the ' Holy Roman Empire ', like the Roman empire before it, depended for whatever validity it possessed, not on universal pretensions, still less on universal recognition, but on force and armed might in a world of contending powers. Can we in our time of crisis build an international order on better foundations? It will not help to draw cheap comfort from the past, to devise shabby formulae for reconciling irreconcilables, or to repeat empty phrases about ' a constitutional co-operative system of world-government '. The middle ages had phrases and theories enough, and they were of singularly little profit ; to achieve anything of value, something more, for which there is no precedent in history, is needed.

[1] Cf. V. H. Galbraith, in *History* XXII (1938), 312.

8. The Mediaeval Empire: Idea and Reality

THE subject of this essay[1] is one that, by general consent, takes a central place in European history in the middle ages. The history of the Empire, it has often been said, is co-terminous with the history of western Christendom; and Lord Bryce long ago described it as a 'universal monarchy', embodying the 'loftiest ideal of human government' and preserving 'the feeling of a brotherhood of mankind, a commonwealth of the whole world, whose sublime unity transcended every minor distinction'. 'From the days of Constantine until far down into the middle ages,' he wrote, ' the Empire was, conjointly with the papacy, the recognized centre and head of Christendom.'

If these words are anywhere near the truth, it may seem strange that no English historian since Bryce has attempted to write the history of the Empire as a whole, and that the English reader, who wishes to gain some idea of the part played by the Empire in mediaeval history, is still thrown back upon the pages of the *Holy Roman Empire*.[2] Bryce's *Holy Roman Empire* is a classic work of historical writing; but the fact remains that it originated in an Oxford prize essay presented in 1863, and the last revision, nearly half a century old, was issued in 1904, by which time the author's interests had long been transferred to other fields and to more recent periods. It is no part of my purpose to criticize Lord Bryce's work; but it would in the circumstances perhaps be a matter for surprise if it were fully abreast of modern knowledge.

For the general reader, on the other hand, concerned less with detail than with the broader conception of what the Empire was,

---

[1] First published in 1950 as a pamphlet by *The Historical Association*; I have made a few revisions in the present version, and added a few references.

[2] These words may seem to reflect upon the value of H. A. L. Fisher's *Mediaeval Empire* (2 vols., 1898); but that is neither my intention, nor is it really the case. Fisher's book was concerned with other things, namely 'to see how the machinery of imperial government worked' in Germany and Italy; and he explicitly disclaimed any intention either of tracing 'the history of the imperial idea', or of 'trespassing upon Mr. Bryce's ground'.

and what it stood for, what is of more importance is the validity of Bryce's approach and interpretation. Here it will suffice to say that whatever the value of the facts which Bryce adduces, the interpretation he places upon them is not one which any longer can claim general assent. It might be said of him, as was said not so long ago of another great historian of his day, Bishop Stubbs : *Zwei Seelen wohnten in seiner Brust*—the one the soul of a scholar, meticulously noting the evidence before him ; the other the soul of an idealist, seeking in the middle ages guidance for a generation racked by growing national antagonisms. If Stubbs had ' a mystic conception of the origins of the English constitution ', Bryce's conception of the mediaeval Empire was no less mystical. Lefebvre's stricture on Stubbs : ' There is no cohesion between his partial conclusions founded on the texts, and his general conception ', might be applied without modification to the author of *The Holy Roman Empire*.

The very title which Bryce gave to his book is characteristic. He chose it, evidently, because it reflected his conception of what the mediaeval Empire should have been ; but he chose it in contradiction to the established facts. ' It is from the year 800 ', he writes, ' that the beginning of the Holy Roman Empire must be dated ' ; but in reality the first known appearance of the title ' Holy Roman Empire ' dates not from 800 (as one might suppose) but from the year 1254, when in fact the Empire had ceased for most purposes to count. Before that we have the title ' Holy Empire ' and we have also the title ' Roman Empire ' ; but the former dates only from 1157, the title ' Roman Empire ' reaches back only to Conrad II, namely to the year 1034 ; even Otto III, whose febrile unhealthy ' Romanism ' was a by-word for the older school of historians, never thought to employ the title ' Roman Empire ' for his dominions. Those being the facts, is it not inevitable that the title of Bryce's book, and the superstructure which it depicts, should mislead and create an erroneous impression? Bryce, of course, was aware of the facts—indeed, he meticulously collected them together and set them down in an appendix. But he chose to disregard them in his interpretation, and to build up instead a mystical picture which, if you analyse it with care, you will see derives largely from writers of the later thirteenth and fourteenth centuries, whose opportunities of knowing what the Empire really was and had been between 800 and 1250, were immeasurably smaller than yours and mine—to say nothing of their lack of critical abilities and of interest in historical truth.

The question that arises—and it is really the only question with which I propose to deal on this occasion—is this : what, if it was not the 'Holy Roman Empire', was the western empire of the middle ages? We must observe immediately that neither the phrase ' western Empire ', which I have just used, nor the phrase ' mediaeval Empire ', which I might have used, is really much more accurate than that used by Bryce. You cannot really speak of ' the mediaeval Empire ' because there were a number of mediaeval empires. First of all there was the Roman empire—what we very often call the Byzantine empire, but that term also is unhistoric, misleading, and far better avoided. The title ' mediaeval Empire ' may in a sense be said to exclude the Roman empire ; for the Roman empire, although continuing in existence until 1453, goes back after all in continuous history to Augustus, and cannot therefore be described with any degree of accuracy by the label ' mediaeval '. But the middle ages knew a number of other empires, using the term not loosely as a mere description, but in conformity with contemporary diplomatic usage. In the east there were the Bulgarian and Serbian empires, and the imperial title was used in Russia from the thirteenth century. In the west the Castilian monarchs were ' emperors of Spain ' ; there was the imperial title of Edgar and others in Anglo-Saxon England ; and from the thirteenth century we find ' emperors ' in Scandinavia also. In view of these facts, the common idea of a ' western Empire' as though there were but one empire in western Europe, is necessarily misleading ; and it is doubly misleading when we consider the fact that, apart from one occasion in 813, of which I shall say more, the term *occidentale imperium* is never officially used.

What, then, you may well repeat, was the Empire about which I propose to write? One answer—and an answer which comes near the truth—is that it was no one thing at all. It was a series of things, different at different times, and most of the salient differences are implicit in the changes of title which I have briefly mentioned. One of the besetting sins of the historian—they are (I fear) many— is to see continuity everywhere, forgetting (as the late Professor Hearnshaw once remarked) that ' continuity is by no means the most conspicuous feature of history '. It is fatally easy to see the whole history of the Holy Roman Empire, down to 1806, unfolding

itself in Charles the Great's coronation in Rome in the year 800.
In reality the story of the Empire, later of the Holy Roman Empire,
is a story of discontinuity. It meant different things to different
men at the same time, and different things to men at different times ;
indeed, it *was* different things at different times. Therefore Bryce's
attempt to depict a self-consistent ' body of ideas on which the
Empire rested ', a set of ' fundamental doctrines ' that ' were in their
essence the same during the whole of the middle ages ', must
necessarily fail. It must fail because it simply is not a fact that what
was ' true for the tenth ' was true ' as well for the fourteenth century '. On the contrary, the Empire in the fourteenth century was
something ' in its essence ' different from the Empire in the tenth
century, just as the empire of Otto I or Otto III was different ' in
its essence ' from the empire of Charles the Great.

It has seemed to me, therefore, that it may be a useful service
if I attempt, in all brevity, to set out the main phases in the history
of the Empire, from 800 to the advent of the Habsburgs ; that is
to say, to draw in outline a clear—perhaps (owing to the exigencies
of space) an over-simplified and dogmatic—picture of historical
change, against which current generalizations about the mediaeval
empire can be weighed. For the mediaeval empire lives to-day
as a force in the minds of men, wherever and whenever political
ideas and ideals are discussed, precisely because of the generalizations which have been formulated about it. Who does not recall
Gierke's brilliant aphorisms, as translated and expounded by
Maitland?[1] But how many of those, who have taken his aphorisms
and applied them to the theory of society and the philosophy of
history, have stopped to check them in the light of the facts established by patient historical investigation? A vast, almost unsurveyable body of work has been done on the history of the Empire
since Bryce and Gierke wrote ; little if any of it, unless my knowledge is seriously at fault, has percolated through into the books
available to us here in England for study and teaching. We are
like a man trying to work by the light of a flickering Victorian
gas-jet, when there are electric arc-lamps available. True, no one
has published, so far as I know, a new history of the Empire covering
the whole ground on the generous scale of Bryce—another vice of

---

[1] O. Gierke, *Political Theories of the Middle Ages* (transl. and edited by F. W. Maitland,
1900).

the present generation of historians is that it fights shy of comprehensive works.[1] But the reassessments which have been made are so wide-reaching that there is no reason why a comprehensive treatment should not now be attempted. What I shall try to do, therefore, without making any pretence of originality, is to set before you the pertinent facts, embodying as much of the results of recent research as I have been able to digest ; and then, so far as space permits, I shall try to suggest some of the changes in interpretation which our knowledge of the facts either warrants or necessitates.

*   *   *

The curtain traditionally rises on a scene of deliberate ceremony set in the basilica of the apostle Peter in Rome on Christmas Day in the year 800.

The question immediately arises whether this traditional starting-point is correct, whether the coronation of Charles the Great really was (in Bryce's formulation) ' the beginning of the Holy Roman Empire '. The answer, I think, is this : that it does, of course, set a train of events in motion, but that it is prehistory, rather than history. The empire of Charles the Great (it has been truly said) ' went with him to the grave ' ;[2] he did not found the western empire of the middle ages, nor was his empire ' revived ' or ' restored ' (as is so often stated) by Otto I. Not so long ago the coronation of Charles the Great was called ' the most important and most puzzling riddle in the whole of mediaeval history ' ;[3] but we may fairly say to-day that the riddle has been solved. We know now, beyond a shadow of doubt, that Charles's coronation was the outcome of a curious chain of events, of intrigues and dissidence, in Rome itself and in Constantinople, reaching back no further than 798. We know also that the events of Christmas, 800, were played out within the framework of the existing Roman empire —the empire we often loosely term Byzantine—of which Rome was still an integral part. All that was intended and all that was done, was to elect a new emperor in the existing empire. There was no

[1] Since these words were first written, a French scholar has published a lucid, compact survey ; cf. R. Folz, *L'idée d'empire en occident du Ve au XIVe siècle* (1953).
[2] F. Schneider, *Rom und Romgedanke im Mittelalter* (1926), 51.
[3] Ibid., 50 ; similarly K. Heldmann, *Das Kaisertum Karls des Grossen. Theorien und Wirklichkeit* (1928), 1. Heldmann's critical survey is unsurpassed, but may be supplemented, from the Byzantine side, by F. Dölger, *Byzanz und die europäische Staatenwelt* (1953), 288 sqq.

idea either of creating a new empire in the west, or of ' restoring ' or ' reviving ' the Roman dominion in the west, which had been obliterated centuries earlier with the rise of the Germanic kingdoms ; nor was there even the idea of ' transferring ' the existing Empire from east to west. All that was at issue was the person of the emperor—the emperor, not the empire.

Consequently we are justified in saying that no tradition, no idea of assuming the imperial title as ' the most appropriate expression ' of the ' universal ' power of the Frankish monarchy, lay behind the events of 800 ; the imperial crown was not (as Bryce maintained) ' the goal towards which the policy of the Frankish kings had for many years pointed '. The initiative in 800 seems clearly to have come from the side of the pope ; but the constitutive act was not coronation by the pope but election by the Roman people. The idea that the pope, in crowning Charles, bestowed the imperial dignity upon the Carolingian dynasty, or even simply on Charles himself, is erroneous ; coronation was a pleasing solemnity, which heightened the effect of the proceedings and surrounded them with a religious nimbus, but it was in no way necessary for the lawful institution of an emperor. Election, on the other hand, though it conferred the imperial title, could not convey it to a dynasty ; for the dignity of emperor was not, and never had been, hereditary ; and though Charles became emperor in 800, no right to succeed was thereby conveyed to his son or sons. That is why it is true to say that Charles's empire died with him. All that happened in 800, therefore, was that Charles, who was already king of the Franks and king of the Lombards, became—in the eyes of those who elected him—Roman emperor. He did not, of course, become sole emperor ; though there might often be a ' senior ' emperor, it had never been the rule that only one emperor could reign over the Roman dominions at one time. Nor, of course, did he become Frankish emperor ; there was not, and never would be, such a person. His Frankish and Lombard kingdoms were, and remained, outside his empire ; and that could not be otherwise, because the empire in which he claimed to be emperor was the existing Roman empire.[1]

But claims were all very well. How were they to be put into

---

[1] W. Sickel, ' Die Kaiserwahl Karls des Grossen ', *Mitteilungen des Instituts für österreich. Geschichtsforschung* XX (1899), is still the best account of the formal and legal situation.

effect? Not unnaturally the imperial government in Constantinople refused recognition to the new emperor, who in its eyes was a pretentious and slightly ludicrous usurper. Charles himself was also in a quandary; for the last thing he wanted was to become involved in hostilities with the imperial government, which might have unpleasant repercussions on his position as king of Lombardy. We can see how ill at ease he was by the fact that, three months after his coronation, he was still cautiously using his old royal title. Five months after the event, he had at last managed to discover a formula—clumsy but not altogether lacking in precedent[1]—which he doubtless hoped would prove innocuous, since it carefully avoided the tried and tested imperial protocol. ' Charles, most serene Augustus, crowned by God, great and pacific emperor, governing the Roman empire ', he called himself.

Thereafter, for a few months—from May, 801, to the end of 802—he seems genuinely to have rejoiced in his new dignity, perhaps even to have felt that it expressed a divine vocation. Disillusion quickly followed. If he thought, by avoiding the title of a legitimate emperor, to disarm the suspicions of the imperial government, he soon discovered that he was mistaken. It is not necessary to weary you with an account of the subsequent events down to Charles's death in 814. Suffice it to say that it needed two costly wars, major territorial concessions, and years of wearisome negotiation, before the imperial government finally decided to recognize Charles' imperial title; and when it did so, it was only because it had just suffered a bloody defeat at the hands of the Bulgars, and was compelled to wind up minor commitments as quickly as possible in order to concentrate all its efforts on the Bulgarian menace. If Chatham won the British empire on the banks of the Rhine, Charles won his in the rugged defiles of the Balkan mountains—or rather that would have been the case, if the peace-treaty he concluded on April 4th, 812, with the emperor Michael I had ever come into force. For on April 4th, 812, the imperial ambassadors, sent to Aachen to conclude a settlement, actually did address Charles as ' emperor and basileus '; it seemed, at last, as though the new empire had become an accepted fact.

But what, you may ask, was Charles emperor of? The answer is—nothing. It is true that Charles himself, in 813, wrote a fulsome

[1] Cf. P. Classen, ' Romanum gubernans imperium ', *Deutsches Archiv* IX (1951).

letter to Michael I, expressing his joy that peace had at last been concluded between the ' eastern ' and the ' western ' empires ; but he was going beyond his brief. The concept of a ' western ' empire found no place in the official negotiations. Charles was to be ' emperor and basileus '—a personal dignity—but not emperor of any specified land and least of all Roman emperor. Characteristically, he himself from this time dropped from his title the inaccurate formula ' governing the Roman empire '—obviously part of the price he paid to secure a settlement. I need hardly emphasize the significance of this. Even those historians who have seen—and rightly—that 812, rather than 800, is the important date, have too often concluded that from 812 there really was a division of the Roman empire into east and west, and that thereafter the history of the Roman empire in the west is continuous. That is not the case. None of the Carolingians—with the possible exception, for a few months, of Louis II—nor indeed Otto I after them, ever thought to use the title ' Roman emperor ', to which (as they well knew) they had no right. The Roman empire was not theirs ; it was the empire ruled over by the emperors in the east. But that is not all. Charles, overjoyed by the outcome of the negotiations of 812, immediately proceeded to a step he could not earlier have lawfully taken, and in 813 he had his son Louis elected co-emperor. But even this was premature. By a curious series of accidents—it was, I think, no more—Charles died before the peace of 812 could be ratified ; and it was in fact never put into force.

Thus in spite of all his efforts and the many concessions he made, Charles never became a duly recognized emperor at all. The bid of 800 to foist the Roman title on him came to nothing—it was a *coup d'état* which did not come off—not least because he himself had the sense to back out ; the negotiations in 812 to secure him an imperial title which was not Roman, were inconclusive. Except that he had (under a genuine misapprehension) had his son Louis raised to the purple, thus ensuring (almost by accident) that the title did not die with him, the whole episode, which Charles had never wanted, ended in fiasco.

*　　*　　*

Such is the prologue—one of those complicated stories of the unexpected and the undesired, too improbable for even the most lively imagination to invent ; it may help to explain why a distinguished French historian once described the events of 800 as ' a comedy improvised by a handful of antiquarian-minded ecclesias-tics '.[1]

We pass now to the first phase, which lasts exactly one hundred and ten years, and ends with the murder of the emperor Berengar in 924. The emperor Berengar—is not the mere mention of that nonentity a sufficient commentary on the significance of the eleven preceding decades? It was not long ; but it was long enough to demonstrate that the imperial title (it was a title only, not an empire) handed on by Charles to his son, Louis, meant nothing to the Franks and was incapable of taking root in Frankish soil.

Nevertheless Louis himself laid great store by his imperial dignity and it is characteristic that, from the beginning, he laid aside the Lombard and Frankish royal titles his father had so carefully pre-served and entitled himself simply *imperator augustus*. But the ques-tion what this title signified, still remained unanswered. It was not Roman, nor (we have seen) was it Frankish ; the idea of a ' Frankish ' or ' Carolingian ' empire is simply a figment of the modern his-torian's imagination. In the years after 800, it is true, Carolingian poets and court-chroniclers, churchmen and philosophers, impressed by the exalted dignity, had begun to attach all sorts of incompatible meanings to it ; but it remained in fact neither more nor less than a personal rank. On the other hand, it is not surprising that Louis the Pious, under the spell of the magic word, tried to give it a mean-ing and content still lacking. There is little reason to doubt that, influenced by churchmen of the calibre of Agobard of Lyons and by the clerical idea of a ' Christian empire ', he really had it in mind to transform all his separate dominions into a unitary empire on a foundation of common Christianity.[2] This is the sense of the famous *ordinatio imperii* of 817, with its programmatic reference to the unity of the empire. But it was too revolutionary a step to succeed. The reaction to the ordinance was immediate and hostile ; and in a few years the whole fragile superstructure came crashing down. The civil wars of the ninth century and the successive parti-tions of the Frankish dominions among Louis' sons and grandsons resulted in a constant narrowing of the territory over which the

---

[1] F. Lot, *La fin du monde antique et le début du moyen âge* (1927), 296.
[2] This phase is well discussed by L. Halphen, *Charlemagne et l'Empire carolingien* (1947), 226 sqq.

I

emperor ruled, until in the days of pope John VIII the imperial title had shrunk to the narrow dimensions of a small Italian principality. The fleeting idea of fusing the empire with the whole complex of Frankish territories and thus making something positive out of it never came to anything.

The civil wars and partitions had, however, a further result of no smaller significance ; they enabled the papacy to establish a hold over the imperial title which subsequently was never entirely relaxed. The pope had had no hand in the elevation of Louis by Charles the Great in 813, nor again when he was re-elected after his father's death in 814 ; he had no part, either, in the elevation of Louis' eldest son, Lothar, in 817. But the conflicts between the members of the Carolingian house, all naturally desirous of securing papal support, made it easy for the popes to renew the link between the empire and Rome, which had snapped between 800 and 812 ; and in fact from 823 onwards, right down to the days of Maximilian, at the beginning of the sixteenth century, no one was emperor who had not received the crown in Rome at the pope's hand. Thus, from about 850, it seems that the empire, which had failed in Frankish hands to acquire meaning and content, was taking shape as an instrument of the papacy. And, in fact, it was in these years that the foundations were laid for the ' papal ' theory of the empire—unhistorical, of course, with no foundation in the facts—which was destined in the later middle ages to wide (though never universal) currency : the theory, expressed in its final form by Innocent III, that it was for the pope to bestow (and therefore, if he thought fit, to withhold) the imperial crown.

But the papacy of the late ninth and early tenth centuries did not know what to do with the empire when it had secured control over it. Its need of an emperor was urgent, as every action of pope John VIII reveals ; but its need involved it in an insoluble dilemma. In a strong emperor it saw the red light of danger, but of what use was an emperor so weak that he could not help the pope to maintain his independence? Faced by this choice of evils, it was not unnatural to play for safety ; but the result was that, unable to save itself, the papacy involved the empire also in its fall and decline—indeed, papal intervention was not least among the factors depreciating the value of the imperial title until in the end it passed out of currency. After the pontificates of Nicholas I and

John VIII the papacy and with it the empire fell under the dominion of the Roman aristocracy. There followed a succession of puppet emperors, chosen from the ranks of the Italian nobility, beginning with Guy of Spoleto in 891. Then in 924 the meaningless title was suppressed. It was suppressed by the rising house of Crescentius, which saw in it merely an impediment standing in the way of its own efforts to build for itself a principality in and over Rome. It died because it incorporated no vital force and expressed no effective principle. When it disappeared in 924 it had no achievement to its credit; nothing had been done in any sphere, material or moral, which was beyond the powers of kingship, nothing which we must attribute to the existence and possession of the imperial title.

And yet, less than forty years later, the imperial dignity which had passed practically unmourned in 924, was acquired by Otto I, and thereafter for three hundred years the succession of emperors is unbroken. Why, it may well be asked, did Otto grasp after a dignity which (if what I have said is true) was empty and meaningless?

The answer takes us back again to the middle years of the ninth century. The Franks knew little and cared less about the Roman empire; but they had, since 813, had an emperor of their own, and inevitably—just like Louis the Pious earlier and like the popes of their own day—they sought to give 'their' empire (as they considered it) a meaning in terms they understood. We can see their view emerging in the passages in which ninth-century writers tried to their own satisfaction to explain the imperial dignity of Charlemagne. He was emperor, they thought—their theory was, of course, as unhistorical as that of the papacy—because he ruled over a number of peoples. In short, his 'empire' was based on conquest and hegemony; and the conflicts between rival Carolingian pretendants provided fertile ground in which such ideas quickly took root. Charles the Bald, we are told, had himself proclaimed 'emperor and augustus' when he invaded the kingdom of Lorraine in 869—six years before he was crowned emperor in Rome—because he was the possessor of two kingdoms. The parallel with the Anglo-Saxon *bretwalda* and the Spanish and Scandinavian 'emperors' is obvious. It is an idea of empire which has nothing to do with Rome—neither with the Rome of antiquity, nor with

the Roman empire as it existed in the ninth century, nor with papal
Rome. But it lives on—while the actual empire, handed down from
Charles and Louis, withers and dies—because it is rooted in popular
ways of thinking, and because of the persistence of the political
conditions which gave it force.

It is here, rather than in the persistence of Carolingian tradition,
that we should seek the link between the 'empire' of the ninth
century and the 'empire' of Otto I. Otto I's policy never left the
lines of late-Carolingian tradition. He reached out east and west
and south ; but his main concern was to secure the lion's share of
the shattered Carolingian realm, and particularly the fragments of
the old middle kingdom of Lorraine. In this his policy represents
nothing new ; it falls into line with that of the many kings who,
amassing bits and pieces of the Carolingian lands, had striven for a
' hegemonial ' position, and the acquisition of Rome and the imperial title was only the culmination of a policy which had already
assured control of Lotharingia and Burgundy and brought Lombardy under his rule. Much effort has been spent on trying to
elucidate the role which the empire played in Otto's policy ; the
only result (it has truly been said) is to show ' that in reality such a
role did not exist '.[1] The old idea that he was seeking to revive
the dominion of Charlemagne is contrary to the evidence ; the west
Frankish lands, now and for all time, stood outside, and no claims
of supremacy or suzerainty or even of hegemony over them was
ever made. Neither was Otto's empire Roman, either in intent or
in fact. His title was the traditional *imperator augustus* ; Rome was
not mentioned. It was only a personal dignity ; it did not weld
his lands together into a unity, any more than Charles the Great's
imperial title had welded his lands into a single empire. After
962, just as before, Otto remained king of Germany and king of
Lombardy ; his imperial dignity brought him esteem and rule over
the diminutive duchy of Rome, but no more. We are back again
roughly where Charles was in 812 and 813—but this time on a far
narrower territorial basis, which excludes the west Frankish lands
and other rising states of western and central Europe.

But Otto I's intervention in Italy and his coronation in Rome
in 962 had one result of major importance. It brought him face to

---

[1] Cf. T. E. Mommsen, *Studien zum Ideengehalt der deutschen Aussenpolitik im Zeitalter
der Ottonen und Salier* (1930)—the best account to date.

face with the Roman empire—and that just at a time when the Roman empire was rising to new heights and preparing to embark, under Nicephorus Phocas and Basil II, on expansion and re-conquest. The conflict which ensues is a capital fact in the history of the western empire. Fears of Byzantine intervention in Roman politics, the conflicting claims of the rival powers in Italy, the desire to stake out a title to territories which might be re-conquered from the Saracens : these are the factors which lead to what now follows, the ' Romanization ' of the western empire. Otto I had been *imperator augustus* and nothing more. Otto II, to substantiate his claims against Basil II, became ' Roman emperor ' ; and the title, once introduced, remained. Furthermore, in order to counter Byzantine infiltration, his son, Otto III, took up and adapted to his own uses the ideas of Roman ' renaissance ' current in the ranks of the Roman aristocracy ; that, we now know, was the sense and practical purpose of Otto III's ' Roman ' policy, which was once dismissed as the romantic foible of an impressionable youth.[1]

Nevertheless the empire itself, even under Otto III, was not Roman. And under his successor, Henry II, when we find the phrase *imperium Romanum* in official use, it means simply the imperial dignity ; the word *imperium* signifies not a territory—in the modern sense of the word ' empire '—but simply the functions and authority of an emperor. But under the next ruler, Conrad II, the designation ' Roman empire ' starts to appear in the charters in a new sense— namely, as a collective term for the lands under Conrad's rule. This is a major innovation and significant in more ways than one. It is significant, first, because there is no ruler in the whole line of emperors from Otto I onwards whose policy was more stolid and realistic than Conrad II's ; and the fact that the Roman designation first appears under him is therefore in itself a sufficient indication that it was not adopted to express a resuscitation of the ' universal ' pretensions of ancient Rome, but for practical reasons of diplomacy and foreign policy. It is significant, secondly, because it means that from Conrad II's time the empire was at last stabilized as a terri- torial *bloc*. It is no longer simply a title, a dignity, which can pass from one ruler to another at will, as it was offered (for example) first to the French king and then to duke William of Aquitaine after the death of Henry II in 1024. From about 1034, on the contrary,

[1] Cf. G. Barraclough, *The Origins of Modern Germany* (1946), 61.

it is the official designation for the whole complex of lands ruled by the emperor. These lands are Germany, Burgundy, and Italy ; and henceforward Germany, Burgundy, and Italy, hitherto independent kingdoms connected only by the personal bond of a common ruler, become subordinate parts of one empire. This connexion was reinforced and made permanent, from 1040, by the introduction of the new title ' King of the Romans ' as a designation for the emperor-elect before his coronation, or for the emperor's designated successor. The institution of a ' King of the Romans ' was important because it settled once and for all the question of succession, and forestalled any further attempt (as in 1024) to sever the connexion between the imperial dignity and the lands with which, since the time of Otto I, it had been associated ; it attached it, once and for all, to a particular territorial complex.

Thus the reign of Henry III, in this as in so many other respects, marks a definite stage ; at the end of his reign the curtain falls— for the first time in two and a half centuries—on a definite achievement. The ' empire ' had lost its nebulous character, the lack of specific meaning and content which had dogged its history ever since 812, and had taken on the significance which it retained henceforward right down to the end of Hohenstaufen times. It is now something quite specific, an actual territorial power, limited and defined. It is this and no more. Beyond the frontiers of Germany, Burgundy, and Italy it does not extend. There is no idea of European hegemony, still less of world-dominion, nor has the empire, as shaped by the process of historical development, anything in common—save perhaps its seat in Rome—with the Christian commonwealth, the *imperium Christianum*, conceived of by ecclesiastical thinkers.

This very fact, so important for assessing the place of the new Empire in mediaeval political society, also explains its instability. Had it been (in Bryce's words) ' an institution divine and necessary, having its foundations in the very nature and order of things ', it might have secured general acceptance in Europe. In reality, it was the product of an almost fortuitous chain of historical circumstances, not even sanctioned by long tradition ; and so it was no sooner formed than it was challenged. In the eyes of the peoples outside its frontiers, it had no claim to sacrosanctity ; and even within its frontiers the ' empire ' meant more to the Germans, who profited from it, than to the inhabitants of Burgundy and Italy, among whom the feeling was never entirely absent, that it betokened their subjection to the German conquerors. The empire was Roman, in the limited sense that there never was any idea of establishing (as would, had it been desired, easily have been possible) a German empire independent of Rome ; but in substance it was German, in the sense that its establishment reflected the preponderance of the German monarchy in eleventh-century Europe.

Such an empire, evidently, was a very incomplete realization— if it was not, indeed, a negation—of the imperial ideas current in the ecclesiastical circles which, on the whole, determined the climate of opinion. It reflected a particular constellation of political power ; but there was no reason why it should outlast the balance of power which was its precondition. Already in the attitude of Suger of St. Denis we can see that ' the imperial metaphysics of the Germans no longer found adherents in the west ' ;[1] and in fact the older and contrary idea of the empire as a title, independent of any particular territorial complex and freely transferable from one ruler to another, which (as we have seen) was still alive in 1024, never completely disappears ; it crops up again—ineffectively and half-heartedly, but sufficiently frequently to show that the ' German' conception of the empire as a territorial unit had not unreservedly carried the day— in 1112, 1139–41, and 1163. In substance, it is true, the empire remained down to the time of Frederick II what it became in the days of Conrad II and Henry III ; no other conception of the empire ever prevailed. But, outside Germany, it was accepted *de facto*, rather than from conviction ; and it was only for a few years in the middle of the eleventh century that the empire stood unchallenged. It was vouchsafed scarcely more than one generation of stability ; then for two centuries, nearly without break, it stood on the defensive, sometimes making a tactical sortie or even a violent counter-attack, but never really advancing the line it held. It was (it has truly been said) ' never so strong as it seemed ' ;[2] and as political conditions and the balance of power in Europe evolved, the relative position of the empire deteriorated, so that in the end it was only by efforts which overtaxed its strength that its position could be maintained against the opposition of the papacy and the

---

[1] Cf. W. Kienast, *Deutschland und Frankreich in der Kaiserzeit* (1943), 102.
[2] J. Haller, *Das Papsttum. Idee und Wirklichkeit* III (2nd ed. 1952), 176.

states associated or allied with the papacy, which had never acknow-
ledged its sway.[1]

It is a remarkable fact that in Ottonian times the papacy—with
the single exception of the pontificate of Silvester II—had played
no part in the formulation and development of imperial ideas ;[2] the
papal view of the empire, formulated in essentials under Nicholas I,
had (as we have seen) ceased to count when the Holy See fell under
the domination of the Roman aristocracy. But the reform and re-
vitalization of the papal court by the agency of the German emperors
of the eleventh century opened up new possibilities, and within a
few years of Henry III's death the initiative passed into papal hands.

We may regard the counter-attack which followed under pope
Gregory VII, as a reaction to the achievements we have just examined
—to the territorial stabilization and the regulation of imperial
succession which deprived the pope of effective influence (such as
he had exercised in the ninth century) over the person of the emperor. But it was also a consequence of fundamental changes in
world-politics. The decline of the Roman empire in the east after
the death of Basil II meant that the pope, now that the threat from
that direction had ceased, could take up a more independent attitude
in his dealings with the emperor in the west ; the appearance of
the Normans in the Mediterranean, potential allies of the papacy,
was another factor working in the same direction. In this sense the
schism of east and west in 1054 marked a turning-point ; and a few
years later Gregory VII turned against the western emperors the
weapons forged by Leo IX against the emperors of the east. In
1075 the outbreak of the so-called Investiture Contest brought
matters to a head. I do not need to retail its course and bearing.
Suffice it to say that it marked a renaissance, on far stronger material
foundations, of the papal theory of the empire, formulated in the
ninth century. For Gregory VII the empire was the secular arm
of the church—a theory no less effective because it did violence to
the whole chain of historical facts which we have followed. But
no less significant was the reaction which the papal attack provoked.
Its result was to force the emperor to seek new foundations. To
meet the onslaught he shifted his ground, built new defences, grasped

---

[1] Cf. W. Holtzmann, *Das mittelalterliche Imperium und die werdenden Nationen* (1953).
[2] Cf. C. Erdmann, ' Das ottonische Reich als Imperium Romanum ', *Deutsches Archiv*
VI (1943), 440.

new weapons. First and foremost among these was the Roman law. Henry IV was not slow in forging connexions with Peter Crassus and other experts in the ' school ' of Ravenna ; and a new and more exalted conception of the empire and its meaning was the result.[1]

These new conceptions, reaching back to Justinian and grasping what was useful from the arsenal of Roman law, were one of the main forces behind the imposing façade which we call ' Hohenstaufen imperialism '. Among other things they explain the adoption by Frederick I in 1157 of the epithet *sacrum*, the ' Holy Empire '. The pompous phrases of antiquity were called in for their propaganda value in the struggle with the church : the empire became the *sacrum imperium* in order to compete on an equal footing with the *sancta ecclesia*. But we must not exaggerate the importance of such innovations, nor suppose that the pretentious rhetoric of Rainald of Dassel or the bombastic verses of the Archpoet reflected the principles upon which the empire was governed any more than we must suppose that Roman law was the only or main source of Hohenstaufen imperial ideas. The example and stimulus of the Roman empire in the east, reviving once again under the Comnenian dynasty, counted for much ;[2] and traditional Frankish notions were there as well, according to which imperial rights were based not on conferment by the pope or by the Roman people, but on conquest. ' Our predecessors ', Frederick I informed the representatives of the Roman senate, ' wrested your city with the lands of Italy from the Greeks and Lombards, and brought it within the Frankish frontiers, not as a gift from alien hands, but as a conquest won by their own valour '. And when asked from whom, if not from the pope, he held his empire, Frederick gave the characteristic reply : ' From God alone ! '

The position thus adopted by Frederick Barbarossa found its clearest expression, a few years later, in the famous legal dictum, formulated by the canonist, Huguccio, and his pupil, Johannes Zemeke : ' He who is chosen by the election of the princes alone is the true emperor, even before he has been confirmed by the pope '.[3]

---

[1] Cf. K. Jordan, ' Der Kaisergedanke in Ravenna zur Zeit Heinrichs IV ', *Deutsches Archiv* II (1938), 85–128.

[2] Cf. above, pp. 84, 87–8.

[3] For this dictum, cf. G. Barraclough, *The Origins of Modern Germany* (1946), 208. There is some further discussion of the legal texts in W. Ullmann, *Medieval Papalism* (1949), 142 sqq.

This conception evidently reflects the actual process of historical development from the days of Conrad II and Henry III to those of Frederick himself. The new arguments from Roman law are interesting, but they contribute little of substance to the imperial case ; they are an answer to the papacy, but little more. The papal theories are similar in character. In answer to the Roman lawyers the popes applied the new-found solvent of Aristotelianism to destroy the old theory of church and state and create another more favourable to their own pretensions. Innocent III's decretals, it has been pointed out, are an essay in the new Aristotelian doctrine of unity, in contradiction to the theory of ' two powers ' which had dominated mediaeval thought down to his time.[1] ' The empire appertains to the apostolic see *principaliter et finaliter* ', Innocent proclaimed, travestying the historical facts ; but even Innocent III could not shake the general belief in the doctrine of two powers, equal and independent; and for that reason alone his theories fail to command respect, except in the remote and arid atmosphere of scholastic speculation.

All in all, the pronouncements of the pope and the fulminating answers of Frederick II—who took Innocent III's weapons from his hand and turned them against the papacy—are of theoretical interest rather than of practical importance. They have echoed down the ages ; but the real issues were different. Innocent III was interested first and foremost in practical questions, the union of the empire and Sicily, and territorial dispositions in central Italy ; and his theory of the empire was shaped not in accordance with transcendental cosmological principles, but as a practical weapon to further his policy in these fields. Moreover, it was as a theory never successful. The poet Walther von der Vogelweide immediately registered his protest : ' die pfaffen wellent leien reht verkeren ' ;[2] and the imperial standpoint, proudly affirmed in the Declaration of Speyer and the Halle protest in 1199 and 1202, and restated within a few years by Eike von Repgow in the *Sachsenspiegel*, was never surrendered. It was taken up again in 1338 at the Diet of Rhens and supplied the keystone for the settlement of the imperial question put through by Charles IV in 1355 and 1356. In so far as the papacy was successful in the practical issue, it was not because it won acceptance for its theory of the empire, but because it was able to enlist the support

---

[1] Cf. E. Eichmann, *Die Kaiserkrönung im Abendland* I (1942), 331.
[2] Cf. C. C. Bayley, *The Formation of the German College of Electors* (1949), 125.

of the national monarchies outside the empire, France to the fore. The union of Germany, Italy and Burgundy had made the empire the preponderant territorial *bloc* in western and central Europe; and the national monarchies, as in the course of the twelfth century they consolidated their position, first resisted and then challenged this German preponderance—a preponderance based not on any specific recognition of imperial hegemony, but on the commanding position of the empire in international politics; they used the conflict of empire and papacy to bring about a major shift in the balance of power, to the detriment of both. After 1197, still more after 1250, the really decisive factor is their policy, rather than the conflicting theories of popes and emperors.

The reaction against German preponderance began to take shape soon after the weakening of the empire and the shift in the balance of power during the Investiture Contest. The new imperialism of Hohenstaufen times, the arrogant imperialism of Rainald of Dassel and of the Archpoet—although itself merely a rejoinder to the œcumenical claims of the Hildebrandine papacy—provoked a hostile reaction in neighbouring lands. When Rainald disdainfully called the kings of Europe *reguli*, seeming to hint their inferiority to the emperor, he was met by John of Salisbury's sharp rejoinder: ' who then appointed the Germans to be judges over the nations? ' The authority of kings and emperors, it was insisted, sprang from the same source: ' the king is emperor in his kingdom '.[1] This was, indeed, a truism; the imperial title had never implied a claim to preponderance. But it was also a necessary defence against the new-fangled theories of empire which Roman lawyers were propounding, which seemed to foreshadow novel and exalted claims. And later the restless, adventurous policy of Henry VI bred further disquiet; it was not (as so often said) a chimerical attempt to realize an idea of ' universal empire ' or of ' world-dominion ', but just the same it was calculated to provoke hostile reactions because it seemed to threaten the security of all neighbouring countries.

Nevertheless the fundamental issue was not the ' equality ' of kings and emperors, any more than it was the papal claim to confer the imperial crown—a claim that could never play more than a

[1] ' Rex est imperator in regno suo.' The famous phrase has a long history, adequately summarized by J. Rivière, *Le problème de l'église et de l'État au temps de Philippe le Bel* (1926), 424–430.

transitory role in politics, because the papacy never possessed the real power wherewith to back its pretensions. What was at issue, fundamentally, was the connexion forged in the eleventh century between *regnum* and *imperium*—the connexion upon which, as an historical fact, the empire was based ; it was against this, the very keystone in the imperial structure, that the attack was directed. After 1250 the question whether this bond would be maintained or severed, became for a century the dominant theme of European politics ; a whole series of contradictory schemes followed each other in rapid succession. There were, first, those who demanded the ' translation ' of the empire ; that is to say, its severance from Germany and its conferment on the strongest continental power, i.e. the king of France. In practice this amounted to a demand for French succession in Italy, Burgundy and Lorraine ; in theory it implied a revival of the old idea of empire as the expression of hegemony, and its most notorious exponent was Pierre Dubois. Then, there were those who advocated the ' abrogation ' of the empire, which in practice meant that Germany, Burgundy, and Italy would go their own way under separate kings. It was an idea with which some of the German rulers of the period played, particularly the Habsburgs ; and it was forcefully propounded by Robert of Naples, who hoped in this way to be left free to extend his sway over Italy. Neither plan was, in fact, put into effect ; the conflict of interests and the danger of raising up another overmighty power were too great for any concrete proposal to survive the opposition among interested parties it was bound to provoke. Hence the imperial question, in the end, was shelved rather than settled.

In the meantime the vicious anti-imperial propaganda had provoked a twofold reaction : the first, a rallying of all conservative forces in Germany, which found expression in the Diet of Rhens in 1338 ; the second, the emergence of pro-imperial theorists, such as Alexander of Roes in Germany and Dante in Italy. The theory of the empire, which no one, so long as it existed as a political force, had thought it necessary to express in set terms, suddenly came into its own ; and there appeared the spate of treatises and pamphlets, some inspired by a genuine idealism but few disinterested, by which —often without our knowing it—our views of the mediaeval empire have been coloured and formed. They have no relation with what the empire had been. Some are the propaganda of professional politicians, trapping out projects of power-politics in fine words with a deceptive moral ring ; others reflect the genuine bewilderment of honest men, dazed by a new political instability, who looked longingly back to an imaginary past, and discovered in an imaginary empire all sorts of qualities the real empire had never possessed or aspired to possess.

Meanwhile, though nothing was done to settle the question on the international plane, the Empire was, in fact, gradually divested of its content. The connexion of Germany, Italy, and Burgundy, upon which the empire was founded, crumbled ; first the one, then the other escaped from effective German control. Except for one year, in 1312 and 1313, there was for a century after the death of Frederick II no emperor ; indeed, between 1250 and 1806 there were in all only five emperors—Henry VII, Charles IV, Sigismund, Frederick III, and Charles V—duly crowned by the pope. Sigismund, strutting large across the conciliar scene, still adopted the postures of an emperor ; he was helped by the uneasy longing of a distracted age, divided by the Schism, for leadership and a greater measure of unity. But who would be bold enough to argue that either he or Frederick III, the only two rulers in the whole fifteenth century to obtain the title, had more than the name and the trappings?

After 1356 the dominion of the emperor was limited by precise undertakings to Germany,[1] and there was nothing to distinguish it in scope and character from the rule of a German king. The wheel had gone full circle ; the empire, which in 812 was a title and no more, ended as nothing more than a title. After 1356, if not already after 1250, meaning and content were utterly lacking. The mediaeval empire had ceased to exist.

*   *   *

And yet, as in the middle ages, an empty title could be given a new meaning and content, once it passed into the hands of a power which saw in it a worth-while investment. That is what happened. After a century and a half the moribund empire was given a powerful ideological injection and put out to earn its keep. It was revived by the Habsburgs, in the Habsburg interest, to give the Habsburg

---

[1] This is reflected in the appearance, under Frederick III, of the new title : ' Sacrum Romanum imperium nationis Germanicæ ', implying—as Zeumer showed—a definite territorial limitation of the emperor's powers to the German lands. Cf. K. Zeumer, *Heiliges Römisches Reich Deutscher Nation* (1920).

dynasty an ideology and a sanction in the eyes of Europe transcending anything it could claim in its own right.

In 1526, upon the field of Mohacs, the ' Holy Roman Empire ' was born anew. Its purpose, now, was to fortify and consecrate Austrian leadership in Europe against the Turks. Yet the new empire, in content, character, and configuration, bears no resemblance to the mediaeval empire ; it is not its heir, nor even its ghost, but a foundling laid at the foot of its tomb. The connexion with Rome, characteristic of the mediaeval empire from 823 to the Golden Bull, has gone ; not one of the Habsburgs from Maximilian to Francis II was crowned in Rome, and none save Charles V was actually emperor, though they all laid claim to the imperial dignity, as though they had been crowned as well as elected. The ' empire ' over which they ruled was a typical product of Renaissance politics and the Counter-Reformation, the offspring of the alliance between Vienna and the catholic church ; but its story, from 1526 to 1806, is a necessary epilogue, just as the story of Charles the Great, from 800 to 812, is a necessary prologue. For the Habsburgs took the mediaeval empire and remoulded it in their own pattern ; they are the real creators of the legendary ' Holy Roman Empire '. Charles the Great was decked out in new robes as a fitting precursor for Charles V and Charles VI ; the empire of the Ottos was remodelled as a pattern of what the Habsburgs wished their ' empire ' to be thought—a bulwark of Christian Europe against infidel and heretic alike, a multi-national commonwealth guided by Christian principles. The conception of the empire as a ' universal ' force, with ' universal ' functions and responsibilities, towering above and providing a bond of unity between the nationalities, was necessary to Austria's political existence, and so it was duly propagated ; the idea of an imperial ' mission ', with which historians of the mediaeval empire have made such play, is another characteristic Habsburg stage-property.

So there came about the first great transformation of the mediaeval empire into a shape which better suited the political needs of the age than did the historical reality. It was only the first. In the nineteenth century, when the ' Holy ' empire was no more, the *Kaiserzeit* was invested with all the yearnings of German romantic nationalism. After the Vatican Council militant catholicism contributed a version of its own, no less strange and perhaps more insidious. In the twentieth century, when the Hohenzollern empire was no more, the empire was once again reshaped : this time, by historians whose political convictions were stronger than their scholarly integrity, as an ideological foreshadowing of Hitler's ' new order '.[1] . . . In some ways the epilogue of the mediaeval empire, the myth and the legend, is more remarkable than its history.

*　　　*　　　*

The historian turning to-day to the mediaeval empire is confronted, first with a *chef d'œuvre* of nineteenth-century ' romantic ' architecture in the Wagnerian style of Schloss Neuschwanstein ; clear this away, and you come to a baroque structure in the Austrian style of Charles VI and Maria Theresa ; then to delicate Gothic built by the hand of Dante and his contemporaries. They are all, in their different ways, imposing façades ; but all have to come down before we can get to the Empire as it was—a small and unpretentious core of simple Romanesque building, primitive and workaday by comparison with the towering superstructure with which later generations have embellished and surrounded it.

I have tried to depict the empire as it was, to give you the blue-prints of the original structure, which you can measure against the later accretions. What, you may ask, is the relevance of this for the historian who is not a specialist in mediaeval history? The broadest answer, I think, is this : that reinterpretation of the history of the Empire cannot fail to influence and modify that wider view of the course of civilisation, including mediaeval civilisation, and (more widely still) the conceptions of the relationship between civilisations, which all of us who claim to be historians are under compulsion to formulate, if only as a working hypothesis or as a framework into which our own more limited fields of study must be fitted. Our conceptions of the nature of mediaeval political society in the west are bound up with our views of the character and content of the Empire, which so often has been considered the pivot of that society. And evidently our conception of the Renaissance, and its place in the historical sequence between the middle

[1] As a typical example, H. Aubin, *Das erste deutsche Reich als Versuch einer europäischen Staatsgestaltung* (Breslau, 1941) ; but any reader who is interested in the pathology of German historical scholarship between 1933 and 1945 may find a veritable anthology of similar titles and sentiments in the sixth (war-time) edition (1943) of F. Schneider's book, *Die neueren Anschauungen der deutschen Historiker über die Kaiserpolitik des Mittelalters.*

ages and modern times, is largely coloured by the ideas we have formed of the guiding principles and essential characteristics of preceding centuries.

The contrasts so frequently drawn by historians and others between mediaeval and modern political ideas and institutions derive very largely from the view that mediaeval society was governed by a principle of ' universalism ' and subject to a ' universal monarchy ' which 'perpetuated the tradition of the universal rule ' and ' imprescriptible rights of Rome '. If (as I have been at pains to indicate) this interpretation of the mediaeval Empire as a ' universal monarchy ' is wide of the mark, it is evident that such generalizations, with their wider implications, stand in need of revision. The same applies to the correlation between ecclesiastical and political society, which is supposed to have characterized the middle ages and to have perished at the time of the Reformation. For Bryce ' the Holy Roman Church and the Holy Roman Empire ' were ' one and the same thing, seen from different sides ' ; and one of the ' essential principles of the mediaeval Empire ' was ' the exact coincidence of the Holy State's limits . . . with the limits . . . of Holy Church '. In Bryce's view ' the emperor was entitled to the obedience of Christendom ' ; ' the connexion of the Empire with religion ' was the characteristic ' which stands out most clearly '. It needs no emphasis from me to convince you that such generaliza-tions, which (if true) would be of the utmost importance in deter-mining our whole view of the course and character of civilisation in the west, cannot for that very reason be treated as dogmas ; they must be tested, and then tested again, in the light of widening knowledge and by the application of sharpened critical instruments.

The view of the mediaeval empire which I have put before you is, on these and many other cardinal issues, diametrically opposed to that of Bryce. It proceeds (in intention at least) from a cool and realistic appreciation of the course of events, and seeks to relate ideas to the particular constellation of events which called them forth. Bryce, on the other hand, sought to ' deduce ' the Empire's content and place in mediaeval society from what he termed ' the leading principle of mediaeval mythology, the exact correspondence of earth and heaven '. For him the Empire was a transcendental unity ; I have suggested that it was a concrete, definable political organization, limited in time and space. But that does not mean that the ideas and ideals which Bryce thought he perceived directing the destinies of the Empire, were non-existent, or that they counted for nothing in the history of European civilisation. That is not true, any more than it is true that the legends and myths which surround the history of the Empire count for nothing. Perhaps Europe owes more, for good and for evil, to the legend of Charlemagne, with its culmination in the *Chanson de Roland*, than it does to the historic Charles. But we must take care to assign the legends and ideals their right place in the historical process, and not attach them to institutions to which they do not belong. The Christian idea of empire, the idea of an *imperium Christianum* or Christian commonwealth, was a powerful force in the middle ages, influential in the minds and actions of many kings and emperors, including Charles the Great, Otto III, and Henry III. We cannot leave it out of our picture. But we shall simply pile up confusion, if we attempt to identify it with the historical empire in the west, or indeed with any other empire of this world. The empire as a historical phenomenon was not, either in intention or in fact, an organization of a kingdom of God on earth ; it was a state among other states, with no higher rights than its neighbours. Dante's ' Universal Christian Commonwealth ' portrayed (as Bryce said) ' a lofty ideal and one never to be forgotten by mankind ' ; but this commonwealth, conceived as a remedy for the ills of the fourteenth century, was not the ' Holy Roman Empire ' of history.

I do not wish to suggest that there is any cleavage in the history of the Empire—or, indeed, elsewhere in history—between idea and reality. But the ' idea ' of the Empire is distinct from the ideas and ideals propagated by individual writers and thinkers about the Empire. It is an idea—only stabilized for an instant in the eleventh century, and then immediately subjected to attack—which developed and took shape in response to specific external stimuli and to particular momentary constellations of events, and what emerges is something which no man ever planned and probably no man ever desired. What I have tried to do is to follow this inter-relation and interaction of idea and reality in its historical context. The resultant picture (as it reveals itself to the student) is as different from that of the political historian, who tends to portray realities that have no value, as it is different from that of the political philosopher and the historian of ideas, who is apt to deal with a scheme of values that

K

has no reality. It has none of the logical beauty which we associate with the latter, and does not easily lend itself to brilliant generalization ; but that is a small price to pay if it brings us nearer—in the spirit of Ranke—to what the Empire really was. From that point—and from that point alone—we can safely advance a step further, and attempt to measure its impact on European society and its significance in the story of European civilisation.

9. *The Fall of Constantinople*

ON May 29, 1453, Constantine XI, last emperor of Rome and descendant in unbroken succession of the Caesars, died fighting in the streets of Constantinople, and Byzantium fell to the Turks.[1]

Few events have made a deeper impression on contemporaries or on posterity. Founded by Constantine the Great in A.D. 330, the 'new' or 'second' Rome held for a millenium a unique place in the civilisation which radiated from the Mediterranean crucible. Not only was it the capital of the Roman Empire which many believed eternal ; it was also the bastion of Christendom, which for centuries had withstood the onslaught of Islam, and the cradle of the missions which carried Christianity to the Slavs ; it was the home of Hellenism, where Greek thought and the Greek language still retained their native freshness and vigour ; and above all else it was 'the great clearing-house between Europe and Asia and between antiquity and all later times'.[2] As Mohammed II surveyed the scene of his victory, it seemed as though Asia had at last taken its revenge on Europe for the victories of Alexander the Great and reversed one of the great judgements of history. The Roman empire which had ruled in Europe, Asia and Africa, had disappeared for ever ; it was the end of an epoch.

But if, for contemporaries, the events of 1453 seemed above all else to draw a line across the ledger of history, for historians of a later generation they were significant less as the end of an old than as the opening of a new epoch, and 1453 was soon picked out as the traditional starting-point of modern European history. The fall of Constantinople, they maintained, not merely left the way open for the rise of the west to pre-eminence ; it also created the essential conditions for its rise. The arrival of Greek scholars, refugees from 'Turkish tyranny', carrying with them precious manuscripts, released the springs which set the Renaissance in motion, liberating

---

[1] Reprinted from *The Manchester Guardian*, May 29th, 1953.
[2] F. B. Artz, *The Mind of the Middle Ages* (1953), 129.

the European mind from its ' mediaeval bondage '. ' The Oxford
lectures of John Colet ', a well-known historian wrote,[1] the humanism of ' Erasmus, perhaps even Luther's historic protest at Wittenberg, may be ascribed, in no fanciful sense, to the Ottoman conquest
of Constantinople '.

In the second place, with the fall of the ancient metropolis, the
Mediterranean ceased to be the axis of civilisation ; the principal
gateway to the east and its riches was closed ; and the search for
new trade-routes ushered in the great period of exploration which
spread European domination across the hemispheres and altered
the economic and political balance of the world. And finally the
very circumstances of the fall of Constantinople, the failure of
Christendom to combine in its defence, were thought to betoken
the new spirit which marked the modern age. They revealed the
collapse of a sense of European community, which soon found its
wider expression in the Reformation, and the rise of national communities pursuing their own ends, in political rivalry and economic
competition—the appearance, in short, of the national states through
whose strivings the immense potentialities of Europe in modern
times were developed.

It may be said immediately that no historian to-day would
accept these judgements in their entirety. Scholars have demonstrated that the leaven of Greek learning began to work on the
European mind long before 1453, and it would be hard to show that
the course of the Renaissance was accelerated or directly influenced
by the fall of Constantinople. Furthermore, we know to-day that
the empire of Mohammed II and of Suleiman the Magnificent was
no mere tyranny, but the most efficient and in many ways the most
civilised government the world of that day knew.[2] For south-east
Europe, which had been unstable and anarchic ever since the
western Crusaders sacked Constantinople in 1204, Turkish dominion
brought substantial benefits.[3] And European rulers were ready to
accept and treat with the Porte on terms of equality. But already
as early as the time of the Second Crusade the sense of European or
Christian unity against the forces of Islam was weak, and there are

---

[1] J. A. R. Marriott, *The Eastern Question* (1917), 64.
[2] A. H. Lybyer, *The Government of the Ottoman Empire in the time of Suleiman the
Magnificent* (1913), paved the way for a more dispassionate view of Ottoman rule ; if
his praise was perhaps too lavish, the main trend of his revision was borne out by
R. B. Merriman, *Suleiman the Magnificent* (1944), and by F. Babinger, *Mahomet II le
Conquérant et son temps* (1954).   [3] Babinger, op. cit., 522–523.

many mediaeval precedents for the alliances with the Turks which Francis I and Henry II of France made in the sixteenth century.

On the other hand, the famous voyages of Columbus in 1492 and Vasco da Gama in 1498 were in no sense a consequence of the fall of Constantinople, but rather a tardy but long-prepared reaction to the stranglehold over oriental trade acquired by the Mamelukes of Egypt after the fall of the last European colonies in Asia Minor in 1291. Moreover, it is an exaggeration to suppose that the discovery of the Americas had immediately revolutionary effects in diverting the axis of European history away from the Mediterranean to the Atlantic sea-board in the west. European colonisation overseas hardly started before the seventeenth century, and down to the defeat of the Turkish navy at Lepanto in 1571 the Mediterranean retained its old central importance.

For all these reasons the historian to-day, who seeks to assess the significance of the fall of Constantinople in the light of five centuries of history, will look further afield than his predecessors in the nineteenth century. For us, who have witnessed in our own lifetime the passing of the ' European age '—who look back over the last five hundred years as a period irremediably past, to which we no longer belong save as its bewildered and disinherited successors —an interpretation which surveys the events essentially from the point of view of western Europe is no longer adequate. We have to try to take the wider view of world history.

It is, of course, true that the consolidation of Turkish dominion over eastern Europe after 1453 left an indelible imprint on European history. The battle of Mohacs in 1526, which established Turkish dominion up to the gates of Vienna, was in a very real sense the date of foundation of the Habsburg empire of modern times, which assumed thenceforward the place of Constantinople as the bulwark of the west against the Islamic world.[1] And it may fairly be said that so long as the Austrian empire lasted, Europe lasted, and that the struggle for the succession to the Habsburgs—itself the sequel to the struggle for the succession to the Ottoman empire—opened the great European civil war, in which Europe crippled itself and destroyed its pre-eminence in the world.

But Austria, because it shared neither the Greek religion nor Byzantine culture, but was linked irrevocably to a German and

[1] Cf. above, p. 126.

Catholic environment, could never be the true heir of Constantinople, or a fatherland for the Slav and Magyar peoples it brought
under its dominion. Its failure and downfall was due to its efforts
to span two worlds. When Constantinople fell in 1453, the last
remaining citadel of Orthodox Christianity was Moscow; and it
was on Ivan the Great of Russia, not on his contemporary, the
Habsburg emperor, Maximilian I, that the mantle of the Byzantine
emperors fell. When Ivan married Constantine XI's niece in 1472
and adopted as his coat-of-arms the double-headed imperial eagle
of Byzantium, Russia asserted its title to the legacy of Constantinople.
For the moment few, if any, practical consequences were drawn,
and nothing done to make the inheritance effective; nevertheless it
was a turning-point in history, the significance of which has only
become fully apparent in our own generation.

' Two Romes have fallen,' wrote the monk of Pskov, ' but the
third is standing, and there shall be no fourth.'[1]   Ever since the
Mongol invasions of the thirteenth century Moscow had been
isolated; now it took its place in the main stream of world-history.
In the centuries which followed, the course of Russian history was
affected by many new influences; and we must not exaggerate the
Byzantine strand in Russian policy to-day. Nevertheless from 1453
the legacy of Constantinople remained an integral part of Russian
tradition. It was not merely that it provided a basis and justification
for Russian claims to the Dardanelles and for Russian expansion into
south-east Europe, and thus dominated the whole subsequent history
of the ' Eastern question '. Far more important—for it was what
gave such territorial aims consistency and purpose—was the new
conception of Russia's universal mission, transmitted through the
Christian church from Byzantium to the ' Third Rome ', which
entered Russian policy after 1453.

Five centuries ago the words of Philotheos of Pskov may have
sounded arrogant and foolhardy; but for us to-day, in the new
constellation of world-forces after 1945, they echo through the
centuries as the prophetic expression of the most momentous consequence of the fall of Constantinople. In western Europe the wheel
has come full circle; but on the wider stage of world-history the
effects of the events of 1453 are only now making themselves felt.

[1] For this famous statement, and the doctrine of ' the Third Rome ', cf. above, pp.
40–1, and below, p. 197.

10. Metropolis and Macrocosm Europe and the Wider World, 1492–1939[1]

EVER since the end of the war a change has come over our conceptions of modern history. We no longer feel that we stand four square in a continuous tradition, and the view of history we have inherited, the history which has western Europe at its centre, seems to have little relevance to our current problems and our current needs. In the Second World War ' the collapse of the traditional European system became an irrevocable fact ', and ' what is called the " historic Europe " is dead and beyond resurrection '.[2] ' The old Europe of the years between 1789, the year of the French Revolution, and 1939, the year of Hitler's War, has gone for ever '.[3]

This fundamental change is bound to have repercussions upon the writing of modern history, in particular upon the inescapable assumptions of historians. There is still, for those who lived through the period beginning with the great depression of 1929, a morbid interest in the *post mortem* type of history, of which Sir Lewis Namier had made himself the master; but such history avails little as orientation among the dilemmas which face us in the post-war constellation of world-affairs, and it is natural and inevitable that a younger generation of historians should turn away from the older preoccupations, which no longer correspond to a living need, and attempt to hammer out a new vision of the course of modern history, to replace the world-picture which the war has torn to shreds.[4]

In some cases this reaction has taken the form of a critique of the assumptions which had become the unquestioned foundations of western historiography—in particular, the assumption, which nineteenth-century economic developments seemed to prove, that Europe, the ' microcosm ' at the heart of an expanding world-economy, was destined to transform all other civilisations and carry

[1] Reprinted from *Past and Present* V (1954), 77–93.
[2] H. Holborn, *The Political Collapse of Europe* (1951), x.
[3] A. Bullock, *Hitler. A Study in Tyranny* (1952), 738.
[4] Some of these views I have attempted to summarize, below, pp. 172 sqq.

over into the hemispheres the system of a balance and concert of
powers, by which it was loosely integrated.[1] The illusory nature
of these assumptions is already common knowledge[2]; it is not
merely that imperialism has produced a reaction in the political
field, the strength of which we are only beginning to feel, but that
throughout Asia and Africa it has been accompanied by rejection
of what are somewhat misleadingly called ' western values ', i.e.
moral and religious assumptions which, in practice at least, the bulk
of the population in the west has already discarded.   European
predominance in Asia is seen to-day as a temporary phase—almost
as a breach in historical continuity—that has now passed.[3] In European history itself the old tendency to exaggerate the role of the
' historic core ', springing from the empire of Charlemagne, has
given way to a better appreciation of the significance for us all of
the enduring factors in Russian history—not merely its impact on
the western world from the days of Peter the Great, but the importance of the period from the end of the eleventh to the middle of
the sixteenth centuries in which the essential features of Russian
culture, distinguishing it from western Europe, took shape.[4] We
realize better that historic Europe includes not only the Germanic
peoples looking to Rome, but the Slavonic peoples looking to
Byzantium and later to Moscow, the ' Third Rome '.[5] And instead
of emphasizing the impact of Europe on the New World, historians
to-day are giving greater attention to the impact of the New World
on Europe, or are at least seeking to treat their history not as that
of separate continents but as directly related elements in the history
of a world which, since the Industrial Revolution, has become ever
more closely integrated.[6]

Underlying this change of orientation is not so much new knowledge as a new vision playing on old facts, and a realization of the
inadequacy of old formulations in a new situation.   The older

---

[1] Cf. L. Dehio, ' Ranke und der deutsche Imperialismus ', *Hist. Zeitschrift* CLXX
(1950), 307–328 ; also ibid. CLXXIII (1952), 77–94, and CLXXIV (1952), 479–502.
[2] Cf. A. J. Toynbee, *The World and the West* (1953).
[3] K. M. Pannikar, *Asia and Western Dominance* (1953).
[4] Cf. W. Philipp, *Hist. Zeitschrift* CLXXVI (1953), 590 ; cf. below p. 187.
[5] H. F. Schmid, ' Eastern Europe in the light of world history ', *Eastern Review*, I
(1948), 7–23 ; S. H. Gross, *Slavic Civilisation through the Ages* (1948) ; H. Ludat, ' Die
Slaven und das Mittelalter ', *Die Welt als Geschichte* XII (1952), 69–84 ; O. Halecki,
Borderlands of Western Civilisation. A History of East Central Europe (1952).
[6] Cf. M. Silberschmidt, ' Wirtschaftshistorische Aspekte der neueren Geschichte,
Hist. Zeitschrift CLXXI (1951), 245–261.

historiography, with its myopic concentration on Europe and on the European powers and—where it looked further afield—its independent treatment of the history of America and the overseas territories as distinct units or spheres moving in a separate axis, had discredited history and denuded it of sense and significance ; it seemed to be lost in a world of nationalities which has disintegrated visibly before our eyes. The effort of the newer writers is therefore directed to blasting a way through the blank wall, against which our previous historiography had come to a halt ; to opening a path for the historian into the future ; and to restoring the connexion between past and present, between history and life, which had perished.

Two main postulates underlie the new view. The first is the realization that what has been called ' the European age ', which may be dated roughly from 1492 to 1914, was not a steady culmination, but a phase with its beginning and its end, lying between the preceding ' Mediterranean ' and the succeeding 'Atlantic ' ages.[1] The second is that the history of this age cannot profitably be studied in isolation, particularly for us who stand outside its limits, and are interested as practical persons above all else in the establishment, during the ' European age ', of the foundations of the period which, after the wars of 1914–18 and 1939–45, was to succeed it ; that, in particular, the distinction between European and American history, as though they were two trams running simultaneously down parallel tramlines, is as unreal and deceptive as would be the attempt to-day to draw a dividing-line between the economic and political problems of the European and the American continents.

There have, of course, from Tocqueville and Burckhardt onwards, always been historians who have perceived the temporal limitations of the ' European age ', and were acutely conscious that it was running to its close ; but they remained eccentric and exceptional, and exerted no clear influence over the tradition of historical writing. To-day it is different. The failure of the old historiography to provide reliable guidance—for example, in regard to the rise of Russia to the rank of a world-power—its extraordinary capacity, which has bred widespread scepticism as to the ' use ' of history, to get the portents wrong, because it failed (if, indeed, it

[1] O. Halecki, *The Limits and Divisions of European History* (1950), 29, 61.

did not often deliberately refuse) to take a wider view, have cleared
the decks. Much of the writing to-day, naturally enough, is still
tentative, a groping after new formulations, and he who attempts
a new synthesis does so at his peril. But already we have from a
German historian a challenging re-examination of the whole course
of international relations for the five centuries following the fall of
Constantinople[1]—a reappraisal which has placed the political history
of modern Europe in an entirely new light by setting it in an extra-
European context—and there is evidence that this work will not
stop short at the political level. The impact of the outer world on
European politics, and the transforming effects of that impact are
now evident. Equally important is the economic impact—considered as a whole, and not merely in relation to isolated incidents,
such as the periodic effects of American slumps—and its transforming effects upon the whole superstructure of ideas and institutions in the modern world. And precisely this is the field which
the American historian, Walter Prescott Webb, has chosen to investigate anew. For Webb, the opening of the frontier lands of
the western hemisphere to a static European society in 1492, is the
beginning of a new epoch in the story of mankind. Thereafter ' in
the history of western civilisation the two are inseparable ', and ' the
interaction between the two ', a ' gigantic process extending over
more than four centuries ', is for him the essential ' drama of modern
history '.[2]

Whatever reservations we may have to formulate as to its positive results, Webb's work deserves recognition as a bold attempt to
re-examine along new lines the fundamental postulates of modern
history ; even where, we may think, it fails to convince, it helps us
to clarify the issues, and above all else to see the present not as a
continuation of, but as a break with past development. For Webb,
as for Halecki—though the terms he uses are different—the
' European age ' is a thing of the past ; and if, viewing it as a past
age, he seeks to re-appraise its character and the elemental forces
which determined its beginning and its end, it is not to discover
guiding lines leading out of it into the future, but on the contrary
to make clear the fundamental differences in environment which

[1] L. Dehio, *Gleichgewicht oder Hegemonie. Betrachtungen ueber ein Grundproblem der
neueren Staatengeschichte* (1948).
[2] W. P. Webb, *The Great Frontier* (1952), viii, 8, 11.

place us to-day before new circumstances, in which the experience of the past offers no sure guide.

*   *   *

The conventional starting-points of modern history, for historians in western Europe, are the Renaissance and the Reformation.[1] Walter Prescott Webb takes another view. There had been other renaissances, a long series reaching back to the time of Charlemagne ; there had been reformers without number before Luther. But the earlier reforms had withered, the earlier renaissances had failed to produce a decisive turning in the human mind. Why was it that the sixteenth century registered a permanent advance, where other centuries had experienced only a transient stimulus? Was it simply the gathering impetus, which now suddenly burst the banks and carried all before it, or was it that a new factor, a new ' propelling force ', so changed the external environment and ' enlarged the field in which the human mind could operate ', that the decisive leap into the future which had baffled earlier generations became suddenly feasible? Webb's answer is clear and categorical. The supreme architect of the modern world, for him, was Christopher Columbus ; the decisive event, differentiating the modern era from all previous recorded history, was the discovery of the New World in 1492, and the series of voyages, explorations and discoveries which followed in its wake. Decisive, because the vast accretion of new territory, ' of gold and silver, of new foods for every empty belly and new clothing stuffs for every half-naked back ', opened up possibilities no previous society had known. Down to 1492, for all its political upheavals, society had been static in essential things. The rise of empires, Persian or Roman or Carolingian, did not add to wealth, but simply transferred it to other hands. Apart from insignificant increments, due to the slow recovery of forest and marsh, ' the land area available to Europeans ' remained substantially unchanging ; and the consequence was that population, pressing hard on the means of subsistence, was stable too. The idea of progress had not been born ; ' heaven alone, which could be reached only through the portals of death, offered hope to the masses '.[2]

The discovery of the New World completely altered this situa-

<hr />

[1] On this periodization of history, cf. above, pp. 59–61.
[2] Webb, *The Great Frontier*, 9, 143.

tion. It added to the old inhabited areas—the ' closed world ' of
the Metropolis—the whole ' frontier ' zone, the unexploited habitable
regions revealed by the explorations of the fifteenth, sixteenth and
seventeenth centuries—' three new continents, a large part of a
fourth, and thousands of islands in oceans hitherto hardly known '.
What this signified figures best make clear. The population of the
' Metropolis ' in 1500, about 100 million, was crowded into an area
of three and three-quarter million square miles, giving an average
density of 26.7 persons per square mile. But now ' to the 100 million
people of the Metropolis was suddenly made available'—in addition
to the exportable wealth, gold and silver, timber, furs—' nearly 20
million square miles of fabulously rich land practically devoid of
population, an area more than five times as great as all Europe '.
The result was that ' the population density was reduced to less
than five persons per square mile, and each individual could have
an average of 148 acres instead of 24 '. In addition, however,—
and far more immediately effective—there was the impact on the
Metropolis of the wealth of the New World. It was American
treasure, and American treasure alone, ' that reversed the long
descent of prices and sent them slanting upwards to such heights
as to constitute a revolution '. It was the ' windfalls ' of the frontier
—those commodities which fell into the hands of explorers and
adventurers almost for the taking—that brought about the capital
accumulation which made the Industrial Revolution possible. As
Webb says, ' it is inconceivable ', that the people of Europe in 1500,
confined to their original area, ' could by any stretch of their genius
or by any invention they might make produce the wealth and create
the boom which they enjoyed during the following four centuries '.
The frontier was ' the matrix of the modern world '. ' Without its
frontier modern Europe would be so different from what it is that
it could hardly be considered modern at all.'[1]

Modern history is therefore the drama of the impact of the
Metropolis on the frontier and of the frontier on the Metropolis.
If Western Europe—the Metropolis—is considered alone, its history

---

[1] Ibid., 7, 10, 16, 17, 144, 174. As instances of the ' windfalls ' of the frontier Webb
cites the examples of the gold and silver brought back by Drake in the *Golden Hind*—
which provided the capital behind the Levant and East India Companies—and the
dividend paid in 1687 by Sir William Phipps—' what is probably the biggest dividend
in business history, 10,000 per cent as against a paltry 4,700 per cent paid by Drake about
a century earlier ' (ibid., 197, 201).

does not make sense ; for ' the story of the Great Frontier and the Metropolis rises high above the fragments of both ' ; it is the unity of which each singly is the imperfect part. It was through contact with the frontier in the New World that the institutions handed down from the Middle Ages disintegrated ; and ' the character of the modern age is due in large measure to the fact that it had a frontier setting, that it grew up in an economic boom induced by the appropriation and use of frontier resources, and that its institutions were designed and modified to meet the needs of a booming society '.[1]

In 1500 ' wherever man turned, some guardian was telling him what to do, what to believe, what to think. All round he was walled in by authority, which saw to it that he moved in a prescribed groove '. The frontier was ' the fifth column of liberty '. It put a premium on the individual, made possible ' his temporary supremacy over institutions '. ' Democracy ', says Webb, ' is a frontier institution, so far as the modern world is concerned '. On the frontier the old-world ' baggage ' of ' ideas about rank, status and relative position ' was jettisoned, because it was useless ; and instead there arose a new creed of equality. The institutions of the old corporate class-conditioned European society of the *ancien régime* ' wore themselves out against the abrasive frontier grindstone '. And in their place—spreading back to the Metropolis—arose the characteristic institutions and outlook of a frontier society : individualism, equality, democracy, the ' religion of work ', ' unbridled optimism ', ' rude manners ', the profit-motive—a mixed bag, indeed, for the frontier ' ruthlessly crushed out many fine qualities which human beings derive from leisure ', but a mixture without which modern civilisation, in the Metropolis as well as in the New World, would be unrecognizable.[2]

It is easy to take these changes for granted ' as merely another logical step in the orderly progress of an endowed people '. To do so is to miss the essential point. We are apt to assume that man ' achieved freedom by his own efforts ' ; in reality, the whole substructure and the whole superstructure of modern civilisation rest upon a ' windfall '. ' The modern age ', in other words, ' was an abnormal age and not a progressive orderly development which mankind was destined to make anyway '. ' The institutions developed

---

[1] Ibid., 11, 140.　　　　[2] Ibid., 5, 30, 31, 34, 35, 49 sqq., 55, 265, 303.

in this exceptional period were exceptional institutions . . . quite different from what might be expected in the course of human affairs '. Like the ideas that went with them—ideas, for example, about the relations of the individual and government—they were ' highly specialized to meet boom conditions ', and as such bound to undergo violent change as soon as ' boom conditions ' passed ' away and history returned to normal.' And precisely that is what has happened. The 'Age of the Frontiers ' is an age which has passed. Between 1890 and 1910 the frontier closed. As we have seen, the ratio of population to land in 1500 was about 27 to the square mile ; by 1900 it was again approaching that mark ; by 1930 it had passed it ; a decade later it was touching 35. There was a ' pause ' lasting about a generation, from 1900 to 1930 ; but ' by 1940 the big house was much fuller than the little house was in 1500 '.[1]

Just as the opening of the ' frontier ' marked the beginning of a new era, so the closing of the ' frontier ' marks its passing. The repercussions are already being felt all along the line. ' Frontier individualism is now old, a thing of history ', something to look back on, representing the ' goal of an extinct period ' ; and the modern individual, ' caught between the closing frontier and the expanding production of the machine ', feels himself ' useless, baffled and defeated '. He sees the economic system he knew in process of falling about his ears ; ' and the case is not much different in our attitude toward democracy '. Even if scientific discovery and technology can maintain the abundance which ' made the profit-motive tenable ' and carried society ' along the road to capitalism ', it will still ' bring with it a new set of needs ' and ' it will be necessary to specialize in another direction determined largely by . . . whatever force dominates society '.[2]

Hence ' we should not be so obtuse as to believe that the means of management are the same as those of conquest, or that frontier institutions will necessarily serve a metropolitan society '. Obsessed by the idea of guarding against the restrictions they had escaped, in the form of absolutism and mercantilism, people failed to see that out of their new condition, out of ' abundance and freedom ', ' new institutions as menacing as the old ones ', were arising. Of these none was more important than the business corporation, ' the pattern-maker of institutionalized modern life '. ' Corporateness is

[1] Ibid., 14, 15, 18, 107, 141, 160, 413.   [2] Ibid., 109, 128, 414.

now the primary fact and the dominant force.' ' Curbed on all sides
by corporations or government agencies or labour unions, or associations ', the individual is ' approaching anonymity in the modern
corporate culture ' ; ' the chief choice left to him is a choice of
curbers '. ' Like the reluctant ox, he comes slowly to the yoke, but
he comes nevertheless.' ' It is not that people are no longer willing
to take risks, but rather that they are overborne by a sense of futility
in striving for what seems unattainable.' Nevertheless the result is
a situation ' which makes it possible for the corporate organizations
. . . to gather their recruits ', and ' gives the few bold leaders their
opportunity . . . to command an army more noted for its docility
than for its courage '. Above all else, it is a situation ' favourable
to the dictator ', who rises from ' the cemeteries of dead hopes and
aspirations '.[1]

This is the new age upon which we are entering ; and of necessity
our entry into it ' will be accompanied by basic changes in the
nature of the institutions which grew up in the earlier one '—
particularly in ' those institutions which best fulfilled the needs of
a frontier society '. ' Society as it thickens will become more closely
integrated and its members more interdependent.   Governments
will tend to become stronger, using more compulsion in order to
meet their obligations. . . . The individual will become relatively
less important and will lose his identity in a growing corporate life '.
' Capitalism of the nineteenth-century type will decline with the
passing of the boom on which it was based '.   Society itself will
' go through a process of devolution and retrogression rather than
evolution and progress ', losing ' much of its dynamic character ',
and 'rural life' will 'tend to become more important' as 'city life'
becomes ' less alluring ', until in the end men looking back will see
' the Age of the Frontier ' and all its ideas and institutions as ' an
aberration , a temporary departure from the normal, a strange
historical detour '.[2]

*   *   *

Such are Webb's arguments.   Their force is due to the fact that
they are based not on chance observation of contemporary trends
but upon a rigorous historical analysis which, if true, is inexorable.

[1] Ibid., 71, 78, 101, 103, 107–109, 113, 118, 119, 131, 418.   [2] Ibid., 414–415.

Few of his arguments are new in themselves. His debt to Turner's famous ' frontier concept ' is obvious ;[1] and scarcely less marked, in his analysis of boom conditions, is his debt to Keynes and to Earl Hamilton, the historian of the sixteenth-century price revolution.[2] His own contribution is to bring familiar concepts and arguments within the fold of an encompassing vision which illuminates them afresh. Nor is it a serious criticism that his narrative—in common with many other great simplifying visions—is sometimes crudely expressed and marred by error in detail. It should nevertheless be noted that he does not hold ' that the frontier originated ideas or institutions, but only that it altered them, often in a spectacular manner ' ; he does not claim that it was the only factor, but simply that it was the formative factor, which provided the impetus otherwise lacking.[3] It might be argued that he exaggerates the role of the ' frontier ' and pays too little attention to economic developments within Europe since the Industrial Revolution, to the coal of South Wales and the Ruhr and the development of the iron and steel industries, as factors in the creation of modern industrial civilisation. To this criticism his answer would be that the capital accumulation and the economic milieu favourable to technical progress, which were pre-conditions of the Industrial Revolution, owed their existence to ' frontier exploitation ' ; that, however formidable in themselves, they were secondary consequences, and the ' frontier ', which ' increased manifold the room over which European people could move, and the body of wealth which they could acquire ', was primary.[4] It is, no doubt, true that the ' fertilization of industry by commercial capital ' derived ultimately from the frontier, was a less straightforward process than Webb appears to suggest ;[5] but whatever nuances might be introduced, it would be difficult to write off his generalization as unfounded. Undoubtedly the historical situation at every stage was more complicated than he indicates ; but this fact does not in itself impair the force of his argument, and we are still entitled to ask,

---

[1] F. J. Turner, *The Frontier in American History* (1920).

[2] Cf. J. M. Keynes, *A Treatise on Money* II (1930), 148 sqq. ; Earl J. Hamilton, 'American Treasure and the Rise of Capitalism ', *Economica* (1929).

[3] *The Great Frontier*, 239 ; cf. pp. 15, 101, 143, 173, 174, 258.

[4] ' The early stages of the Industrial Revolution were the middle stages of the frontier revolution ' ; *The Great Frontier*, 129. Cf. ibid., 75, 101, 238, 410. Cf. M. Dobb, *Studies in the Development of Capitalism* (1946), 207 sqq.

[5] Cf. for example Dobb, op. cit., 195.

what is its validity, not at this or that particular point, but as a comprehensive view of the course of world-history since the age of Columbus.

To this fundamental question—all criticism in detail apart—the answer must be that Webb illuminates part of the scene, but does not illuminate the whole scene because his vision—though wider than that of the average western European historian—is still not world-wide. His study, he says, ' is confined to the empty lands of North and South America, Australia, and that portion of the Dark Continent comprised in the Union of South Africa ' ; Asia ' has no part ' in his ' exposition '.[1] The limitation is arbitrary ; for it rules out a phase in the relations of Frontier and Metropolis comparable in scale to, and no less heavy in consequences than those with which he deals : the history of the Russian frontier. It may be true that, relatively, the extent of European colonization, beginning in the Middle Ages—in Prussia, for example, and other trans-Elbean lands—is too small to set beside that of the New World, though the repopulation of the Hungarian plain in the eighteenth century, after the expulsion of the Turks, was so vast a movement that Hungary at that time has been compared with America.[2] But all historians are agreed that in Russian history the ' frontier ', moving across Asia to the Pacific, has been as important a factor as it was in that of the United States ; and in excluding Russia and Russian expansion from his scheme, Webb not only violates the unity of history, but also vitiates his own conclusions.

The elementary geo-political facts are sufficient to demonstrate this limitation. The Soviet Union is as large both in extent and numbers as the whole of the North American continent ; it is four times the size of Europe, and yet has less than half its population.[3] This itself implies a ratio of land and population radically different from that upon which Webb's whole argument rests. In fact, where Webb establishes for 1940 a figure of approximately 35 inhabitants per square mile, the figure for the Soviet empire is no more than 22—a figure, significantly, still below the European ratio

[1] *The Great Frontier*, 9.
[2] Nevertheless we should remember that two-fifths of modern Germany—estimated by its pre-war frontiers—was added by colonization in little over two centuries, between 1125 and 1346 ; cf. G. Barraclough, *The Origins of Modern Germany* (1946) 251.
[3] B. H. Sumner, *Survey of Russian History* (1944), 9 ; ' throughout Russian history ', he adds, ' one dominating theme has been the frontier '.

L

of 1500.[1] In addition we may take into account—by contrast with the 'ruinously rapid rate of soil exploitation' in North America—the slow tempo of Russian colonisation in Asia, which only got going on a major scale after 1891.[2] If we accept Webb's postulates, only one conclusion is possible : namely, that the turn of the wheel which he claims to have been completed by about 1910 in the western hemisphere, has not yet occurred in the Soviet Union, that the Soviet frontier is not yet ' closed ', and therefore that the decline, the ' devolution and retrogression ', that set in in the west with the closing of the frontier, does not apply in the Russian orbit.

It is, however, another question whether we can accept Webb's postulates, and in particular the statistical basis upon which he works. To throw together the land area and population of Europe and the New World, as he does, may illuminate certain facts in their relations, but it obscures others. Even if ' the influence of the frontier on the Metropolis was indivisible ', if ' it exerted its influence on non-owners as well as on the proprietors '—if, for example, ' Spanish gold prospered England and Holland and France ', and we should not allow ' the concept of colonies and empires ' to ' obscure its common characteristics and the unity of the force it exerted '[3]— the fact remains that its impact was uneven. It is certainly worth emphasizing that the wealth of the New World was not canalized by political frontiers ; but that does not mean that political frontiers counted for nothing. When, for example, Webb states that the discoveries ' made available nearly 20 million square miles ' for the inhabitants of the Metropolis,[4] it is fair to point out that this availability was largely theoretical, and that in many directions it became illusory when political action in the form of immigration laws checked and even halted the flow of population. When Hitler in 1939 drew President Roosevelt's attention to the fact that the United States, with a population scarcely one-third greater than that of Germany, possessed more than fifteen times as much living space,[5] he unerringly put his finger on the inherent weakness of any argu-

---

[1] Assuming a population of 192 millions ; cf. A. Mousset, *Le monde slave* (1946), 8. The figure of the 1939 Soviet census is 170 millions, but this covers an area smaller than the Russian empire ; cf. Sumner, op. cit., 391.

[2] Cf. Sumner, op. cit., 17, 55.

[3] *The Great Frontier*, 11, 21, 410.   [4] Ibid., 17.

[5] *Documents on International Affairs*, 1939–1946, I (1951), 255. ' In this state', he had already remarked, ' there are roughly 140 people to each square kilometer—not 15, as in America ' (p. 254).

ment comprising the European metropolis and the New World in one formula. To treat either the New World or the Metropolis as a ' unity ', as Webb postulates, is itself of dubious validity ; but it will suffice for present purposes to emphasize the broad distinction between the two ' colonial ' regions, the Asian and the American, and Europe. Europe, with its relatively small land-area and its high population, stands apart from the one as it does from the other ; and the only safe course, for the purpose of analysis, is to treat each area separately.

This fact becomes even clearer if we turn to the political and institutional developments, which Webb associates with the influence of the frontier. It is a plausible (though by no means new) argument that the values of individualism were born on the frontier and ' that democracy is a frontier institution so far as the modern world is concerned ' ; but a finer analysis—particularly if, unlike Webb's, it is extended to include Russia—will not stop at this point. Democracy, as a descriptive term, has been used from the time of Aristotle to denote a variety of ills, a number of different political systems ; and it is important—not in order to make moral judgements, to castigate the one or the other as merely ' a semblance of democratic forms ',[1] but simply in order to secure a sound basis for historical analysis—to distinguish between the democracy of the frontier lands, of Russia and the United States, and that of Europe. There are adequate reasons, if we so wish, for describing all three forms of government as democratic, provided that we realize that such a description does not imply identity between them, or even identity between any two. Neither Russian nor American democracy—despite obvious inter-connexions and cross-influences—is the type of democracy we know as a historical fact in western Europe, if only for the reason that they are products of a totally different environment. For Webb the class structure of modern Europe, the privileges of groups and local communities, the corporations which existed to bolster and defend these privileges, constitute both restraints on liberty and the antithesis of democracy. For the European historian who is in a position to compare both the United States and Russia, they are likely, on the contrary, to appear as the very core and kernel of European democratic institutions. Whether we like it or not, Cromwell's famous dictum : ' Where is there any bound or limitt

[1] *The Great Frontier*, 165, 166.

sett, if . . . men that have noe interest butt the interest of breathing shall have a voice in elections? ',[1] is an essential ingredient of European democratic practice; and 'liberty' and 'privilege' in European political tradition are historically not antitheses but co-ordinates, at some periods even synonyms.[2] In western European experience democratic practice has resulted from the action of estates and—on the continent, if not in England—of provincial groupings, fighting for their 'rights';[3] it is for that reason and in that sense that it has so often been described as 'empirical' or 'pragmatic', the product of historical circumstances rather than of systematic theory.[4] We do not need to nourish any illusions about the limitations of democracy of this type, still less—as is now so common in Germany —to entertain nostalgic longings on its behalf; but it would be blindness to ignore the historical force of the traditions upon which it rests.[5]

From this point of view the historian in western Europe is more likely to contrast Europe with America and Russia, the two societies of the great open spaces, than to range Europe and the United States together as one type, in contrast to Russia.[6] In America, the dismantling of the corporative structure introduced by the early settlers—the collapse of guild-organisation and apprenticeship, the destruction of the village-community, the disestablishment of the church, and the introduction of a free system of land-tenure in place of entail and primogeniture—had occurred before the end of the eighteenth century.[7] In Russia, except perhaps on the western frontiers, such a social structure had never existed.[8] As in America,

[1] Cf. C. H. Firth, *The Clarke Papers* I (1891), 309. I have cut out the double negative of Cromwell's statement in the defective copy of the shorthand notes. The text is reprinted in A. S. P. Woodhouse, *Puritanism and Liberty* (1938), 59.

[2] Cf. G. Tellenbach, *Church, State and Christian Society at the time of the Investiture Contest* (1940) 16 sqq.—an important statement of the relations of *privilegium* and *libertas* which, no doubt because of the special context in which it is found, has not received the general attention that it deserves.

[3] It is sufficient to refer to Mill's classic statement in the historical introduction to his essay *On Liberty* (Everyman's Library edition, 66).

[4] Cf. G. H. Sabine, *A History of Political Theory* (1938), 665 ; M. Oakeshott, *The Social and Political Doctrines of Contemporary Europe* (1939), xviii ; C. E. M. Joad, *Guide to the Philosophy of Morals and Politics* (1938), 770, 788.

[5] Cf. for the whole of the above paragraph and for what follows, D. Gerhard's impressive study, 'Regionalismus und ständisches Wesen als ein Grundthema europäischer Geschichte', *Hist. Zeitschrift* CLXXIV (1952), 307-337.

[6] Cf. M. Beloff, 'Is there an Anglo-American political tradition?' *History* XXXVI (1951), 77, and passim.

[7] Cf. Gerhard, op. cit., 327-328 ; for primogeniture and entail, cf. Webb, op. cit. 259-268.   [8] Cf. Gerhard, op. cit., 312.

the open spaces, the moving frontier, the flow of population, stood in the way of the formation of stable social and regional groups comparable to those of the west; even the provincial and district assemblies of the nobility were weak.[1] And, as in America, the open frontier and the existence of free land created possibilities for the sudden rise of the individual, which find their parallels in America rather than in western Europe.[2] Indeed, in Russia, as in America, the open frontier has been the source of liberties—the history of the Cossacks is the best evidence of that[3]—but these liberties were never incorporated in fixed institutions in such a way as to withstand the extension of state power and the transformation of the structure of frontier society.[4] Here, in fact, we touch the essential difference between the ' democracy of the frontier ', and the historically conditioned democracies of western Europe ; and it may be argued that 'the democracy of the frontier ', for Webb the only true democracy, is a fragile growth precisely because it lacks the support of ingrained institutions, because it is related to a theoretical structure of individual rights and based on the atomized individual standing alone in society, whereas western democracy has its roots in groups and associations which effectively bind individuals together as a counterpoise to the power of Leviathan. ' Take away corporations and communities ', wrote Bodin, ' and you ruin the state and transform it into a barbaric tyranny '.[5] Not the least significant feature in the situation in Germany leading to the rise of Hitler was the undermining, by economic and other factors, of the old-standing corporate associations, from the *Länder* to the trade unions and the Christian churches. We may well think that Russian history is evidence of the fragile nature of ' frontier democracy ', that the weakness of local institutions and the mobility of the population go far to explain the triumph of autocracy. And if that is so, we may attach particular importance to Webb's chance remark, that ' if totalitarianism comes, it will come hardest among the people who made the most of individualism, the Americans of the United States '.[6] In spite of contemporary political and ideological diver-

---

[1] Sumner, op. cit., 76.   [2] Cf. Gerhard, op. cit. 329–33.

[3] Cf. Sumner, op. cit., 49 sqq.

[4] Cf. A. von Schelting, *Russland und Europa im russischen Geschichtsdenken* (1948), 274–278.

[5] J. Bodin, *Les six livres de la république* (Geneva, 1629), 502 (bk. iii, cap. 7) ; cf. *Six Books of the Commonwealth* (transl. M. J. Tooley, 1955), 107.

[6] *The Great Frontier*, 122.

gencies, there may well, in short, be fundamentally more affinity between the two extremes than between either extreme and the mean.

*   *   *

The foregoing reflections, summary as they are, may serve to throw into relief some of the main limitations of Webb's arguments, as a comprehensive picture of the development of modern society. They indicate three main reasons why his thesis fails to convince, although it helps to illuminate certain aspects of modern history. The first is that he exaggerates the influence of frontier institutions, and seriously underestimates—indeed, virtually ignores—the effects of industrialization and of the shift of population from the land to the great urban centres, which is so outstanding a feature of more recent American history. Even in the United States, in short, there are good reasons to think that the frontier was not the sole or even the main factor in the evolution of political and social democracy,[1] while it still has to be satisfactorily explained why, if decisive, it failed to produce parallel results in South or Latin America.[2]   Secondly, he fails to perceive that, in the Metropolis, what we may call ' frontier values ' have never been accepted as the norm of human existence, and that their influence has been limited historically by counter-currents coming from the heart of western society.   European historians are accustomed to see this reaction—with its ideal of an organically articulated society, built up of groups and associations, in contrast to the ideal of a uniform egalitarian society—as finding its outlet in the Romantic movement after 1815 ; indeed, many would regard it as the essence of the Romantic movement, and it is of the deepest historical significance that, whereas European rationalism of the eighteenth century had powerful repercussions in America and in the Russia of Catherine the Great, the Romantic movement remained, in its political aspects, a western European phenomenon affecting Russia only in so far as it was diverted into Slavophile channels, and thereby sharply differentiating the temper of European thought from that

---

[1] This has rightly been emphasized by P. Marshall, ' The Great Frontier ', *Past and Present* VII (1955), who effectively assembles American criticism of Turner's ' frontier ' thesis.

[2] Webb's summary treatment of this problem (pp. 87–89), in which he emphasizes exclusively the ' rigidity and stability of the Catholic church ' as a differentiating factor, is inadequate and unsatisfactory.

of Russia and of America alike.[1] We may, if we like, call this temper conservative, provided we realize it is not the conservatism of political parties ; and it is again of the deepest historical significance —wherever our personal sympathies may lie—that the force of this conservatism in Europe, as events since 1945 have demonstrated, is not spent, and that it still exists as a powerful check to the levelling and atomizing influence of ' frontier civilisation ', though in what direction its influence will be exerted no one can foretell.

But Webb does not merely exaggerate the influence of the frontier and underestimate the strength of contrary forces. His third major error is to misinterpret the role of frontier institutions, which historically have weakened the safeguards of individual rights and so have marked a dilution rather than an advance of the democratic tradition which Europe inherits from its Middle Ages. It is another question whether the new ' democracy ' is, except in the most indirect way, a product, as Webb supposes, of the frontier ; whether it is not more simply the result (as indicated above) of the growth both in the United States and in Europe of an amorphous urban proletariat which, inadequately represented by the older political associations, gave rise to a new political machinery to cope with its requirements and implement its aspirations. Nevertheless, no one would deny the force of the institutions and ideas which Webb, rightly or wrongly, has identified with the frontier. But to admit their force does not imply that we must welcome their advance as progress. On the one side, we can see all too plainly —for all the obstacles have been torn down—the wide road leading from ' frontier democracy ' to totalitarianism. On the other side, we can assert with a good deal of conviction that diversity, regional differentiation, and stability—the very things that the levelling force of the frontier attacked—are part and parcel of the indispensable foundations of civilisation.[2]

Nevertheless, it remains true that Webb is right in emphasizing the importance of the closing of the frontier, the cessation of the boundless opportunities for the individual which it betokened, and the problems of a frontierless society. Even in Russia the time cannot be far distant when the frontier will have closed. But whereas

[1] Cf. for example G. Ritter, ' Ursprung und Wesen der Menschenrechte ', *Hist. Zeitschrift* CLXIX (1949), 233–263.
[2] Cf. Gerhard, op. cit., 337, and Oakeshott, op. cit., xix.

Soviet Russia claims to have its own answer to the problems of a frontierless society, western society, in Europe and in America, is still entangled in the 'philosophy of a free and unfettered world', still 'trying to harness the dreams of yesterday . . . to the machines of to-day and to-morrow', and searching among the debris of the old for new or 'substitute' frontiers.[1] On these 'unreal images of new frontiers' Webb is caustic and astringent; in particular, he is sceptical of the common assumption that the problems of a frontierless society can be circumvented by science which, in place of the open frontier that has gone, can give us the infinite possibilities of a 'scientific frontier' stretching indefinitely ahead, and a new abundance produced by scientific means.[2] Science, he insists, cannot create abundance; it may 'speed up the rate at which resources already in existence' can be 'utilized', but its end-effect is destructive. Indeed, by fostering 'a population that is expanding with explosive force all over the world', it is more likely to add to our problems than to solve them. The solution to these problems, if they are to be solved, can only come on the political level.

But this solution is complicated by the fact—to which Webb scarcely refers—that the conquest of the frontier, for good or for evil, has made the whole world one. There is no 'overspill' area left, no outlet for surplus population, not even room for manoeuvre. Precisely because the unification of the world—in every sense save the political sense—is something unique in history, it has created a situation without parallel in the past.[3] The question to-day is whether we can devise new means of coping with this new world-situation. One of the virtues of Webb's analysis is that—parting company from most of his compatriots—he realizes that the newness of our situation leaves no room for the classical individualistic remedies, and makes no attempt to fob us off with the empty clichés —'the middle way', 'constitutional co-operation', 'spiritual rebirth', and the like[4]—of threadbare liberalism. It is a cardinal weakness, on the other hand, that he ignores the achievement of Communism and the fact that Communism—whether we like it or not—provides the only alternative to date which has not lost constructive force and imaginative grip; it offers at least a plausible solution for the

---

[1] *The Great Frontier*, 121, 133.   [2] Ibid., 280–302.
[3] Cf. A. J. Toynbee, 'The Unification of the World and the Change in Historical Perspective', *Civilisation on Trial* (1948), 62–96.
[4] Toynbee, op. cit., 27, 39, 40, 142, and passim.

countless millions of ' under-privileged ' in Asia and Africa as well as in Europe, to the problems of a frontierless society. But there is another way out, of which Hitler has given us a foretaste,—the conquest of ' living-space ' at the expense of others. It is the classical solution and probably the line of least resistance in a world of contending powers, with a resurgent Asia looming ever larger in the background ; but it is a solution which entails famine, blood-shed, want, destruction, and its result can only be the survival— of which past history gives us so many examples—of the least fit, and the crudest, the earthiest and the least civilized.

11. *Inquest on Europe*[1]

IN 1945, when the mists of battle cleared, a corpse was found lying, naked and despoiled, in a corner of the field. It was the old familiar Europe we knew so well—the Europe of the Congresses, the urbane Europe, well-nourished and prospering, which tasted with equal zest French wine and Gallic wit; which laughed at itself as it grew fat, but which grew fat and laughed; civilised, humanist Europe, for which the pleasures of youth were as nothing compared with the pleasures of middle age; self-satisfied, self-sufficient, with God discreetly in reserve, but its own world, the world it had contrived in its own image to its own liking, never out of view; sometimes with twinges of conscience, which may often have disguised spasms of indigestion, but never without ready cash to assuage conscience in the name of charity; tolerant, in its affluence and security, of cranks and heretics and doleful Jeremiahs, whose admonitions flattered and amused without endangering its anchored stability. We knew, before 1945, that it was getting short in the wind, this Europe of ours, that it suffered from occasional bouts of arthritis; we suspected that its teeth were false, and that round its middle it wore a masculine body-belt. But we cherished it, not least for the occasional grey hair; and it was an unpleasant shock to find the dishevelled corpse lying in the dirt, and two youthful giants disputing the spoils.

And so, out of piety, with a view to a decent burial, a jury was summoned to review the whole unhappy incident; for it is an old and laudable custom, in a case of sudden death, to summon a Coroner's Inquest, a jury of neighbours, good men and true, to enquire into the circumstances, to determine the causes, and to pronounce a verdict. Was it murder? Was it suicide? Was it ' natural causes '? An answer must be found, a clear decision reached, without prevarication, and without fear or favour.

And now, after a seemly interval, we have the findings, in three handsome volumes, decked out in the modern style with appendices of unimpeachable documents.[2] Four Englishmen, three French, a

---

[1] First published, in an abbreviated form, in *The Listener*, July 8th, 1954.
[2] *The European Inheritance*, ed. by Sir Ernest Barker, Sir George Clark and **Professor** Paul Vaucher, 3 vols., 1954.

Scot, a Belgian, an American of Norwegian extraction : it may
seem, at first glance, an oddly constituted jury, since all are implicated
in one way or another, and some may even be beneficiaries under the
will.   Surely it is the essence of the jury-system that it should be
composed of neighbours with no axe to grind, and not of blood-
relations? If it was to be confined to Europe, what of the proud
Spaniard, whose contribution to civilisation, in Europe and beyond,
has never been negligible, what of the German, what of the denizens
of eastern Europe, Poles or Russians, who assuredly have something
relevant to say? But we should not stop there, if what we really
want is the verdict of neighbours standing outside the fray.   A
philosophic Brahmin, a wise Confucian, a learned doctor of Islam,
an intelligent Kikuyu—how refreshing their autopsy would be, how
quickly they would strip off the smartly-tailored suit and expose the
fat paunch and the yellow streak of primitive humanity beneath.

And yet we should not make too much of this. The outsider
has his prejudices as well as the inhabitant of the house, and there
are things he does not see. Above all, he will judge by external
actions and results and know little of the conflicts of the soul, the
silent struggles of good and evil at dead of night, which have so
persistently accompanied the pilgrimage of European man. If we
criticize the jury, it will not be because, as blood-relations, they
have sought to conceal the truth, but rather because they have been
so anxious to avoid the charge of prejudice that they have left us
in the dark. It is sometimes as though they have thought it a sufficient explanation of death, to give us a recital of the life and works
of the deceased, and of his father and grandfather before him, and
of his ancestors back to the seventh generation.

Nor is one helped by the fact that the jury, so far as one can
penetrate behind their polite reticence, seems far from unanimous.
Professor Vermeil is the most forthright ; if I understand him right,
he would bring in a charge of murder, and indict Germany as the
culprit.[1] Sir Ernest Barker, on the other hand, will not have it
that the corpse is a corpse at all ; the body of Europe, like Juliet
in the tragedy, is stiff and pallid in a deathlike trance, but thee is
life in it yet ; it only needs an injection of federalism to ' endure
and prosper, and maintain the perpetuity ' of its ' inheritance '.[2] But
the others, so far as they feel called upon to venture an opinion at

[1] III, 190–192.   [2] III, 348.

all, diagnose a chronic internal malady as the cause of death ; and
theirs, it would seem, is the majority verdict.   Professor Vermeil
himself speaks of ' the undeniable decadence of Europe ', its ' failing
spiritual resources ', the ' bankruptcy ' of ' liberal humanism ', and
' moral exhaustion '.[1]   But it is to Professor Bruun that we must
turn for a masterly diagnosis of the sickness (as he calls it) that
began to assail Europe towards the close of the nineteenth century.

What are the causes and symptoms of this sickness? First, like
a galloping consumption, carrying endless secondary complications
in its train, Professor Bruun singles out ' a runaway technology ',
the ' most unmanageable factor ' of all, which soon ' outgrew
control '.   Next, there is the ' implicit contradiction ' at the heart
of ' liberal philosophy '—the unresolved contradiction between
' political equality in theory ' and economic inequality in fact.
Then there is the ' cleavage ' between ' those with property and those
without ', between ' employers and employees ', between ' the
bourgeoisie and the proletariat ', and following hard at heel the
' emergence of the masses ' on the one side, on the other the twin
maladies of ' dehumanisation ' and ' depersonalisation '.   The
suppression of the Paris Commune in 1871, the murder by Frenchmen of 10–20,000 other Frenchmen, marked the turning-point in
the illness : a confession that there was no physic to cure the internal
malady, that the surgeon must be called in. Thereafter the ' confident
premisses ', the optimistic philosophy which had carried the old
Europe along, were no more.   European man ' still obeyed an inherited pattern of conduct, but he was an exile from his own past '.
He beheld ' in cloudy vision the coming disintegration ', ' caught
the pale reflection ' of his own ' disenchanted face ', sought in vain
' the riddle of his inner real self ', and felt ' the weight of his desolate
and incommunicable singularity '.   When the end came, old Europe's
last breath was a sigh of relief, as it concluded the unequal struggle,
cast aside its burden, and gave up the ghost.[2]

It is obvious from this diagnosis that the European malady was
an internal malady, the sickness a sickness of the European soul ;
that ' the disruptive forces ' lay ' within European society '.[3]   On
the other hand, it is, of course, true that the sickness may have been
brought on by external events ; and if so, those events are relevant.

[1] III, 229, 257, 258, 261.
[2] III, 17, 57, 58, 81, 89, 98, 101, 107, 122, 123, 124.   [3] III, 128.

But a mere recital of external events can never explain anything so intimate, so subtle, so personal. As J. B. Bury, no enemy of factual history, long ago pointed out, no ' collection of facts ' has ' the slightest theoretical importance ', unless we can ' determine their vital connection in the whole system of reality '.[1] Surely, it is fair to ask, some things were more important than others in this long spiritual pilgrimage? Surely there were turning-points, such as we all recognize in our own lives? But, if there were, it is hard to find them in a narrative which advances with measured tread from the Ice Age, 600,000 years ago, to the half-century after 1914— the time (as Professor Vermeil calls it) of the ' second Thirty Years War '. Where are the peaks and the headlands, the hills which we climb to survey the long vistas behind us and in front? How, except from such eminences, are we to relate each ' period ', as it passes by, to ' the whole system of reality '? Perhaps this is the vaunted ' objectivity ' which modern historians have adopted as their ideal ; perhaps it springs from the belief that the historian's function is to narrate, not to relate and still less to judge. If so, it is worth pondering the remarks of another distinguished contemporary historian, Sir Keith Hancock. Historians, he says, who refuse to judge, ' do not succeed in refraining from judgement. They simply succeed in concealing from themselves the principles upon which their judgement is based '.[2]

Without judgement we cannot, in fact, advance one step. Consider for a moment the various occasions when (so our jury tells us) Europe, or European civilisation, or western Europe, or western civilisation, was ' saved '—saved, that is, from itself or from foes without. First, ' the whole future of Europe ' was saved in 480 B.C. when Themistocles defeated the Persians ; it was saved again in 1529 by the defence of Vienna, when the Turks ' threatened ' ' the survival of western civilisation ' ; it was saved again by William of Orange in 1688 when he took the lead against Louis XIV of France.[3] What strikes one first about these judgements, thrown out without explanation or justification, is their supreme assurance. They assume that the writer knows what would have happened if the fortunes of battle had gone the other way. In reality, of course,

---

[1] J. B. Bury, *Selected Essays* (1930), 47.
[2] W. K. Hancock, ' Machiavelli in Modern Dress : an Enquiry into Historical Method ', *History* XX (1935), 100.
[3] I, 168 ; II, 15, 16, 51, 81 ; II, 142.

there is no possible means of proving that any of these ' threats '
(as they are called), if they had come to pass, would have been more
than temporary, mere episodes in the life of European man. The
Huns swept across Europe and vanished without a trace. Are we
really to suppose, had Vienna fallen, that the Turks would have
marched across Europe and mastered England, France and Spain?

But what is more important and more in need of emphasis is
the obvious fact that judgements such as these—valueless as I think
they are—could not be made at all, unless the writers already had
some conception of Europe, to which they were related. You
cannot claim that Europe has been ' saved ' until you have decided
what Europe is. But here, at the decisive point, we are left suspended
in mid-air. Is Europe, for example, a purely geographical conception? Sometimes one suspects it is ; yet that can scarcely be the
case, for, as Sir Ernest Barker says, Europe is neither ' a fixed
quantity ' nor a ' determinate area ', and ' history does not move
according to continents or geographical divisions '.[1] And in fact,
when Professor Gordon Childe says of early Cretan art that it is
' quite European ',[2] he is evidently setting up a criterion which is
not merely geographical. He is postulating the existence of a specifically European style which has persisted in distinct and recog-
nizable form from the nineteenth century B.C. to the nineteenth
century A.D. That seems to imply some unity of civilisation, some
common durable elements and characteristics.

But what, in fact, is the evidence of such unity? ' The Europe
of antiquity ', Sir Ernest Barker says, ' was not a unity ' ; ' there
was no united Europe even in the days of the Antonines '.[3] Sir
George Clark claims that in spite of all variety there was ' one
civilisation ' in the fifteenth century ; but not much later he speaks
of a ' revolution in the relations between the eastern and the
western-central civilisations '.[4] Yet, for Professor Vaucher, Sir
George Clark's ' western-central civilisation ' does not exist. The
river Elbe, for him, marks a ' cleavage of European society into
two opposing worlds ', and in the Wars of the French Revolution
(he says) ' two different Europes confronted one another '.[5] Moreover, does not Sir George Clark's own statement that William of

[1] III, 296.   [2] I, 122.
[3] III, 297, 301.   [4] II, 4, 150.
[5] II, 237.

Orange 'saved western Europe', itself imply dichotomy? For
France—from which the Dutchman saved the west—was after all
a part of Europe, and Louis XIV a western European man. William
of Orange, it would appear, 'saved' western Europe because he
gave a lead to the opponents of 'authoritarian government'.[1] Are
we, then, to understand that 'authoritarian government' is non-
European, or at any rate not 'western European'?[2] If so, we have
moved away from the geographical criterion and from the artistic
criterion to one that is political and ideological. And, of course,
there may, for all we know, be good reasons for this change of
attitude. It may be true that Europe, without being either a political
or a geographical or even an historical unit, constitutes in some way
a spiritual entity. But if so, we are entitled to know where we stand.
It is not good enough to slip in among a series of facts, as though
it were a fact itself, a bland assertion which is neither self-evident
nor irrefutable. Themistocles 'saved the whole future of Europe',
Alexander of Macedon 'proclaimed' the 'idea of the European
inheritance' :[3] here is no simple fact, but the subject-matter for a
book. To clarify a single statement such as either of these, would
do more to explain what we mean by Europe and by the European
inheritance than a thousand pages of tightly narrated events.

*   *   *

The history of Europe is not a sequence of happenings but a
series of problems—fundamental, inescapable problems. Every
accretion of knowledge, instead of simplifying, complicates them,
makes it less easy to reach a clear-cut solution ; but it is precisely
the *Problematik* (as Germans call it) that has engrossed the best
minds in every generation, and it is by returning again and again
to the central problems that history has renewed itself by discovering
new impulses, new perspectives, a new vision.

By general consent three great problems dominate the history
of Europe : the problem of late antiquity ; the significance of the
great revolution at the close of the eleventh century, so inadequately
called the 'Investiture Contest' ; the problem of the eighteenth-
century Enlightenment. These are the three great turning-points,

---

[1] II, 139, 142.
[2] When the lord of Knossos made himself master of the whole of Crete around
1500 B.C., it was (it seems) an 'attempt to establish despotic monarchy in Europe',
which was providentially 'frustrated' (I, 132).
[3] I, 168 ; III, 335.

the three stages in the pilgrimage of European man ; we shall not
go far wrong if we compare them to birth, to manhood, and to
the onset of middle age.[1] They were shaped, of course, as our own
lives are shaped, by the manifold impact of external events, and of
these events every historian must take due notice. But it is not enough
to recount the events themselves ; what matters in the long run is
the effects they produced on the European spirit. If we are to understand the long pilgrimage of European man, we must take account
of the great spiritual crises through which he passed, and come to
grips with the reality that what determined the course of his life
was less the impact of outside events than his responses to the great
spiritual challenges by which he was confronted.

The first great crisis—what I have called the problem of late
antiquity—comes in the fourth and fifth centuries of the Christian
era. It is fundamental, for in it is contained the whole problem of
the relations between Antiquity and modern times, the problem
whether ancient civilisation should be termed ' European ' at all.
As Sir Ernest Barker concedes, there are reasons for questioning
such an identification. Greek history, in its Hellenistic phase, had
seen ' a fusion of Greece with the Orient ' ; civilisation became
' Hellenistic-Oriental instead of Hellenic and western '.[2] The Roman
world was a Mediterranean world rather than a European world,
in which Asia Minor and North Africa, as well as parts of Europe,
were integrated. Evidently there is no inherent reason to term such
a society or such a civilisation ' European ' ; and it is obviously
important, if we are to know at all what we mean by ' European '
and by ' the European inheritance ', for this problem to be discussed.
Merely to travel, in linear progression, from Rome to ' the dis-
location of Roman unity ',[3] without pausing on the way to ask what
has happened in between in men's souls, is not enough. In the third
century, says Dr. Tarn, ' pagan literature fell away ' ; but ' one
beautiful Latin poem has survived, the *Pervigilium Veneris* '.[4] One
beautiful Latin poem ! Here, in this bare phrase, is masked the
startling fact that the poem in question, the ' Vigil of Venus ', shows
us with astonishing clarity the break-through in late antiquity of a
spirit quite distinct from the classical spirit—a ' yearning aspiration '

---

[1] For reasons for rejecting the view that ' the middle of the fifteenth century ' was
' the beginning of a new age in western civilisation ' (II, 14) or that the sixteenth century
marked ' a great divide in history ' (III, 306), see above, pp. 59–61.

[2] III, 201.   [3] I, 313.   [4] I, 246.

and ' tints of living movement ' which reveal at once a turning-away
from the ' forms of integration which satisfied the ancient world '
and ' potential co-ordinations ' from which were to come things
' far richer than antiquity could compass '.[1] It is the same in art.[2]
Somewhere, on an unknown date, back in the fourth century of our
era, a new civilisation was born : a civilisation different from any
that had gone before, a civilisation which for the first time we may
rightly term European.

Seven centuries later, in the spiritual turmoil at the close of the
eleventh century, it came to manhood.[3] If we look only at the
events, this turmoil—the Investiture Contest, as we call it—seems
merely a tedious clash between kings and popes over episcopal
appointments.[4] And yet other historians, looking deeper, have seen
further. They have seen how, beneath this narrow concrete issue,
it ' was in reality a conflict between two violently opposed conceptions of the nature of Christian society ' ; and for that reason they have
singled out the crisis as ' a great revolution in world-history ', ' the
greatest—from a spiritual point of view perhaps the only—turning-
point in the history of Catholic Christendom '. It was the time
when ' the world was drawn into the church ', when in the west
the attitude of ' converting the world gained once and for all the
upper hand over the policy of withdrawing from it ' ; it was the
time when the practical aim was enunciated—the aim which is still
with us to-day—of establishing a moral order, God's ' right order ',
in this world.[5] Of this great decision, which has so powerfully
affected the whole subsequent history of Europe, a mere survey of
events can provide no glimpse ; and yet the failure to explain this
turning-point in the history of western Christendom—while eastern
Christianity remained faithful to earlier Christian traditions—
precludes any satisfactory explanation, at a later stage, of the undoubted divergencies between eastern and western Europe, in spite
of the fact that both are parts of one civilisation. Many external

---

[1] Cf. J. Lindsay, *Song of a Falling World. Culture during the Break-up of the Roman
Empire* (1948), 52, 54, 237, 282–3. There is an English version of the poem, ibid.,
64–68.

[2] Cf. E. Kitzinger, *Early Medieval Art in the British Museum* (1940), and the work of
Max Dvořák, cited above, p. 36.

[3] For a fuller account of this turning-point in the history of Europe, cf. above,
pp. 78–84.   [4] I, 368–370.

[5] Cf. G. Tellenbach, *Church, State and Christian Society at the Time of the Investiture
Contest* (1940), v, 111, 164.

M

reasons may be adduced, adequate partial explanations, for the
divergence of east and west; but the fundamental spiritual divergence, which goes back to the close of the eleventh century, is the
essential clue.[1]

The next great turning-point in the history of the European
spirit, the eighteenth-century Enlightenment, the Age of Reason,
is too near to be neglected in this way. But the profundity of the
revolution, and above all, the problematic nature of the inheritance
of the Enlightenment—these things are less obvious, and neither
Professor Vaucher nor Professor Mornet succeeds in conveying
their full implications. The displacement of dogma, the discovery
of God not (as in Christian theology) towering above nature, but
immanent in nature, the explanation of the universe as a rational
order in the light of its own indwelling laws, the confident belief
that man is the measure of all things and that the highest ideal is
the greatest happiness of the greatest number : all these are there
as facts of intellectual history.[2] But their revolutionary effects on
the whole cosmogony of European man—the total change in mental
outlook which Troeltsch expounded so brilliantly[3]—and above all
the critique of this brave optimistic humanism, with its firm belief
in progress : these are missing. No one reading Professor Mornet's
pages will realize that here European man came to a parting of the
ways ; that here he substituted a secular ethic for a Christian ethic,
or even worse, that Christian ethic itself was secularized ; that here
he jettisoned once and for all the dogma of original sin, and with it
the dogma of Grace, upon which the whole of Christianity rested ;
that here he decided that he could dispense with the mystery of
the universe, and of humility in face of that mystery.[4]

This was the time, we are told, when ' young pastors were freed
from the bigotry of a narrow pietism ; instead of preaching strict
doctrine they began to preach the principles of rational ethics '.[5]
But are we so sure to-day of the superiority of ' rational ethics ' over
' narrow pietism '? Are we so sure that the piety of Francke and
Zinzendorf, with its deep perception of the limitations of Reason,
its call for the dedication of the whole man to Christ, its unqualified

---

[1] Cf. below, p. 188.   [2] II, 294.
[3] E. Troeltsch, *Gesammelte Schriften* IV (1925), particularly pp. 338–374, 834–844.
[4] All this is brilliantly portrayed by T. Steinbüchel, *Zerfall des christlichen Ethos im
XIX. Jahrhundert* (1951), particularly caps. 3–6 (' Die Aufklärung als Erbe des 18. an
das 19. Jahrhundert ').   [5] II, 215.

search for God's Grace, was mere 'bigotry'? No one doubts the advances registered by the Age of Reason; they are all around us. But no one should ignore, either, its shortcomings. And the shortcomings were as heavy with consequences for the future as the advances. It was not merely that humanism and rationalism ignored realities which were as powerful as reason and stronger than man. The more fateful shortcoming was that the Enlightenment, the cult of a leisured moneyed middle class, assumed automatically that its beliefs were universal truths, applicable to all humanity—truths which only needed disseminating through education to provide a valid philosophy for democracy. Less than a century was needed to expose this illusion. The optimistic belief that it was only necessary for all citizens to receive the franchise for governments to become truly popular and harmonize all divergent interests, proved—optimistic. Napoleon I, and after him Napoleon III, showed Europe that democracy was more likely to lead to dictatorship than to Reason enthroned. ' Things are in the saddle and ride mankind ', wrote Emerson. But it was not the machines and technology of the nineteenth century that were responsible. The eighteenth century discovered the worship of things, turned the universe into a huge mechanism, a vast clock which God existed merely to wind up ;[1] and so it implanted the germ of the mortal sickness, which soon beset European man and laid him low. Without doubt, the new cosmogony of the Age of Reason cleared the way for the stupendous progress of the natural sciences in the nineteenth century; but to gain these riches Europe, like Faust, sold its soul. That is the twofold legacy of the Enlightenment to Europe.

*   *   *

It is only when we have analysed these great spiritual crises in all their depth and breadth that the history of Europe comes into perspective, and we can start to assess its heritage. If they have not been analysed in all their breadth and depth, the findings of our autopsy cannot but fall flat and be unconvincing. Why was it, for example, that, after 1914, Europe (in Sir Ernest Barker's words) ' went into the melting-pot in which it is still immersed '? ' What had been the flaw that led to the cracking and rending? ' The

---

[1] But later, when Napoleon asked Laplace, Newton's successor, why he nowhere mentioned God in his greatest work, the *Mécanique céleste*, Laplace answered : ' Sire, je n'avais besoin de cette hypothèse' (Steinbüchel, 62).

answer, he says, can be summarized 'in a word'; it was 'the dissolution of two empires, first the Turkish and then the Austro-Hungarian '.[1] Can the explanation really be so simple, we ask in wonder. What has this external fact to do with the spiritual crisis, the onset of which we have traced back to the time of the Enlightenment? And would that crisis have been any less real and threatening, had Turkey and Austro-Hungary never existed? Or consider again Sir Ernest's claim that by establishing ' some new and experimental form of federalism ', Europe can still ' retain ' its inherited ' riches '.[2] What relevance, we may ask, has federalism to the violent internal tensions—the conflict, for example, between middle-class liberalism and working-class democracy—which (as Professor Bruun shows)[3] rent and tormented the body of Europe until, in despair, it came to prefer death to life? The problems, we can see, go far deeper than this; they are in the last analysis spiritual problems; and mechanical explanations and mechanical remedies can neither clarify nor solve them.

Nor is it possible to solve the problems by saying, quite simply, that at one or other of the spiritual crises in its history, Europe took a wrong turning. We cannot say that the reform papacy of the eleventh century, in determining to shape the world in accordance with what it believed to be God's design, led Europe down the wrong road. We can say that in so doing it shifted the perspective and shaped the future of Europe. We can say that the evident benefits of the noble attempt to build a kingdom of God on earth were offset by a weakening spirituality, a tendency to forget that the kingdom of God is not, and never can be, of this earth. We may even say that the conception of a transformation of the world, affirmed in this way for centuries, prepared men's minds for the humanist ideal of a world shaped by man to his own purposes, which came to fruition at the time of the Enlightenment. But we cannot condemn the attempt for that reason. Nor can we condemn the orthodox Christianity of eastern Europe because it did not make this great leap; we can only say that the other-worldliness and spirituality which it preserved, were offset by a far weaker influence over social ethic than that exerted by Latin Christendom in the west. It is not, in other words, a question of praise or blame, for the gains

[1] III, 340.   [2] III, 348.
[3] Cf. above, p. 156.

and losses on both sides are obvious, but of historical differences
which go to make of Europe what it is.

And is it not the same in regard to the Enlightenment of the
eighteenth century? It is all too easy to condemn it for its spiritual
deficiencies, to say that here European man took the wrong turning
down a materialist road. It is easier still to cling to its exploded
values—its uncritical faith in the virtues of formal education, its
fallacious belief that democracy is the antithesis of autocracy, rather
than its seed-bed, its rationalist conviction that human passions and
social antagonisms can be harmonized by neat philosophic or political formulae. But the reality was not so simple as that. The defects
and the values, both real, were complementary ; each depended on
the other : and they cannot be neatly separated out like sheep and
goats. For the historian the Enlightenment is simply a stage through
which European man passed. It brought greater opportunities,
greater efforts, greater rewards, but also greater strains, greater
risks and greater temptations. We cannot say that the risks were not
worth taking, the achievements vain ; but we can point to the price
at which they were bought—particularly the vast consumption of
energy which left Europe, after the crisis of the French Revolution,
too weak to achieve again a comparable synthesis.

If that is the case, it must be obvious that any attempt to draw
up a balance-sheet is bound to fail. We cannot pick out of the past
certain elements, rejecting others, and claim that they, and they alone,
constitute the European heritage. Sir Ernest Barker, for example,
includes ' parliamentary democracy ' in the European inheritance,
but makes no mention of autocracy in its various forms, from the
tyranny of Greece and of the Italian city-states of the middle ages
down to the dictatorships of modern times.[1] In reality the European
inheritance comprises both forms of government, and both have
proved their value and constructive powers, in different circumstances, just as both, in other circumstances, have failed and been
superseded. History gives no clear brief in favour of either.

It is the same with the other ' elements ' (as they are called) in
the heritage. It may be that Sir Ernest Barker is right in emphasizing
the contributions of Israel, of Hellas and of Rome—the personal
God of Judaism and Christianity, the Greek conception of an
ordered, intelligible cosmos, the Roman system of law and order

[1] III, 354.

binding the members of a human society.[1]   But there are so many
possible permutations and combinations of these elements, so many
possibilities of attraction and repulsion, that no clear picture of a
specific inheritance emerges.   And, in fact, none can emerge, because
these things have each borne different interpretations and provoked
different reactions at different stages in the pilgrimage of European
man.   To say that they have been fused and absorbed by the European
mind, sounds plausible, but it is scarcely true.   On the contrary—
as an eminent Catholic scholar has recently said[2]—the significance
of Greece and Rome in European history lies in the fact that they
have never become an integral part of the European inheritance,
have always remained a ' foreign body ' which Europe could neither
digest nor expel.   The struggle to grapple with them led to no
definite results ;   but it was supremely important nevertheless.   It
was supremely important because it helped to create and stimulate
the spiritual tension which carried the European spirit to dazzling
heights never before attained.   This, precisely this, is the European
inheritance :   not concrete achievements, which can be counted up
and handed down, but the spiritual exaltation, the incomparable
soaring of the human spirit, the opening of new horizons, even
though they have left behind (and were doubtless bound to leave
behind) unsolved and insoluble problems.   Success or failure is not
the only criterion ;   and we may respect, and look back with pride
on the strivings of European man, because he never hesitated, no
matter what the cost, to reach out to the stars.

What matters in the end is not the precise elements—varied,
undefinable, many-complexioned as they are—of the European
inheritance.   Nor is the important thing (as Sir Ernest Barker seems
to imply)[3] to ' preserve ' that inheritance, to ' guard ', ' maintain ',
' transmit ' it to the future, like a precious fossil in a museum.   What
matters is the ability to re-shape the elements into a new and living
pattern, the capacity to adapt the inheritance to new and ever
changing conditions ;   otherwise it can only become like a millstone
round the neck.   It was the failure to re-shape its inheritance, the
failure, after the eighteenth-century synthesis, to create a new idea
of man and his existence and activities, the weary plodding along

[1] III, 310.
[2] M. Seidlmayer, *Das Mittelalter. Umrisse und Ergebnisse* (1949), 29, 31.
[3] III, 353, 354, 355.

the overgrown humanist paths with no new vision, that brought the old Europe to its end. Back in the fourth century of our era, when Europe began its life in the crisis of the ancient world—its first cry echoing ' the world's chaos ' and ' the discord at the heart of things ' [1]—the future lay with those who had ' a new idea of man ' to propound, a new vision in place of a bankrupt inheritance and a sterile philosophy. Their inspiration was God's glory, not man's past. And so it is to-day. The European inheritance is a tangle of unresolved contradictions, a thicket of dead ends, offering no direct line of advance. Only a new inspiration, a new idea of man and his place in the universe, can open a clear vista into the future. Perhaps it is there already—so Professor Vermeil appears to suggest[2]—in the ideals of communist society; more probably (you may think) we shall have to wait long weary nights before it comes. We do not know. But inspiration will not come to those who look back, only to those who look forward and look up. There the future lies—not in the heritage of our European past, but in the vision of a new world in God's image.

[1] Lindsay, op. cit., 236–7.   [2] III, 201.

12. Europe in Perspective
New Views on European History

EVERY thinking man and woman to-day—in England or in Germany, in America or in Russia—who seeks an answer to the dilemmas of the modern world, turns inevitably to the past, hoping to discover in history a clue to modern trends and tendencies.[1] Our thinking about practical problems of current politics is bound up with the patterns we have formed in our minds of the course of historical development, particularly the historical development of modern Europe. We look at the issues facing us to-day with analogies from the past in our minds—assessing Russian aims (for example) in the light of what we know of the policy of czar Alexander II—so that the present appears to us very largely as a prolongation of the past, a continuation on logical, foreseeable lines of developments we can trace back (say) to the Congress of Berlin in 1878, and beyond that to the Congress of Vienna, or even further. This is natural enough, and within limits useful, since there is a certain continuity in the policy of all the Great Powers. But, rigidly applied, it is also very dangerous, since it makes no allowance for what H. A. L. Fisher once described as 'the play of the contingent and the unforeseen'—that is, for newly emerging factors outside the range of our historical experience. And it is doubly dangerous, if the conceptions of historical development on which we draw for comparison and analogy are partial, one-sided, or simply ill-founded. What I am going to suggest is that very many of our historical conceptions are ill-founded and one-sided, and that consequently there is a great deal of confusion in our assessment of current international problems. I am going to suggest that our current views of European history need radical revision, and I am going to put before you some of the criticisms which have been levelled against them since 1945.

[1] First printed, in German, in *Merkur* VIII (1954), 401–414, under the title : 'Abschied von der europäischen Geschichte?'; an abbreviated version appeared in *The Listener*, March 5, 1953, under the title : 'Farewell to Europe ?'.

The conception of European history which underlies all standard accounts in England and Germany (though not perhaps so predominantly in France) goes back to the great German historian, Leopold von Ranke.[1] It was first sketched by Ranke in 1824 in the introduction to his *History of the Latin and Teutonic Nations*, was developed in a famous essay on *The Great Powers*, and set out more fully in his lectures *On the Epochs of Modern History*. For Ranke the foundation of European history lay in the 'unity' (as he called it) and inter-connected development of the 'Romano-Germanic peoples'—that is to say, of the mixed stocks which emerged, as a result of the Germanic migrations into western Europe, in the fifth and sixth centuries. They constituted, he said, 'a world for themselves'; and this world was the foundation upon which 'the whole development of our conditions down to the most recent times has depended'. The 'unity' of which Ranke speaks must not, of course, be misunderstood. Each of the 'six great nations of the Romano-Germanic world—French, Spanish, Italian; German, English, Scandinavian—was a distinct unit; they never formed one society, and 'they were almost always at war among themselves'. Wherein, then, is their unity to be perceived? It was not merely that all sprang 'from the same or a closely allied stock'; their real unity, Ranke says, is revealed 'in idea, in action, and in development'. 'Their internal histories precisely coincide', and their 'common development . . . necessarily produced the same ideas in all'.

The 'unity' of which Ranke speaks is therefore unity in plurality —perhaps better, unity in diversity. And this conception of 'unity in diversity' is characteristic for the whole conception of European history which he bequeathed to western historical thought. The immense potentialities of Europe, and still more the freedom to develop these potentialities, are unthinkable without the diversity, the free interplay in political rivalry and economic competition between the constituent nations. And the practical means by which this free interplay is secured is the system of Balance of Power, which time and again in the course of modern history maintained the essential character of European civilisation by preventing the hegemony of any one among the Great Powers. Therefore in

[1] On Ranke, see the excellent short sketch and appreciation by H. Liebeschütz, *Ranke* (Historical Association, 1954).

Ranke's thought, and in that of succeeding generations of historians, the Balance of Power takes a central place ; it is the pivot upon which the fabric of European society depends.

For Ranke himself it is characteristic that he chose, in his earliest major work, to deal precisely with the years 1494–1514, the period when (as he thought) the mechanism of the Balance of Power was perfected. This was the foundation for all his subsequent writing, and (more important still) a framework for practically all that was written by succeeding generations on the political history of Europe. From the starting-point at the beginning of the sixteenth century, when the Balance of Power centred round the struggle for domination over Italy, the circle gradually widened, as the older Powers in the heart of Europe, in their efforts to preserve an equilibrium, called in new areas and new forces to counterbalance the old. Ranke himself showed how, as a result of the strivings of the Powers to prevent French hegemony, Russia at the time of Peter the Great was brought into the European Concert. The discovery and colonisation of the New World carried the Balance of Power overseas, as was demonstrated in the Anglo-French rivalry in the New World in the eighteenth century. And so what began as a European system gradually merged into a world-system.

But it was after Ranke's own day, at the close of the nineteenth century, that the change from European to world-wide perspectives became ever more important, providing the setting for the next generation of historians, the generation which experienced the struggle for power in Africa and the ' new imperialism ' which set in after 1870. What is remarkable is that their fundamental attitude, their belief in the validity of the principles established by Ranke, remained unchanged, in spite of the altered conditions. They did not feel called upon to criticize Ranke's theories in the light of new circumstances, but rather they interpreted new circumstances in the light of Ranke's principles. To historians of this generation, who had imbibed Ranke's ideas from their early school-days, it seemed axiomatic that each nation should have its share in the spoils of Africa, for fear lest its relative standing in the Concert of Powers should be diminished ; but still more it seemed necessary that Africa should be partitioned in order that the Balance of Power should continue to function as of old, on both a European and a global plane. In their eyes Ranke had established a universal rule, which the whole course of European history endorsed : that an intricate, self-adjusting mechanism of political forces was always in existence, spontaneously operating to counteract any threat to the liberties upon which the fabric of civilisation rested—a mechanism parallel in the political sphere to the principles of *laissez-faire* economics postulated by Adam Smith as the condition of the functioning of economic society. Both the war of 1914–18 and that of 1939–45 were wars fought to preserve the Balance of Power ; and although both were evidently world-wars, it still seemed clear that it was the delicate issue of the Balance of Power in Europe that touched them off, that the world-balance still operated from a European centre and responded to reactions from the heart of the old continent. Ranke's ' Romano-Germanic peoples ', their possessions and influence and sphere of action now embracing the whole globe, still seemed to dominate the field.

*　　*　　*

And then, in 1945, when the dust of battle began to clear, the blitzed and bomb-scarred face of Europe revealed a very different prospect. Where were the great Powers, upon whose ' unity in diversity ' the whole working of a European civilisation which had become global seemed to depend? What survived of the system through which equilibrium had been preserved by adjustment between a multiplicity of nations? Instead of a concert, there were two Great Powers, Russia and the United States,[1] neither essentially European, and following at a distance—because it had been bled white by the Second, much as France had been bled white by the First World War—there came the British Commonwealth, the sinews of which lay also outside Europe. The rest, overshadowed by continent-wide empires, had shrunk to provincial status, more like the principalities of the German Confederation before 1871 than the Great Powers we had known.

It was not difficult, on a practical plane, to draw immediate political conclusions from the new configuration ; the apparatus of international power-politics was soon adjusted to the altered circumstances. It was less easy to draw long-term deductions in the historical field, to see the immediate events in historical perspective ;

[1] At this stage China, which subsequently has attained equality of status (at least militarily) with the U.S.A. and the U.S.S.R., had not yet made its power and influence felt

and most of current political speculation has suffered from this
failure. First of all, the two victor Powers had no need for introspective historical analysis; they simply resorted to bold simplifications. Russia undertook to re-write the history of eastern Europe
in its own image; and certainly it was not wrong to insist on re-
writing—eastern European history had too long been seen through
western (and mainly German) spectacles—but the Russian version
tended to be as one-sided as the western version it replaced. The
United States, with magnificent audacity, but with a surprising
disregard for the inherently different circumstances governing
American history, simply laid claim to the European heritage, posing
as heir of a civilisation different in formative conditions and in
historical evolution from its own.[1] In Great Britain, perhaps
because its place amongst victors or losers still hangs precariously
in the balance, there has been singularly little attempt to take stock
or reconsider accepted historical theories; and it has been left to
the losing peoples, the decimated and disinherited as well as the
vanquished, to re-examine the foundations of European history and
the implicit assumptions underlying the work of three or four
generations of historians. As evidence one may cite the work of the
exiled Polish historian, Oscar Halecki, now fairly well known in
this country; acute, far-seeing, penetrating, if only it were not
warped by political motivation. But it is appropriate that it should
have been among German-speaking historians, above all others, that
the most thorough attempt was made after 1945 to criticize and
revise the standard formulations which originated in Germany
itself over a century ago. It is this criticism of which I mainly wish
to speak.[2] I shall not say more than a word or two about its less

---

[1] This significant trend in recent American historiography requires further discussion
than is here possible; cf. however, below, p. 219 (and particularly note 2) for a few
indications.
[2] Among the writings in which, since 1945, a real endeavour has been made to arrive
at a new conception of history, the works of Ludwig Dehio are outstanding: first
his book *Gleichgewicht oder Hegemonie. Betrachtungen über ein Grundproblem der neueren
Staatengeschichte* (1948), and then a series of articles in the *Historische Zeitschrift*, vols.
CLXX, CLXXIII, CLXXIV, of which the article ' Ranke und der deutsche Imperialismus ' (*Hist. Zeitschr.* CLXX, 1950) seems to me particularly illuminating. The American
impact on Europe is well delineated by Max Silberschmidt, ' Wirtschaftshistorische
Aspekte der neueren Geschichte ', *Hist. Zeitschr.* CLXXI. Traditional views of eastern
European history, derived from Ranke, are criticized by H. Ludat, ' Die Slaven und
das Mittelalter ', *Die Welt als Geschichte* XII (1952). For the interactions of Europe and
Asia, see particularly R. Grousset, *Bilan de l'Histoire* (1946). Noteworthy and stimulating
also, if not always convincing, is O. Halecki, *The Limits and Divisions of European History*

immediate and more academic aspects ; it is better to use the space I have to develop the points which come nearest to the bone of modern contentions.

*   *   *

The first and perhaps the central question is whether the evident collapse of the old system of Balance of Power is simply the result of World War II—the implication being, if so, that it may only be temporary, and that, given time, we may get back to the traditional equilibrium, and so prevent the world from being dominated by one or divided between two Great Powers. Can the international political system of 1939 be restored, not of course exactly as it was, but with different pieces in play and different combinations, yet still in principle the same game with the same basic rules? The optimists answer yes, and pin their faith in the organisation of a ' Third Force ' as a political fulcrum to weight the balance between the opposing *blocs*. The pessimists say no ; and their arguments were cogently set out by Alfred Weber in his book, *Farewell to European History*.[1] But Weber spoke as philosopher and prophet rather than as historian ; and both the opposing contentions rest more upon political speculation than upon historical analysis, are concerned more with prognosis, the prediction of the future, and with present action, than with diagnosis. As such they fall outside the historian's field of vision. But the historian is entitled to examine the historical arguments upon which they depend, to see whether they are historically valid or simply the reiteration of old assumptions ; and this is where historical criticism may legitimately be brought into play. Its first task will be to examine the situation in 1939 ; then the functioning of the Balance of Power between 1919 and 1939 ; and finally to analyse the historical development of the system of Balance of Power through the course of modern history.

It is unnecessary to do more than state briefly the results of such an analysis as they affect the immediate issue, in order to work out their implications for our views of European history. In the first

---

(1950).—These are the writings which I have chiefly had in mind in compiling the present survey, and my debt to their authors, particularly to L. Dehio, requires no emphasis.

[1] Cf. A. Weber, *Abschied von der bisherigen Geschichte* (1946), translated into English under the title *Farewell to European History or the Conquest of Nihilism* (1947).

place, it is true that down to 1939—and, indeed, right down to 1945—the Balance of Power in Europe was the decisive element in international politics ; the reaction to Hitler's bid for hegemony falls into line with the reactions, earlier, against those of William II, Napoleon I, Louis XIV, Philip II, Charles V. But it is true also— and this in the long run is far more important—that the differences were greater than the similarities, and that the preponderance of Europe after 1919 was more apparent than real. Already as a result of World War I the role of the European powers in international affairs had withered and shrunk ; but this consequence was hidden, almost accidentally, by the absence of the two great world powers, Russia and the United States, the former as a result of the 1917 revolution, the latter in consequence of the American withdrawal into isolation after the fall of Wilson. Thus the old system of Balance of Power appeared to go on, led and directed by France, but it was a pitiful shadow of its former self, quite incapable—as the meteoric recovery of Germany under Hitler showed—of performing its essential functions.

The fact was that already, by 1918, power had moved from the continental to the great flanking powers ; the total defeat of Hohen- zollern Germany, precluding a negotiated compromise peace, was due to the crushing superiority of the United States, just as in 1945 the total defeat of Hitlerite Germany was due to the United States and Russia. I do not mean, in either case, to underrate the part played by Great Britain and the Commonwealth, or to suggest that without the United States and Russia there would necessarily have been a total German victory ; only that the actual result was achieved within a relatively short period of time as a result of their inter- vention, and was unthinkable without it. Europe alone, even if we include Great Britain in Europe, was unable to solve its problems; it required the pressure of extra-European forces to prevent a hegemony that would have been fatal to the values of European civilisation, which owed their existence to a multiplicity of free nations.

If we look back to earlier struggles against other powers striving for hegemony, we can see that this recourse to extra-European forces is the rule, not the exception. It is common still to emphasize the revolt of nationalities as a prime factor in the defeat of Napo- leon : the War of Liberation in Germany, and the ' Spanish ulcer '.

But the exaggeration in both cases is patent.[1] There would have been no War of Liberation unless Napoleon had previously been defeated in Russia, and the only significance of the ' Spanish ulcer ' was the loophole it provided for Wellington's armies. Napoleon was defeated not by an uprising of the continental peoples but by powers which drew their strength from outside Europe, Russia from its vast Asiatic reserves beyond the Urals, England from the wealth of the New World. And even earlier the same was true. It was the maritime powers, England and Holland, which defeated Louis XIV by employing their naval supremacy and their colonial resources ; and in the sixteenth century the bid by the emperor Charles V for control of Europe was brought to nothing by the Turks. France alone, with its European allies, was not strong enough ; it required the external pressure of the Ottoman Empire to save the ' liberties ' of Europe.

If these facts meant simply, as the traditional view would have it, the extension in an ever-widening circle of the principle of Balance of Power from its European centre, their significance would be small. But closer inspection shows that is not the case. The flanking powers, particularly the maritime powers, whose strength derives from non-European resources, obey rules of their own, which are not the rules of the European Balance of Power. It was characteristic already in the seventeenth century that England and Holland, in spite of commercial and colonial rivalries which had already given rise to armed conflict, drew together against France ; it is characteristic again, in spite of the ' Russian bogey ' haunting British policy throughout almost the whole of the nineteenth century, that there has never been a serious conflict between England and Russia ; and it is most characteristic of all that the conflict of interests between England and the United States, upon which continental statesmen speculated for a century and more, hoping that America would provide a counterpoise to England's naval supremacy, never materialized. The plain fact is that policy moved in two distinct spheres, global and European ; and though England provided the link between the two, the circles did not overlap, still less merge.

[1] The tendency of German historians to romanticize the *Befreiungskrieg* has been criticized, rightly in my opinion, by A. J. P. Taylor, *The Course of German History* (1945), pp. 44–46.

The effect of the Balance of Power in Europe over four centuries has been a steady break-down into ever smaller units, culminating in the creation of the post-Versailles states of eastern Europe, which were too small, too weak, and too divided to maintain their independence against attack either from west or from east. Liberty, in short, was paid for by loss of power, which has now assailed Europe as a whole. How different is the process in the extra-European sphere! Here the tendency throughout has been to the formation of ever greater areas of domination, and the deliberate exclusion of fragmentation. Every European war has resulted in greater division, every colonial war in greater cohesion. This was evident already in the seventeenth and eighteenth centuries; it became even clearer in the nineteenth century. The promulgation of the Monroe Doctrine in 1823 meant definitely the exclusion of the principle of the Balance of Power from the Americas. In Asia, England and Russia, in spite of their rivalries, have stood firm at every crisis to exclude the entry of a third power—Germany or Japan—which would have introduced the possibility of counter-balancing combinations, such as are familiar in Europe. In Africa, Belgian and Portuguese possessions are a mere survival, tolerated because they do not affect the Anglo-Saxon preponderance, guaranteed by English control of the sea. Inside Europe, any threat of preponderance has always been combatted and brought to nothing ; outside Europe, the principle of preponderant Powers is securely established.

These facts have wide implications for current politics ; they also cast radical suspicion upon standard theories of the course of European history. If, in fact, the European Balance of Power has not been transposed to a global plane, if world-politics follow quite a different modality from those of Europe, where do we stand to-day, when Europe is like a burnt-out volcano, the cone of which has fallen in? And of what use, in such circumstances, are the ' lessons ' (as they are commonly taught) of European history? If the values upon which European civilisation is built, depend upon the co-ordinated existence of a multiplicity of small sovereign nations, what is the future of those values in a world in which three or four Powers at most retain their sovereignty in the old sense? And if the liberties (and therewith the values) of Europe have depended always upon the mobilization of non-European forces for their defence, what are we to think of a theory of history which has not only placed the western European nations at its centre—'an incomparable association ', as Ranke described them—but has also treated European history as separate and distinct, operating according to its own rules, reacting upon the world, of course, but not in its essence impinged upon by factors from without?

*   *   *

The first conclusion I would draw is that the old conception of western Europe as a ' world in itself ', a complex of closely-related peoples pursuing its own distinct course of development ever since the collapse of the Roman empire, must be abandoned. The history of Europe—a peninsula of Asia, as Paul Valéry called it—cannot be considered in isolation. Contrary to the views popularized by A. J. Toynbee, for whom ' western society ', taken alone, is ' an intelligible field of study ', it is the connexion of Europe with the wider world that we shall see as the decisive factor shaping European history ; without this impact from outside no phase of European development, still less of western European development, would be intelligible. That is true not merely in the present, as all of us can see, and in the recent past, but throughout European history. If I understand the French historian, Grousset, aright, it is the essence of his teaching that Europe in the middle ages—in other words, at the time when, through lack of adequate communications, it seemed most isolated from the outside world—was never free from pressure coming from Asia ; at every turn of mediaeval history it was the impact of Asiatic peoples, Huns, Avars, Bulgars, Magyars, Turks, that forced forward new developments. And if this is true of the impact from the heart of Asia, how much more true of the influence of the flowering Arab civilisation, which reached from North Africa into Spain and Sicily ! Nor, of course, can we in the whole period which we call ' mediaeval ' separate the western lands from eastern Europe ; the cross-currents running not only to and from Byzantium, but also between the peoples of the west and the Slavs were powerful and continuous.

These may seem remote and academic aspects of the question ; but they cannot be ignored, if we are to get our perspectives right ; for the same lack of perspective that has led to the neglect of the Byzantine strand in mediaeval European history, has led also to the neglect of outside influences, particularly of American influence,

N

in European history in the nineteenth century. We shall err, in other words, if we assume that our standard accounts of modern history are correct so far as they go—let us say, down to 1914—andsimply need bringing up to date, in view of current developments, by the addition of a couple of supplementary chapters under the headings ' Russia ' and 'America '. On the contrary, we are dealing with a conception of European history which is out of focus and therefore misleading, because of the false emphasis and isolated prominence it gives to western Europe, and which therefore needs revising not merely in its recent phases, but at every turn from the early middle ages onwards.

How is it misleading? Two examples will show. The one is our attitude—the attitude of our history-teaching—to the two great revolutions at the close of the eighteenth century : the French Revolution and the American Revolution. No one to-day can fail to see that the American Revolution, the establishment of the first great independent power in the New World, was the starting-point for the new era of global politics in which we live ; and as such we shall not be tempted to underrate its importance. And yet who would deny that, of the two, it is the French and not the American Revolution that looms largest in our history-teaching? We hear a great deal of the effects of the French Revolution ; but how much do we know of the effects, so important for us, of the American Revolution? It is true, of course, that American history is no longer neglected, either in the schools or in the universities ; but that is not the point. To teach American history in isolation, as a separate branch of study parallel to European history, is to commit the very errors of which our teaching of European history has been guilty. What we require is a history which will reveal the impact of the new American republic upon the world at large and upon Europe in particular ; for the United States, although it stood outside the concert of Great Powers for almost the duration of the nineteenth century, and thus appeared to exercise no immediate political influence over international affairs, exercised so powerful an economic influence, from the time of the Napoleonic Wars onwards, that its effects upon European development, including European political development, can scarcely be exaggerated.

Who, for example, would deny the political importance of emigration to America, the drawing-off of vast, potentially revolutionary population-surpluses, as a factor in the history of nine-teenth-century Europe? And who can fail to speculate upon the political effects of the reversal of American immigration policy, the closing of the European safety-valve, after 1918? And yet what place have such factors in any of the standard accounts of nineteenth-century history? It was precisely because our history-teaching turned a blind eye to such things, treating the history of Europe as an independent chain of events operating according to laws of its own, that the American predominance, when it came about, took us unawares, seeming rather a revolutionary change than the culmina-tion of a secular trend.

Historians had spoken so long in European terms that it seemed impossible to conceive that the European era was at an end. They spoke, for example, and still speak—and herewith we come to our second example—of the years between 1870 and 1890 as the 'Age of Bismarck'. Yet in what sense is this description true? In an exclusively European sense, yes ; in any other sense, no. Bismarck had raised Germany to front rank among the continental powers ; but front rank among the continental powers no longer denoted— as it had in the days of Louis XIV or Napoleon—a title to rank among the world-powers, as Germany learnt to its cost after Bismarck's fall. One historian—exceptional, if not unique[1]—saw the true position ; and characteristically he is a historian whose reputation has suffered an eclipse. J. R. Seeley, describing the inter-national system in 1883, at the height of the so-called ' Bismarckian era ', mentioned Bismarck not at all and Germany only in paren-thesis ; for him there were, outside the British Empire, but two Great Powers, Russia and the United States—' enormous political aggregations ', which (he foretold) would in fifty years ' surpass in power the states now called great, as much as the great nation-states of the sixteenth century surpassed Florence '.[2] Who can doubt to-day that Seeley was right? Bismarck was a great statesman ; but he was the last great statesman of the European age, the last

---

[1] A correspondent in the *Listener* kindly drew my attention to the parallel words of the American historian, Henry Adams, who wrote in 1899 : '. . . America and Russia. These are the two future centres of power ; and of the two America must get there first. Some day, perhaps a century hence, Russia may swallow even her ; but for my lifetime I think I'm safe '. A year later he wrote : ' Europe is done ! The hand is played out. We are now playing a new suit, and when I see the stakes I feel my poor old bald head creep with horror at the chances.'

[2] Cf. J. R. Seeley, *The Expansion of England* (1897), 350.

great statesman who played according to the rules of the European
Balance of Power. Limit your view to Europe, and Bismarck seems
a dominating figure ; extend it to the world, and he falls back into
second rank. Once the purely continental task of German unification was achieved, once the new Germany began to press for a
place, alongside England and Russia and the United States, in the
universal sun, Bismarck was like a fish out of water, and there began
the long series of desperate, hopeless expedients which showed only
too clearly that the so-called 'Age of Bismarck ' was an age Bismarck
neither understood nor dominated. Only a historiography obscured by European blinkers, and unable to scan the horizons, could
get the portents so utterly wrong.

*   *   *

The conception of European history which still holds sway
to-day reflects the attitudes of a period when, to all appearances,
predominance and leadership were in the hands of the western
European powers. It was a period when the expansion of the European powers into the New World, into Asia and into Africa, seemed
to betoken the beginning of European mastery of the world, the
beginning of a world-order which was merely an enlarged version
of the European order and regulated like that by the tested principles of the Balance of Power. Ranke, writing in the ' Indian summer '
following the Napoleonic Wars, regarded the defeat of Napoleon
at the hands of England and Russia as a confirmation of the old
European system, and failed to see that the French Revolution
within and the preponderance of the extra-European powers without
represented the first stage in its collapse. His vision was limited
by a false sense of continuity, a mistaken devotion to purely historical
factors, which led him to concentrate almost exclusively on the
Powers which had dominated the scene in the past, as though it
were God's law that they should dominate for all time. How
characteristic that, writing in 1833 of the Great Powers, he omitted
to include among them the United States! And, on the other side,
his attitude of almost contemptuous dismissal for the eastern
European peoples, as though they stood outside and had contributed
nothing to European development, must be regarded as a reflection
of the prejudices and preconceptions of an age when eastern Europe
was either submerged under Turkish dominion or partitioned
between Russia, Austria and Prussia.

What we have to do, first of all, is to realize how limited in time and circumstance this conception of history is. It was not true of mediaeval Europe, and it was ceasing to be true of modern Europe precisely at the moment when Ranke wrote. It represented at best a particular historical situation, and it was this situation that Ranke perpetuated, as though it were a ' still ' picked out of a cinematograph film and enlarged. There are, without doubt, periods, when owing to a particular constellation of world-events, which can in each specific case be analysed and defined, western Europe has been left in relative independence to develop in accordance with a rhythm of its own ; just as there are times also when the pressure of Europe on the outside world has been stronger than the pressure of the outside world on Europe. But such periods are not to be taken as a standard. They may be compared with the troughs between the great breakers beating upon the shores of time. We can postulate our history upon neither the one nor the other ; neither upon trough nor upon wave. But we can observe the succession and alternation of wave and trough ; and we can perceive, if we look back over European history, how the troughs get shallower and the waves more overpowering, until in the end the last projecting rocks are submerged. That, without doubt, is the result of technological advance, which has quickened the rhythm. Not only was the defeat of William II and of Hitler far more rapid than that of Napoleon ; but the intervening period, the trough between 1918 and 1939, was far shorter than that between 1815 and 1914.

*   *   *

This survey started from the conviction that the Russian victory at Stalingrad in 1943 made a total revision of European history imperative. It may seem paradoxical that, from such a starting-point, I should end with a reiteration of the old belief that history which is least political, which looks the past most objectively in the face, is the history which will be of greatest value in the present. But the paradox is more apparent than real. If it needed the shock of Stalingrad to open our eyes to the limitations of our western historiography, it was because the political prejudices underlying our history-writing had blinded us to the actual distribution of power in 1943. No doubt those prejudices were largely unconscious ; but they were not for that reason any less real or any less misleading. But it is no remedy to go from one extreme to the other ; to sub-

stitute—as Russian and American historiography seem to be attempting (in opposite ways) to substitute—one political interpretation for
another. It is easy for the historian to be wise after the event; it
is terribly difficult for him to be wise in his own day; but we can
say with safety that the more universal his point of view, the more
he strives to free himself from national or regional preoccupations,
the nearer he will approach to a conception of the past which is
valid for the present. There were plenty of indications long before
1939—as Seeley saw, and Tocqueville before him—of the direction
in which events were moving. In an objective history they would
have had their place; but they did not fit in with our preconceived
views, and so they were jettisoned. The result was a history which,
confronted by events, was fumbling and helpless.

To-day it is obvious that this history will not do. The key no
longer lies, if ever it did, in the west. The war of 1939–45 was the
last European war of the old style, the last of the struggles, reaching
back to Charles V, for European hegemony; already the global
contest between the United States and Russia, the struggle for world-
hegemony, has transferred the centre of gravity from Europe to
the Pacific. The historian cannot probe into these new political
circumstances; they incorporate too many factors outside historical
experience. All he can do is to warn that our knowledge of European
history is no sure guide in the situation which confronts us to-day;
that conditions in the wider world are so different from those in our
European past that any ' lessons ' or analogies we may derive from
European history are more likely to deceive and blind than to illuminate.

The maintenance of the European political system, and of the
values which that system of counterbalancing power guaranteed,
have depended always upon the fact that Europe was only part of
the wider world, and that forces could always be recruited from
beyond Europe to maintain the European equilibrium. Evidently,
in a political system which embraces the whole world, that is not
the case; there are no outside powers, and consequently the whole
mechanism must be different. And what we know of the history of
the world-powers to date reinforces the warning. Taken all in all,
the relations between England, Russia and the United States show
far more differences from than similarities to those of the continental powers. Furthermore, while the whole trend of European

history has been to maintain a concert of equal powers, and to preserve small national units, the whole trend of world-history has been the contrary : the building up of 'enormous political aggregations', none of which is in a European sense a 'national' unit. Who would dare, in such circumstances, to draw a line from the past through the present to the future, to assume that the political constellations of the future will repeat, on a larger plane, those of our European past?

And there are other circumstances upon which I have not touched. One is the problematical position of the British Commonwealth, which is no more easy to fit into the new world we see arising around us, than into the old world which is passing. But overshadowing all else we have the startling change in relations between the white and the coloured races. May it not be that, in a couple of centuries, the war of 1939–45 will appear not as the last in a long succession of successful struggles to prevent a European hegemony, but rather as the decisive conflict in which Europe, committing suicide, surrendered mastery to the coloured peoples?

I do not wish to end upon a speculation ; it is not the historian's function. And I cannot end with a fanfare of trumpets, or even with the plain announcement of a formula for a new historiography. But we may perhaps say that our basic attitude, our basic question, has changed. The historian to-day no longer asks, with Ranke, ' how it was ', but ' how it happened ' ;[1] our vision has travelled from the static and continuous to the dynamic and revolutionary— to the new which continually forces its way into the stream of history and disturbs the steady flow of events. Beyond that the historian can only advance his purpose by avoiding the mistakes of his predecessors, not merely their mistakes in the interpretation of historical fact, but also—and still more important—the mistaken assumptions and preconceptions with which they approach their task. First among these is the tendency, still so rife, to treat the past as the root of the present and to project it into the future ; an attitude which distorts the past because it ignores those aspects which seem to have no present relevance, but which—more seriously still—distorts the present because it makes no allowance for what Nietzsche called ' the mighty impulse to a new deed '—an impulse

---

[1] Not ' wie es eigentlich gewesen ', but ' wie es gekommen ', as Ludwig Dehio has phrased it (*Gleichgewicht oder Hegemonie*, 9).

which breaks through, untrammelled by the past, at every great turning-point in human history.

The second error is to expect too much of and claim too much for the study of history. To expect from the past a key to current problems, a series of patterns which we can immediately transpose into the context of contemporary politics, goes far beyond history's limits ; no present-day issue is, or ever was, intelligible in terms of its origins or history. If those are the questions we ask of history, we must not be surprised if it deceives us. But that does not mean that history is useless or irrelevant, or has no contribution to make to the present. For the individual who, somehow or other, has to find his own values in a shattered world, a history that is truly universal—that looks beyond Europe and the west to humanity in all lands and ages—can fulfil a basic need : it can help him, as perhaps in our generation nothing else can, to know where he stands and to understand his situation as neither good nor evil in itself, but as necessary. Beyond this it cannot go, and if the historian attempts more, he may mislead not only individuals but whole peoples ;[1] but to do less is to fail—as so much of our history has failed—in its most vital function.

[1] No one has better described the responsibilities in this regard of German historians between 1900 and 1918, than Ludwig Dehio ; cf. *Hist. Zeitschr.* CLXX (1950), 307–328.

13. Russia and Europe

THE question of Russia and Europe stands in the forefront of discussion to-day ;[1] but that very fact is more conducive to quick political appraisal than to careful historical analysis, and stands in the way of an examination of the problem in all its aspects. It is obvious that the historian's approach to any such question must be different from that of the politician ; that he must consider factors which perhaps may appear to possess no immediate relevance to current political preoccupations.

For that reason, and because it is not my purpose to talk about current politics, I hope you will not expect to find here views and facts related in any immediate way to contemporary political events. The question 'Russia and Europe' which seems so formidable to us to-day, did not arise in, and after, 1945 ; it did not arise after and in consequence of the Russian Revolution of 1917. Already a hundred or a hundred and twenty years ago it was being hotly debated by Russians in Russia ; and the great debate—as it was called—between the 'Slavophils' and the 'Westernizers', between those who asserted the independent, autogenous roots of Russian and Slavonic civilisation and wished to preserve its distinct character, and those who regarded it as a part of a common European civilisation and wished to develop its contacts with the west, was pursued throughout the nineteenth century, and found a lasting reflection in Russian literature—most clearly, perhaps, in the novels of Dostoievsky. It is probably significant that the advent of the Communist regime brought this great debate to an end, or—perhaps it would be more correct to say—brushed it aside as a purely theoretical argument, without relevance to the practical problems of day-to-day politics. 'Westernization' was, and is, a practical necessity ; and Communism itself is a western doctrine. But under the surface the question still remains alive. It is still a question whether Communism, derived in the west from western conditions by Marx and Engels, has on Russian soil fused with specifically

[1] A public lecture delivered in the University of Liverpool on February 2nd, 1955.

Russian characteristics to produce a type of civilisation different from that in the rest of Europe, or at least from that in Europe beyond the ' Iron Curtain '. Unfortunately, if understandably, this question is bogged down in a sea of prejudice and propaganda, which makes the task of the historian difficult and dangerous. ' Scratch a Russian, and you will find a Tartar '! How many accounts of Russian history are befogged and bedevilled by quick, pithy, and yet misleading, simplifications such as that! I shall try here to pursue a more patient path, not because I can claim any special competence in the matter, but because it seems to me self-apparent that, for all of us, there is need to-day for a fuller and deeper understanding of at least the main strands in Russian history.

' Russia and Europe ' : the very title, it might be argued, begs the question, for is not Russia itself part of Europe? And if, particularly in the course of the last century, it has carried out a vast colonial expansion into Asia, does that make it any less a part of Europe, sharing in European life and civilisation, than England itself after it became the centre of a colonial empire? And yet of course the question is not so simple as that. The civilisation of eastern Europe had its origin, like that of the west, in the Graeco-Roman civilisation of antiquity ; both stem in that degree from the same source, and the contacts of early Russia with the west were far more considerable than we used to think. But, against that, a few facts of decisive importance for the future must be set. First of all, the unity of Graeco-Roman civilisation, at any rate in its later phases, was not absolute. Already, for example, in the hands of St. Ambrose, St. Leo and St. Augustine, western Christianity was something different from the orthodox faith of the east,[1] and we must not therefore simply assume that the inheritance transmitted to the Slav peoples from Constantinople was identical with that transmitted to Germanic Europe from Rome. Secondly, in different environments there is bound to be different development. That is obvious enough within western Europe ; the position in England or Germany, where there was little, if any, direct connexion with ancient civilisation, is very different from that in Italy or France or Spain. Much the same is true in respect of Russia. Russia, as it has developed in later centuries from the principality of Moscow, has no direct connexion with Byzantine civilisation ; it was not land which had been ruled

---

[1] Cf. above, p. 41.

by Byzantium and so had received a Byzantine imprint. But then neither was Scotland, nor Denmark, nor Prussia, directly connected with Rome. Differences necessarily there are : but they may be— and in my view they were—differences in one common civilisation ; one has only to compare Russia with China or India to see that it belongs to the European family. In fact, we can say with a great deal of truth that Russia's position on the Asiatic ' march ' or frontier of Europe, and (arising therefrom) the sense of differentiation from the peoples who swept across the steppe from Asia, was, over centuries, a factor cementing Russia's attachment to Europe.

I have emphasized straight away these common factors, the traditions and circumstances which accentuate the integration of Russia with the rest of Europe, because, from the point of view which we are considering, it will be necessary to give more attention to the process of differentiation. That process of differentiation had already gone far by the time of Czar Peter the Great ; and for that reason alone it is a serious error to suppose that we can—even for the purpose of understanding the modern world—safely take as our starting-point the so-called ' westernization ' of Russia under Peter the Great. First of all, it is really a question for debate how far Peter did ' westernize ' Russia. B. H. Sumner wrote of Peter that he did not seek ' to build upon entirely new foundations or to sweep away the essentials of the old Muscovite social structure ' ;[1] and consequently any appraisal of Peter's work must take account of the Russia he found in existence. One of the best of living historians of Russia recently emphasized—and I think rightly emphasized—that it was in the five preceding centuries, from the eleventh to the sixteenth, that the characteristics which mark off Russian history from that of western Europe took shape and root.[2] Therefore no analysis of modern Russian history which leaves this formative period out of consideration, can hope to provide us with a really serviceable picture.

Let us, then, try briefly to review the main differentiating features in the history of Russia which were already evident by the time of the accession of Peter the Great, at the close of the seventeenth century. The first is in the field of religion, and it is without doubt the most important. The church was the main agent in form-

[1] B. H. Sumner, ' Peter the Great ', *History* XXXII (1947), 43.
[2] W. Philipp, *Hist. Zeitschrift* CLXXVI (1953), 590.

ing the Russian character. Russia, as is well known, received its
Christianity from Byzantium, and was particularly closely influenced
by the Bulgarian church. It would be an error to suggest (as has
often been done) that this connexion imparted a special character
to Russian Christianity from the beginning. At the time of the
conversion of Russia, in the middle of the tenth century, the differences between Byzantium, or East Rome, and West Rome, were—
from the point of view of religion—not very considerable ; they
were latent rather than explicit. To begin with, Christianity seemed
to form another bond with the rest of Europe, and at the turn of
the tenth and eleventh centuries the links between Russia and the
west were closer than ever before. But this phase was brought to a
close by the development of the doctrine and practice of papal
supremacy in the church. Against the Roman claims the eastern
church reacted, and the result was the schism of 1054. This schism
—and its consequences during the succeeding four centuries—
turned Russia, to a greater degree than Byzantium itself, against
the Latin west. As a Christian state Russia felt itself a part of Europe,
and had in fact many common interests with it; but as the living
exponent of the orthodox eastern tradition, it was driven—and this
by its church—into opposition to the line of development in the
rest of Europe.

What this meant in practice a few examples will show. First of
all, Russia did not undergo the immense spiritual ferment which so
decisively affected the whole of western Europe at the turn of the
eleventh and twelfth centuries.[1] Secondly, it did not experience
the revival which sprang out of that ferment—the ' Renaissance of
the Twelfth Century ', as it is often called. Nor, indeed, did it
participate in the stimulus to political thinking—and to other
intellectual speculation—which continued from the twelfth century
through the age of Petrarch to the Renaissance of the fifteenth
century. That fruitful debate with the thought of classical antiquity
which did so much to shape and invigorate men's minds in the west,
was lacking in Russia. And finally, the two great revolutionary
movements of the sixteenth century, the Reformation and the
Counter-Reformation,—though they were an explosive force elsewhere in eastern Europe, particularly in Poland—came to a halt at
the frontiers of Russia. These few facts, barely stated, are perhaps

[1] For this movement, see above pp. 79 sqq.

sufficient to show how different the climate of thought, the very approach to the world and its problems, and the unconscious assumptions of both literate and illiterate, had become in Russia by the seventeenth century. That does not imply, of course, a judgement of values. The Russian approach to life was different, but not by any means necessarily inferior.[1] The eastern church had its own scheme of values, which it impressed on Russian character ; and we should be very foolish to assume that orthodox Christianity had not discovered—and impressed on Russians—some of the most precious facets of God's eternal truth.

Political developments also produced differentiation. In the middle of the thirteenth century the last wave of invasion from Asia passed across Russia, and resulted in a two-centuries-long domination by the Tartar or Mongolian bands of the Golden Horde. It is, I suppose, the best known fact in the history of old Russia. Nevertheless, I do not propose to say much about this phase ; only to warn against exaggerating its effects. It did not, as sometimes has been suggested, leave an Asiatic imprint on Russia. The Mongols exercised a loose tributary overlordship ; but, provided the tribute was paid, they left the Russians pretty well alone to run their own affairs. In particular, they did not interfere with the church. And this being the nature of their dominion, there was little intermixture of stocks—too little, by far, to leave a Mongol strain in the Russian people. The results, so far as the relations of Russia and Europe were concerned, were mainly negative. There is no doubt that relations with the west slackened in this period, and only revived again under Vassili II in the middle of the fifteenth century ; and if relations slackened, the result was a setback to the towns and to the commercial middle class in the towns. With the sole exception of Novgorod—and Novgorod also was on the decline before the end of the fifteenth century—the towns played no part in Russian life ; and at the beginning of the seventeenth century nowhere in Europe, from Poland westwards, was the middle class weaker or of less political importance. Here again, if we take our comparison with the age of the Fugger, or with the great patrician families of the Netherlands, or the Medici in Florence, the contrast with western Europe is very marked. In this respect Russia was backward without any doubt, and remained backward down to the

[1] Cf. above p. 164.

last decades of the nineteenth century, when industrialisation at last began to make headway.

The weakness, even as late as the seventeenth century, of the middle class brings us to a further sphere in which great differences are observable ; what we may call the social basis of Russian life. Here very briefly, we may say that what is lacking, in Russian development, is the growth of organized groups and associations capable of holding a balance against the power of the state.[1] For this, without doubt, the basic attitude of eastern Christianity—its indifference to the world, its emphasis not on the Christian's duty to reform and to reshape the world, but to flee from its clutches —was in no small degree responsible. But there are also other factors. First of all, there was no national spirit, such, for example, as infused the Scots against England or prevented France from absorbing the Netherlands. The three great divisions into which Russia fell after the decline of the first Russian state, the empire of Kiev, in the twelfth century—White Russia, the Ukraine and Great Russia—were not nationalities and never became nationalities, though down to very recent times—and perhaps even to-day—hostile foreign powers have played with the idea of a separate Ukraine. The old Czarist empire (and to-day, the Soviet empire) included many national groups, but outside Russia. Russia is, in Russian thought, not the Russian people but the Russian land, the *russkaja zemlja*— the whole Russian land ; and this has been a factor of great influence in Russian history, which from the time of Ivan the Great may almost be brought under the heading : ' the reassembly of the Russian lands '—lands which, in the anarchy caused by the Mongol dominion, had fallen apart, but which essentially were one. It is, however, sufficient for the moment to emphasize that regional loyalties, local loyalties, the narrower patriotism of the homeland, were never—even in a country so vast—strong enough to act (as, for example, in pre-revolutionary France they acted) as a check on the central government, on the ruler, on the state.

Nor, secondly, can we find any such check—as we do very markedly in western Europe from the fourteenth to the eighteenth centuries—in an articulated and politically organized class-structure. The Russian aristocracy, from the earliest times, was an aristocracy of service, a *noblesse de la robe* ; and when Paul I, at the end of the

[1] Cf. above, pp. 148-9.

eighteenth century, made his famous remark : ' only he with whom
I speak is noble, and that only so long as I speak with him ', he was
only expressing what had, in effect, been true from the middle ages.[1]
That does not mean, of course, that the Russian aristocracy was
devoid of political power ; on the contrary, it is well known how
important a part it played not only in the ' Time of Troubles ' at
the beginning of the seventeenth century, but also a century later
in the confusion after the death of Peter the Great. But they did
not act together as an estate, and were too lacking in corporate
feeling to appreciate the need for any kind of constitutional framework to alter the basis of government. The assembly of the whole
land, an institution analogous to the estates-general of western
Europe, had been called into existence for his own purposes by
Ivan the Terrible in the middle of the sixteenth century ; a century
later it was dead of inanition. Because the Russian nobility had
never, from the earliest times, established fixed, hereditary rights,
like the feudal nobility of western Europe, it never (not even in
the eighteenth century) formed a separate estate, conscious of and
determined to defend its inherited rights against the crown. No
institutional bulwarks were raised against the principle of autocracy,
which was hallowed by the church, and after the fall of Constantinople in 1453, by Byzantine tradition.

When during the ' Time of Troubles ' in the seventeenth century
the Poles suggested union with Poland so that Russia should have
freedom from its autocratic Czar, the answer they received was
characteristic. ' Your way '—the Russians replied—' is freedom for
you, but for us it is the opposite of freedom. You do not have
freedom, but licence. . . . If the Czar acts unjustly it is his will ; it
is easier to suffer injury from the Czar than from one's own brother,
for he is our common ruler '. And at a later crisis this attitude
remained unchanged. ' God grant ', said a Russian nobleman, ' we
don't get ten powerful and despotic families instead of one autocratic ruler '.[2] The antithesis : ' despotic '—' autocratic ', is significant. They are not the same thing. Autocracy is not arbitrary
rule ; it implies responsibility to God, and Ivan IV, when he said
that he bore responsibility before God for the deeds of all his sub-

---

[1] Cf. A. von Schelting, *Russland und Europa im russischen Geschichtsdenken* (1948),
271, 274–280.
[2] Cf. B. H. Sumner, *Survey of Russian History* (1944), 83, 85.

jects, was not uttering an empty phrase. Nevertheless there is never in Russian history anything to set off against this autocracy—unless, perhaps, one may offset its inefficiency—and the great stimulus to political thought and action, and the richness of political life, which arose in the west from opposition to absolutism, was lacking in Russia—and yet the lack was scarcely felt. We must bear that deep-rooted attitude in mind in trying to understand the attitude to-day of the Russian citizen to the Soviet government.

*   *   *

Those, very briefly, are some of the factors which had affected Russian development, and differentiated it from that of the west—not of this or that country in the west, but of the west as a whole—before Peter the Great came on the scene. I am very well aware how inadequately I have described them, how much I have left out, how much more could—and ought to—be said. But as an indication they may suffice. What is important, I think, about all these things is that they produced a state of mind which was not transitory, but lasting ; they continued through Peter the Great's time, and can scarcely be written off as uninfluential to-day. The great question about Peter the Great is, indeed, how far he modified the conditions he found existing, and how far they modified what he did.

This is neither the place nor the occasion to summarize the work of Peter the Great, or to pass a verdict on it.[1] Two observations must suffice : the one on the relations of Russia with the rest of Europe, the other on the effects of Peter's policy within Russia.

As to the first, it is certainly true—indeed, it is a platitude—that from Peter's time, Russia was ' definitely a part of the European state-system '.[2] As a matter of fact, that was nothing essentially new. From the time of Ivan the Great at the close of the fifteenth century, we can easily trace the growing connexions of Russia with western Europe ; in the seventeenth century the efforts of the Protestant powers, particularly Sweden, to gain the support of orthodox Russia against the forces of the Counter-Reformation, the urgent need at a later date of the Habsburgs to find allies to confront the

---

[1] It is sufficient to refer to the two most recent studies : B. H. Sumner, *Peter the Great and the Emergence of Russia* (1950), and R. Wittram, *Peter der Grosse. Der Eintritt Russlands in die Neuzeit* (1954), and to the classic study of V. Klutchevski, *Pierre le Grand et son oeuvre* (1953)—a French translation conveniently abstracted from Klyuchevsky's great *History of Russia* (Engl. transl., 5 vols., 1911–31).

[2] O. Halecki, *The Limits and Divisions of European History* (1950), 98.

eastern powers (including the Porte) in league with Louis XIV, and finally the attempt under pope Innocent XI to build a common Christian front against the Turks, all quickened political relations.[1] In this respect Peter the Great's reign brings no sudden change. But it remains true that the impression on the minds of people outside—and no doubt also within—Russia was henceforward very different. We can see the change best of all perhaps in the case of the philosopher Leibnitz.[2] One of his early writings is concerned with the perennial conflicts over the Polish succession. At this stage, for Leibnitz, Poland is the rampart of European Christianity, while the Czar—he calls him the ' other Turk ' (*alter Turca*)—is its enemy; Europe, he maintains, would be surrendering itself to Asiatic hordes, if it allowed a Russian to take the Polish throne. Then Leibnitz went to Russia, met the Czar, was honoured by him, and a new picture takes shape. Russia is now no longer the strange, unknown, threatening power beyond the frontiers of Europe ; it is rather (for Leibnitz) the land of the centre between east and west, and Leibnitz visualizes Russia carrying forward—by missions and schools and otherwise—the frontiers of Europe to Kamchatka, to the Aleutian islands and to the borders of China. At the same time, in his plans for Christian reunion, he thought to use the Russian church as an intermediary to reconcile the Protestant and the Roman churches of the west. For Leibnitz, therefore, Russia was not simply a factor in European politics ; it was an integral part of Christian Europe.

With the passage of time, by the reign of Catherine the Great, this attitude was general. It would not be difficult to imagine seventeenth-century Europe without Russia ; but to imagine eighteenth-century Europe without Russia is impossible. And, in equal degree, it would be impossible to imagine Russia without Europe. The role of a great European power, gained by Peter, and confirmed when Frederick the Great of Prussia was defeated in 1759, and when in the following year Berlin was occupied by Russian troops, became—perhaps at times to the disadvantage of Russia—the foremost consideration in Russian policy ; and we must, in all fairness, concede that it was used scrupulously in a European

---

[1] Cf. G. von Rauch, ' Moskau und die europäischen Mächte des 17. Jahrhunderts ', *Hist. Zeitschrift* CLXXVIII (1954), 25–46.

[2] Cf. E. Benz, *Die Ostkirche und die Russische Christenheit* (1949), 124–5.

O

sense. If there was any one constant factor in Russian policy, it was the attachment of successive governments to the idea of a European system of which Russia formed part, and which it was a duty to maintain.[1] Paul I, sending Suvarov to preserve Europe from the French Revolution, Alexander I planning and working for the Holy Alliance, Nicholas I defending Denmark from Germany in 1848, and suppressing the Hungarian revolution without any attempt to exploit the situation for the profit of Russia : of course, in all cases, we can, if we so wish, say that action was in the Russian interest, but it would be a partial and tendentious view. It is not necessary to accept their idea of what constituted a true European order ; but it would be wrong to deny that they took the idea seriously, and served it all in all disinterestedly. It was their wish and intention to put the power of Russia—naturally not to Russia's detriment—at the service of Europe. That such were Peter the Great's ideas is doubtless not true; but they were—and that is surely more important—the consequence of the new turn he gave to Russian policy.

The effects of Peter's policy within Russia were more complex. Most people to-day would agree that his aims were essentially practical, and not inspired by a new ideology, or by a conscious attempt to impose on Russia a new ideology. He knew—what was true—that Russia could not compete on an equal footing with the powers of the west—or, indeed, even with the Turks and the Tartars of the Crimea—without great change ; and so far as change was necessary for that purpose—and above all else to increase military potential—he did not hesitate to enforce it. But change for its own sake was not his object. As one historian has said, his positive achievement is traditional in character—a maintenance and continuance of Russian tradition— not revolutionary.[2]

Nevertheless, in forcing forward abruptly an assimilation which had been going on more slowly at any rate since the time of Ivan IV, Peter produced an internal tension—we may even say a dichotomy —which remained characteristic of Russia down at any rate to 1917. In the west, the world which Peter the Great saw had been produced slowly by the transition of the Renaissance and the Reformation, and by a gradual adaptation of social forms, in particular the growing

---

[1] Cf. W. Weidlé, *La Russie absente et présente* (1949), 75.
[2] P. Kovalevsky, *Manuel d'histoire russe* (1948), 204.

preponderance of the bourgeoisie and of bourgeois standards and bourgeois ideals.[1] The world of Newton and Locke, of Bayle, Voltaire and Montesquieu, was rooted in these preconditions. Russia, on the other hand, stepped into the Enlightenment without going through any of the intermediate stages, and without having developed the social foundations on which the values of the Enlightenment rested. Of this Peter was acutely aware. The development of a healthy middle class, to underpin his innovations was, for him, a cardinal point. But the long Swedish wars threw his plans out of gear ; and here—as often later in Russian history—what were regarded as the necessities of foreign policy, cut across the real needs of internal development.[2]

The result was what has been called the ' tragic duality of Russian life '.[3] The most notorious aspect of this—thanks to Masaryk's famous analysis[4]—is the cleft between the westernized aristocracy (and later the westernized intelligentsia) and a peasantry living in primitive conditions, sometimes called ' mediaeval ' but in fact constituting a servitude the middle ages had never known. In reality, however, the dichotomy went deeper and affected every class, most of all the aristocracy. ' Westernization ' produced a reaction in all spheres. The domination over the church established on the German Lutheran model by Peter the Great, led by reaction to the rebirth of Russian spirituality through such notable personages as St. Seraphim of Sarov (1759–1833) and St. Tychon of Sadonsk (1724–1783).[5] Similarly the peasant risings of the eighteenth century, directed basically against the crushing servitude imposed since Peter's day, were conservative in character rather than revolutionary ; they symbolized old Russia rising against the new westernization.[6]

Such was the tension which came into existence with Peter the Great, and which the eighteenth century heightened ; it came to a head in that famous decade, between 1835 and 1845, when ' westernizers' and ' Slavophils ' ranged themselves in two camps, and de-

[1] Cf. W. Treue, ' Zerfall und Einheit. Zum Wandel der europäischen Führungsschicht seit dem 17. Jahrhundert ', *Die Sammlung* VI (1951), 19 sqq., 111 sqq.
[2] Cf. I. Neander, ' Russische Geschichte im Unterricht ', *Geschichte in Wissenschaft und Unterricht* ' III (1952), 609, 617.
[3] B. H. Sumner, ' Russia and Europe ', *Oxford Slavonic Papers* II (1951), 13, 15.
[4] T. G. Masaryk, *Russland und Europa* (1913) ; Engl. transl., *The Spirit of Russia* (1919).
[5] Cf. Seraphim, *Die Ostkirche* (1950), 259 sqq.—A French translation of the metropolitan Seraphim's illuminating book appeared in 1952 under the title : *L'Eglise Orthodoxe. Les dogmes, la liturgie, la vie spirituelle.*
[6] Cf. W. Philipp, *Die Wandlung* III (1948), 451.

bated Russia's past and Russia's future. St. Petersburg—Peter the Great's new capital on the Baltic—or Moscow : which was the true capital of Russia, its spiritual core, its heart and soul, and not merely its administrative centre?

And yet this great debate, so exciting in itself, is in many ways deceptive ; for the strands constantly cross, and there are not two parties, but many. Nicholas I governed in the name of ' Orthodoxy, Autocracy and Nationality ' ; and yet the Slavophils were as hostile to the government as the westernizers.[1] In fact the government, and the whole vast bureaucracy, was forced into a western mould, because *raison d' état,* if nothing else, imperatively required that Russia should have ' the efficient machinery of a progressive western state '.[2] The greatest of the ' westernizers ', Herzen, was scathing about the society he found in exile in the west.[3] The Slavophils, on the other hand, derived their thought from German philosophers, Fichte, Schelling and Hegel. Everywhere, in short, there are contradictions. The Slavophil reaction was not simply a blind reaction against Europe : it was rather an attempt to establish an equilibrium, after the precipitate, excessive, all too rational 'reforming' activity of Peter and his mediocre successors ; to establish a balance between values too sunk in Russia's past to be rooted out, and new values which were essential for Russia's future.

What is remarkable is that nineteenth-century Russia did achieve in some degree this balance ; it did integrate itself with Europe. But it integrated itself with a Europe which was in the midst of an all-engulfing process of transformation—and thereby it was caught up in the ferment and the doubts, the uncertainties and the agonies of this vast transformation.[4] That, in all probability, is the essential point in the debate of Slavophils and westernizers. The so-called ' revolt against Europe ' was not a repudiation of Europe ; was it not Dostoievsky himself who said that ' Europe is our mother, to whom we owe much and shall owe more '? It was not a repudiation of the European inheritance transmitted through Byzantium from antiquity, and through the Christian church. But it was a protest

[1] As Herzen, for example, conceded ; cf. A. Herzen, *La Russie et l'Occident* (ed. A. Prudhommeaux, 1946), 160.
[2] Cf. D. Obolensky, 'Russia's Byzantine Heritage', *Oxford Slavonic Papers* I (1950), 41.
[3] See, for example, the passages in E. H. Carr, *The Romantic Exiles* (1949), 36–7, 51, 239 sqq., or the excerpts from Herzen's *My Past and Thoughts,* assembled by A. J Toynbee, *A Study of History* VIII (1954), 701–703.
[4] Cf. Weidlé, op. cit., 85.

against the encroaching rationalism and materialism of western 'bourgeois' civilisation, as it was visible in France under Louis Philippe; against the cult of the individual, unbridled competition, class-conflict, private property and the primacy of technique, and against the tacit assumption that these were 'the *sine qua non* of historical progress in the future'.[1] There is nothing 'anti-European' in this; and one reason—perhaps the greatest reason—for the extraordinary impact of nineteenth-century Russian literature on western Europe was that it expressed, with a cogency lacking elsewhere, similar doubts which beset all reflecting people in the west—from John Stuart Mill to Nietzsche—and still beset us to-day. For Dostoievsky, Russia is a better Europe, purged of the defects and disharmonies which had entered the west after 1815, or after 1789; and his ultimate hope and vision is of a messianic Russia regenerating and enriching a Europe of which it is not (so to say) a new recruit, but an essential part.

You may think what you will of this vision; but two things about it are clear. First, it stems from roots deep in Russian life and experience, from the messianic spirit of orthodox Christianity, from the belief in the succession of Moscow to Rome taken over after the fall of Constantinople in 1453, from the vision of Moscow as the 'third' (and last) Rome—for (said the prophet) 'there shall be no fourth'.[2] And secondly: it is an affirmation of Russia's place in Europe, and faith in Europe. What is important is that those who believed in Russia's mission turned their faces to the west, not to the east, and confident in Russia's future, believed that the future would be a European future. They believed that Russia had a contribution to make to Europe, that Russian values—different from those of the west but no less a part of the European inheritance—were a key unlocking the gate out of the contradictions and dilemmas of the present.

*   *   *

Such, as I see it, was the attitude of thinking Russians to Europe at the close of the nineteenth century. Has it—as is not uncommonly asserted—changed in any fundamental way since 1917? I am not

[1] Cf. Obolensky, op. cit., 47.

[2] The best account of the doctrine of 'the third Rome' is in H. H. Schaeder, *Moskau das dritte Rom* (1929). The political implications should nevertheless not be exaggerated; they only begin to play a role, through the efforts of J. Križanić, in the middle of the seventeenth century; cf. Rauch, op. cit., 28, 38.

going to attempt to answer that thorny question ; but in conclusion I shall venture a few summary observations, which may indicate perhaps some of the considerations an answer would have to take into account.

First, Marxism was—outwardly at least—a triumph of western rationalism and technique, of the acceptance of the world as a rational order, which men could shape to their own will, which was the mark of the eighteenth-century Enlightenment. It was, one may say, the spirit of Peter the Great imposed by a far more powerful machinery of government. It marks the ending, in official policy, of the dichotomy which the conflict of Slavophils and westernizers had expressed. But—and the ' but ' is important—Soviet Russia formally and officially sanctioned this western doctrine, stemming directly from the western Enlightenment, almost exactly at the moment when it was losing its hold in the west, and when in the west the values of the Enlightenment had come under attack. Thus, instead of the contrast with the west being resolved, that contrast persists in reverse. The values of Soviet communism, as expressed in Marxist doctrine, are western values ; but they are not those western values which at present hold sway in the west.

Nevertheless we may well ask further how far the official doctrines of the Soviet state—though certainly a very substantial part of the truth—represent the whole truth about Russia to-day. The significance of the revolution of 1917 was not merely that it introduced Marxist doctrine and made it the basis of the state. Its significance in Russian history was also—perhaps more profoundly—that it bridged the chasm between government and people—above all the vast submerged peasant population—which had grown wider and wider between the time of Peter the Great and Catherine the Great and 1917. It is, of course, true that this profound change is often denied. The Soviet hierarchy, it is said, is simply a dominant minority, as far removed from the people as the dominant minority of Alexander III's or Nicholas II's time. But it is difficult to accept this view. One of the outstanding results of the revolution, a writer who is no friend of the Soviet regime has written, was to give the country ' a ruling class far less separated from the people than the preceding one ' ;[1] and he adds that the revolution accomplished what the old regime had signally failed to bring about—the integra-

[1] Cf. Weidlé, op. cit., 183.

tion of the peasantry in the nation.[1] How it accomplished it, and
at what cost, does not concern us here and now. What is important,
rather, if these views are correct—and I think, as a generalisation,
that they are correct—is to ask what effects, if any, the new ' integration ' had in Russia and on Russian policy and the Russian attitude
to Europe. That question has often been put in the form of the
statement that Leninism or Stalinism is an adaptation of Marxism
to Russian circumstances ; that Russian Communism is not Marxism,
but Marxism modified in a continuous historical process so as to
combine with other elements coming from Russia's past. And we
may at least say that there are fruitful lines of enquiry here. Ten
centuries of orthodox Christianity cannot simply be expunged from
Russian history. The messianic faith, usually associated to-day with
the world-mission of Marxism, stems more profoundly from the
idea that the Russian church, the last repository after 1453 of orthodoxy, is destined to save the world. And again, as I have already
indicated, the biting criticism of western bourgeois society is older
than Marxism and independent of it ; it reflects Christian contempt
for a society that has made its peace with Mammon.

All these things live on in Russia and are important in shaping
Russian thought and attitudes. But it is important to see also what
does not live on ; and there I would suggest that the old, deep,
popular hatred of the west, rooted in religious prejudice—the blind
animosity against the ' schismatics ' and ' heretics ' of the Latin rite,
which is sometimes regarded as Russia's ' Byzantine heritage '—no
longer counts. I doubt, and most historians to-day seem to doubt,
whether it ever did count for as much as has sometimes been supposed. The issues between Russia and the western powers to-day
are based on concrete political causes, arising from conditions in
the modern world ; they are not, as too often is assumed, the expression of a deep, historical antipathy of the Russian people to the
west—or, as is sometimes said, to Europe.

The view that Russian policy expresses hostility to Europe is
based very largely on the fact that Russia, in the nineteenth century,
carried through a great colonization of contiguous Asia—a movement of colonization so vast in scale that only the opening of the
American continent can compare with it. Russia, it is sometimes
said, may have been a European power until the Crimean war ; but

[1] Ibid., 161.

then it turned its back on Europe, and became an Asian or at least
a ' Eurasian ' power. But if few will be found to deny that Russian
colonization in Asia is a cardinal fact in modern history, it is wide
of the mark to suggest that it has produced an 'Asiatization ' of
Russia, or fusion with the eastern peoples she subdued. Indeed,
considering the extent of Russia's Asiatic interests, it is remarkable
with how few exceptions Russian policy has continued to move in
a European orbit and be anchored in Europe. Russian expansion
into Asia, beginning in the sixteenth century with the ' discovery '
of Siberia by Yermak in 1582 and the astounding advance to the
Pacific by about 1640, was ' a gigantic frontier extension ' of Christian
Europe,[1] in which the orthodox church played a leading part ;[2] and
I know of nothing which would indicate that it has lost this character
in more recent times. It is an extension of the frontiers of European
civilisation because Russia, in making it, considered itself a part of
Europe, and carried with it values, techniques, standards, human
attitudes, which had their origin in Europe.

Against this background, I would suggest in conclusion that we
shall do well to examine with caution assertions so frequently met,
that Russia is opposed, root and branch, to all that European civilisation stands for. Russian history proclaims the effectiveness in
Russia of European values ; to say that to-day this situation has
radically and finally changed, is equivalent to slamming shut the
gates of history, and denying all possibility of further development.[3]
It is, of course, true that Soviet Russia is hostile to the particular
social forms, and many of the values arising from those social
forms, which are predominant in western Europe to-day. It regards
them, justifiably or unjustifiably, as perversions, or (more accurately)
as decadent forms—a criticism in which (though, of course, from
a different point of view) the Roman Catholic church would concur.
In Russian eyes to-day western society is a weary decadent society,
the relict of a dying bourgeoisie, which has lost faith in itself and is
incapable of renewal from within. To you, luxuriating in the manifold
delights of the ' welfare state ', this may seem a curious and perverse
judgement. But perverse or not, criticism of a particular form of
society—which none of us, I suppose, imagines to be the final

---

[1] The description is Sumner's ; cf. *Oxford Slavonic Papers* II (1951), 8, 15.
[2] Cf. the impressive account by Benz, op. cit., 63–77.
[3] Thus E. Hölzle, ' Russland und Europa ', *Die Welt als Geschichte* XIV (1954), 179.

manifestation of God's dispensation for mankind—is not the same thing as a fundamental rejection of European civilisation, or a deliberate severance from Europe. The historian who looks back only so far as the twelfth century has many examples of movements, springing from the heart of European society, which in their day were bitterly assailed as frontal attacks on the fundamental values of European civilisation, yet were then assimilated and defended as part of the inalienable European order. To conservatives and traditionalists the upheavals of the French Revolution seemed to mark the dissolution of all social bonds and to portend the imminent collapse of European civilisation. But civilisation did not collapse, and to-day the conservative Frenchman takes his stand on the French Revolution and the defence of its achievements. It was the same at the time of the Reformation ; and we should be foolish if we asserted, here and now, that the same might not be true at some future date of the Russian Revolution. It is no part of my purpose to argue that this will necessarily be the case ; it might, I imagine, be maintained that the instances are not parallel. But of one thing we should be clear. The relations of Russia and western Europe to-day are not parallel to those of Islam and western Europe in the middle ages ; and to suggest—as Dr. Toynbee, for example, has suggested—that Russian communism, in spite of its roots in Marxism, is ' a non-western ideology ' and that Russian policy since 1945 constitutes ' one of the first moves ' in a Eurasian ' counter-offensive ' against Europe, is certainly misleading.[1]

The relations of Russia with western Europe are not simple ; they comprise very varied elements of attraction and repulsion—but so, of course, do those of Germany. To start off, as Spengler did and as Toynbee does, with a dogmatic assumption that European civilisation and Russian civilisation are two distinct entities, only hides the real questions and problems, as they meet the historian on his journey through the centuries. For that reason, I have not sought to discuss the manifold theories about the character of Russia —for example, the ' Eurasian conception ' of Russian history—which permeate not merely speculative works such as the writings of Spengler and Toynbee, but have affected the interpretation of scholars such as Vernadsky.[2] But I hope the few points I have been

---

[1] A. J. Toynbee, *Civilisation on Trial* (1948), 221.

[2] Cf. P. N. Savickij, ' La conception eurasiste de l'histoire russe ', *Résumés des communications présentés au VIIe Congrès international des sciences historiques* II (1933), 210 sqq.

able to make, as dispassionately and uncontroversially as I can, though they cannot (and are not intended to) give a complete answer, will help at any rate to clarify a question which is certainly not without practical importance for the world in which we live. It is not enough to take Russia as, on the surface, we find it ; we must look also for the deeper roots and the less transient forces, which have made Russia what it is.   Even to-day, in a rapidly changing world, they have not lost their potency, and we must expect them to continue to influence the course of events.   Forty years are too short a period to bring about fundamental changes in the human component of any people ; for that reason alone, it is imperative to consider the relations of Russia and Europe, not simply as they have developed since 1917—or still less, since 1945— or to limit our vision to the narrow confines of diplomatic exchanges and foreign policy, but to see them as a process of give and take, in religion and literature, in art and in the whole realm of ideas, as well as in economic contacts and in political relations, from which, over a thousand years, we in the west, like the Russians, have derived benefit, and the common stock of European civilisation has been enriched.   Even when the result has been tension, the profit has been great, and is not likely to diminish with time.

14. The End of European History

WHEN I announced that I was intending to give this lecture,[1] the immediate response was : 'Oh yes, space-ships, I suppose?' It was a fair criticism, an implicit warning not to don the mantle of Mr. Lyndoe and get lost, like Arnold Toynbee, in fortune-telling and prophecy. It is significant enough that historians to-day all too frequently get themselves enrolled, as dreary upholders of current orthodoxies, in the minor orders of chivalry ; but it will be even worse when they join the inner circle of the Magicians' Union, and start pulling gloomy prognostications (instead of white rabbits) out of their hats. The historian's business is with what has happened, not with what may (or, more likely, may not) happen.

Nevertheless I think the question implicit in the title of this lecture is one we are justified in asking ; I have even the suspicion that, if we shut our eyes to it, we shall be shirking a pertinent issue. For anyone who has tried to follow the main guiding lines in European history, who has observed the turning-points when (so to say) it swung away, out of its former track, on to a new plane, who is aware of the unsolved contradictions and inner tensions which, at the end of a long course of development, seem to persist as a legacy from the European past,[2] it should be possible—with all the necessary reservations—to draw some tentative conclusions, not as to where we shall be to-morrow, but as to where we stand to-day. The phrase : 'The End of European History', if you take it as a bland assertion, is—I must admit—provocative and even question-begging. But it is worth asking whether European history has reached what we may call a 'term'—provided that you observe very carefully the necessary precautions.

Those precautions are, I think, four in number ; and it is perhaps desirable that I should set them out summarily straight away. The first—we all know it, but it is very hard to act on it—is to remember

---

[1] A public lecture delivered in the University of Liverpool on February 16th, 1955.
[2] Cf. above, p. 166.

always that the present is not the culmination of the past. It is human nature—but for the historian it is a fatal error—to assume that the efforts of past generations were concentrated with single-minded devotion on producing the unenviable situation in which we find ourselves to-day. Rather we had better assume that in the eyes of the Almighty, and in future history-books, 1955 will loom no larger than 423 or 1731, or any other date about which, if you scratch your head, you can remember nothing in particular. In other words, seeing that we cannot possibly range 1955—or, indeed, 1945—in historical perspective, we had better beware of attaching any particular importance to it; and that means, in a practical sense, that we had better not put any very great weight, in attempting to describe the present situation, on developments of the immediate past, such as the Paris Agreements. They are not yet susceptible of historical appraisal; may, in fact, turn out to be scraps of paper. You only need to recall the number of books written between the wars, which regarded the League of Nations as the final achievement of human endeavour, to realize the dangers.

In the second place, it is very important to be aware of the limitations of historical method. It is comforting, particularly for politicians, to suppose that the past leads through the present, in a fairly orderly and logical way, into the future, and therefore that if you can find some line leading from 1815 to 1870, or from 1870 to 1945, and prolong it into the future, you will have a pretty good idea of the shape of things to come. Unfortunately—or perhaps fortunately—the past is far too complicated and there are far too many lines leading out of it, and usually it seems to be the most unexpected one that matters. Who, in 1788, for example, would have anticipated Napoleon? History moves forward, no doubt; but it moves forward like a crab skirting a boulder. There is always something turning up, and we must leave room for that: the new which unexpectedly impinges, and swings things off in a direction no one anticipated and no one wanted.

In the third place, let me clear up what, if I say ' the end of European history ', I may reasonably mean by ' end '. It does not mean, of course, that European history will come to a full stop; it means rather that it will cease to have historical significance. For example, under the Roman empire Greek history, the history of the Peloponnese, went on; but what—unless we are a rare specialist, do

you or I know of it after the death of Philip V of Macedon? Turn,
for example, to Fisher's *History of Europe*, and there (you will find)
for 1500 years Greece disappears from the scene, which a couple of
centuries earlier it had dominated. Its history is, in Fisher's words,[1]
the history of men and women who have ' lived, worked and died,
leaving no memorial, contributing nothing to the future '. In that
sense Greek history—though it goes on—comes to an end ; and it
is in that sense—and in that sense alone—that we can speak of an
' end ' of European history. For 800–900 years Europe has been
the chief centre of political experiment, economic expansion and
intellectual discovery in the world. Is it losing—or has it already
lost—this position to-day? Have the values established by European
civilisation, which were certainly the dominant values down to the
close of the nineteenth century, exported afar to the New World,
to Asia and to Africa, ceased to be the dominant values?

That, as I see it, is the question implicit in the formula : ' the
end of European history ' ; and in answering this question—that
is my fourth and final point—we must be very careful to guard
against a purely subjective answer. It is a great temptation for the
middle classes—and nowadays all historians belong to the middle
classes—to identify the end of middle-class predominance with the
end of European civilisation. The result is the fashionable pessimism
of the intelligentsia, which is so rife to-day. But that pessimism
may easily be false. Time and time again in European history
pessimists have predicted the dissolution of all social bonds and
the imminent collapse of European civilisation ; time and time again
they have proved wrong. Europe survived the disappearance, and
was even glad to be rid, of the feudal nobility and the aristocracy
of the *ancien régime* ; it may survive the disappearance, and even
be glad to be rid, of the old *haute bourgeoisie*, the Forsytes, the Swanns,
the Buddenbrooks. Social change, however profound, may be a
sign of renewal, not of collapse. Therefore—and that perhaps is the
important point to make—in discussing the ' end ' of European
history, we must look for trends and changes which go deeper,
which have altered the very preconditions upon which European
history has rested, and without which it is impossible to envisage
its continuing, however much its form and structure may be changed.

One such change—I think we can say with all certainty—is a

[1] *A History of Europe* (ed. 1936), 1219.

matter of historical fact, and not of mere surmise. That is the change
in Europe's position in the world. I do not need to say as much
about that as I should have done twenty, or even ten, years ago.[1]
Writers such as the American, Eric Fischer,[2] the Pole Oskar Halecki,[3]
or Arnold Toynbee in England,[4] have made us familiar with the
idea of the ' passing of the European age '. As Halecki says, historians have given a lot of thought and effort to describing the
' making of Europe ' ; now we have to ' seek similar dates ' for
' the un-making of Europe and what is undoubtedly the end of a
whole age '.[5] And that involves, probably, a reconsideration—
which I do not intend to embark on here and now[6]—of the whole
established chronology of European history. It is evident that the
conception of ' modern history ' has become meaningless ; [7] that
what is usually called ' modern ' is by no conceivable standard
' modern ' ; that the phase which is usually called ' modern '—from
the Reformation to Bismarck or the First World War (which is a
very dubious division anyhow)—has been superseded by a 'post-
modern ' period—a period which is sometimes called ' contemporary
history ', but which we had better not call ' contemporary ', because
there is nothing very contemporary about Bülow or Tirpitz or Lloyd
George, or even Stanley Baldwin.[8] The very fact that people so
near in time are separated by a gulf so wide in thought and reaction,
is perhaps itself the best evidence of a decisive change and of the
onset of a new period. Already attempts have been made to find new
names, more appropriate to current thinking, for the successive ages.
It has been suggested that a ' Mediterranean age ' was followed by
a ' European age ', which is now being succeeded by an 'Atlantic
age '.[9] It is not necessary to discuss those appellations now. They
seem to me to be better than the old ones—although the term
'Atlantic age ' begs a lot of questions : if we consider that to-day
Russia and America face each other across the Bering Straits as
England and Germany once faced each other across the Straits of
Dover, then we may wonder whether what is called the 'Atlantic

---

[1] Cf. above, pp. 135 sq., 171.
[2] E. Fischer, *The Passing of the European Age* (1943).
[3] O. Halecki, *The Limits and Divisions of European History* (1950).
[4] A. J. Toynbee, *The World and the West* (1953).
[5] Op. cit., 46.   [6] But cf. above, pp. 57–8, 61.
[7] D. P. Lockwood speaks of the ' ex-modern age, the now nameless age, the period
of the fourteenth to nineteenth centuries ' ; cf. *Journal of the History of Ideas* IV (1943), 63.
[8] Cf. Halecki, op. cit., 165 sqq.   [9] Ibid., 41, 54, 61, 168, etc.

age' may not turn out, after all, to be 'the Pacific age'. That, however, is incidental. The important thing, whatever we call the new age, is to see that it is a new age.

There is not, of course, any sudden break. Just as Europe arose from the ancient world by stages which are exceedingly difficult to pin down, so that you cannot really put any fixed date to the change in predominance, and can only say that it took a period of four or five hundred years to complete, so in the transition from 'modern' to 'post-modern' history there is a long period in which the two ages, the declining and the rising, co-exist or overlap. It would be an error to say, even now, that that period of overlap was finished ; the extraordinary recovery since 1945 shows that Europe cannot, even at this late date, simply be written off as an extinct volcano. But two facts point to a fundamental change. 'Modern history', as we know it, seemed to be given unity by two things : first, what is called 'the expansion of Europe', and secondly the predominance of the European powers. Both are too obvious and well known to require elucidation : what is important is that they no longer hold good. For three centuries, following the voyages of Columbus, Da Gama and Magellan, the shadow of European hegemony moved across the oceans ; between 1815 and 1914 the world entered a new era of global integration under the compulsion of western techno-logy, and seemed to be receiving a European imprint, not merely in material things, the cotton shirts of Lancashire and the shoddy trousers of Dewsbury, railways, electricity, architecture, but also in political organisation and political ideas. Predominance and leader-ship were in the hands of the European powers. To-day that is no longer true. Down to 1914, it seemed that the relations of the Euro-pean powers would settle the future of the world, and that European expansion was simply carrying the principle of Balance of Power, on which the relations of the European states were based, into the other continents. In fact, well before 1914 that had ceased to be the case. When the tottering Ottoman empire was admitted to the European Concert in 1856, and when, a little later, the United States and Japan were recognized as 'great powers', in addition to the six nations which happened at the time to be the strongest in Europe, it was clear that world-leadership was no longer a European privilege. To-day, after the war of 1939–45, two great powers survive : Russia and the United States, both with European roots and origins but neither at this date essentially European—and following at a distance there is the British commonwealth, the sinews of which also lie outside Europe. The rest, as we have seen,[1] have sunk to provincial status. It is too early yet to speak with certainty ; but the indications are that in the late twentieth or in the twenty-first century Europe is destined to enjoy (if that is the right word) something not unlike the colonial status which in the eighteenth and nineteenth centuries it imposed on Africa, much of Asia and the New World. Already the Soviet Union and the United States have their European satellites ; already eastern Europe can only defend itself with Russian help against American domination, and western Europe can only defend itself with American aid against Russia.

The German historian, Ludwig Dehio, in what is probably the most remarkable and prescient study of modern history to appear since the war, has shown how and by what stages the old ' historic core ' of Europe (as it is sometimes called) was overtaken, dwarfed and is now in effect divided between the two great flanking powers in east and west.[2] As his analysis makes clear, the struggle of first one power and then another to secure hegemony in Europe forced the defenders of European liberty to call in the aid of outside powers, or to mobilize for their defence non-European or extra-European resources. Napoleon's attempt to unite Europe in a French empire was defeated not by the efforts of his opponents and victims in the heart of Europe, but by the resistance of the two great flanking-powers, England and Russia. And it is evident, however high we rate the defensive effort of Great Britain in 1940, that Hitler was defeated by the overseas resources of the U.S.A., on the one hand, and, on the other hand, by the Asiatic resources which Soviet Russia drew from its empire beyond the Urals.[3] These wars, fought on European soil, devastated Europe, with the result that the extra-European powers drew ahead. The war of 1914–18 resulted, as everyone knows, in the economic and financial supremacy of the U.S.A. But another result, though less obvious, is no less significant. The successive defeats of successive powers seeking hegemony in Europe meant that European national divisions were not only

---

[1] Cf. above, p. 171.
[2] L. Dehio, *Gleichgewicht oder Hegemonie. Betrachtungen über ein Grundproblem der neueren Staatengeschichte* (1948).
[3] Cf. above, pp. 174 sqq. for further detail.

preserved but increased. Few people in Europe would regret that result ; few would prefer unity under French or German hegemony to the relative liberty assured by a system of small counterbalancing powers, none strong enough to enforce its will against a combination of the others. The diversity of the nations, it is usually held, has been the source of the richness of European culture and civilisation. But if we emphasize that important fact, we must recognize also that these divisions meant, and were bound to mean, weakness in the face of outside powers. They were one of the main reasons why the U.S.A. and the U.S.S.R. drew ahead. Even to-day, though in area far smaller, in population Europe (excluding the U.S.S.R.) is considerably larger than either Russia or the United States of America. The present population of Europe is around 400 million. Western Europe alone, including western but excluding eastern Germany, to-day contains over 275 million people ; yet Russia's population is only about 220 million and that of the United States less than 165 million. There is therefore no absolute European numerical inferiority. And in addition, relative to its size, Europe can still claim to rank as the most highly industrialized continent of the globe.[1] If, therefore, Europe has been overtaken and outstripped politically by the U.S.A. and the U.S.S.R., this is due in part at least to conditions within Europe itself. It was because Europe failed to solve its own problems, that it lost its predominance. Hence, in considering the position of Europe to-day, we must take into account not merely the change in world-conditions, but also the changes in European conditions.

Why, in the war of 1939–45, do we find non-European forces fighting on European soil, and deciding the issues most vital for the future of the continent? Why, at the end of the account, did Europe find that, far from having a primacy or setting a general pattern, it was not even sufficient for its own problems, but needed the aid of the new and great powers outside itself to ensure its defence and sustain its economy? The answer may be put in this form : that historical Europe, during the protracted revolutionary crisis which began with the French revolution, lost its last oppor-

---

[1] Cf. H. Holborn, *The Political Collapse of Europe* (1951), 191. The present annual output of western Europe is ' more than half the production of the United States '. But there is no reason to doubt ' that ' under certain circumstances ' it ' could approximate in the future ' to ' that of the United States '. The circumstances envisaged are, of course, political unification.

P

tunity to work out a satisfactory solution of the problems which had
been the main concern of the whole European age. First of all, the
diversity of Europe proved stronger than its unity. The result was
that its potential strength, economic as well as political, was wasted
and dissipated by division, whereas both Russia and America have
the great advantage of unity over a very extensive area. It is this
unity, evidently, which has enabled them to outstrip Europe.
Secondly, the concentration of a vast population in a small area has
imposed limits and created problems which are not—or at any rate
are not yet—operative either in the U.S.A. or the U.S.S.R. Both
are still lands of unlimited opportunity with vast scope for development, as the industrialization of California since 1939, or of Magni-
togorsk or more recent centres beyond the Urals, sufficiently shows.
Europe, on the other hand, is ' saturated ' ; there are obvious limits
on new development ; and further industrialization, for example, is
less likely to add to, than to displace, older industry ; ' rationali-
sation ' and improvement may still add to output and wealth, but at
disproportionately greater cost and effort. Thirdly, this basic
difference in conditions has necessarily produced a radically different
outlook, a different attitude to political and social questions. It
is evident, for example, that the whole attitude to employment and
unemployment must be different in the great ' frontier ' lands with
vast unexploited resources—and both Russia and the United States
are ' frontier ' lands in this sense[1]—and in Europe where opportunities are limited. What happens—what has happened—above all
else, is that the tensions, which in the U.S.A. and the U.S.S.R. could
be turned outwards, and deflected into the struggle to subdue and
exploit nature, in Europe are turned inwards, and produce struggles
and conflicts within society itself.

   This was already evident by 1848. The fundamental cleavage in
European society had ceased, by the middle of the nineteenth
century, to be the old historical distinction between a privileged
aristocracy and priesthood and the great body of unprivileged
commoners. It had become instead a cleavage between those with
property and those without, between those who owned the machinery of production and those who worked it—in a word, between
the bourgeoisie and the proletariat.[2] And this cleavage was reflected

[1] Cf., above pp. 145 sqq.
[2] Cf. G. Bruun in The European Inheritance III (1954), 58.

in the conflict of principle and idea between liberalism and democracy. So long as the European peoples could use the resources of
their overseas dominions, and overseas markets, to bolster up their
own standard of living and maintain employment, this unresolved
conflict could be held at arm's length, staved off, glossed over.
Hence the imperialism of the last quarter of the nineteenth century,
when one-fifth of the land area of the globe and one-tenth of its
inhabitants were gathered into the expanding domains of the European conquerors within a generation—a rate of imperialist encroach-
ment unsurpassed in history.[1] On this basis, it looked, about 1880,
as though Europe might find equilibrium in the framework of a
number of middle-sized, industrialized, democratic, national states.
To-day, it is obvious that this expectation of equilibrium on the
basis of the national unit, was illusory. First the reaction, economic
as well as political, of the non-European world, destroyed all the
preconditions. Secondly, nationalism—far from stabilizing the European order—proved to be an explosive force, which blew it sky
high. And so, the internal conflict came to the surface again. During
the nineteenth century, partly through pressure, partly to forestall
conflict, partly for merely tactical reasons, the franchise had been
extended step by step, in the belief that the electorate, enfranchised
in this way, would accept the current liberal beliefs and postulates,
and could be absorbed into and assigned a place in the established
system of parliamentary liberalism. In fact, this did not occur.
Instead, the extension of the franchise made the old system of
parliamentary democracy unworkable—in the sense that it produced fundamental structural changes in the machinery of government, of which the most obvious was the emergence of the highly
organized mandatory political party, supported by press and propaganda.[2] Thus the liberal world fell to pieces under the pressure of
demographic factors, and gave way to what is often called the ' age
of the masses '. The victory of 1919 appeared, in 1919, to be a
victory for liberalism ; in fact that victory was temporary and
superficial. Universal suffrage resulted not in the entrenchment of

[1] Ibid., 112.
[2] The classical analysis of these changes is M. Ostrogorski, *La démocratie et l'organisation des partis politiques* (1903 ; Engl. ed. 1903). Probably the best modern account
is in G. Leibholz, *Der Strukturwandel der modernen Demokratie* (1952) ; cf. also T. Schieder,
' Das Verhältnis von politischer und gesellschaftlicher Verfassung und die Krise des
bürgerlichen Liberalismus ', *Hist. Zeitschrift* CLXXVII (1954), 49–74.

liberalism, but in a reaction against liberalism, and outside England,
—which, for historical reasons, was in an exceptional situation—
parliamentary institutions, though still functioning and in existence,
had almost everywhere changed their form and purpose.

The movement was practically universal throughout Europe ; it
was found under left-wing governments as in Russia, and under
right-wing governments as in Poland ; it was found in Catholic
countries such as Spain ; in Italy and in Germany ; in the France of
Pétain ; as well as in a host of little countries in the Balkans. Whatever their acclaimed political and ideological associations, Communist, Fascist, Catholic, pagan, whether they reflected the alleged
interests of the working classes or the alleged interests of the middle
classes, all these movements had certain things in common : for
example, the predominance of one party, and the suspension of the
civic rights of the individual, such as freedom from arrest without
trial, or freedom of conscience, which were the very foundation of
the liberal political philosophy, upon which, up to this date, the
civilisation of modern Europe seemed to have been built.

The nature and extent of these changes is not always fully understood. It is still common to group them under the heading ' totalitarianism ', and to write them off as abnormalities produced by the
economic crisis of the 1930s, which a more expert handling of economic difficulties might have avoided. And that, no doubt, is a partial
explanation of what occurred. But in reality the changes went far
deeper, and affected—and are still affecting—all regimes, whatever
the political slogan by which they are called. It is not necessary that
the features which we commonly associate either with Fascism or
with Communism should be involved. The mere fact of organizing
a mass political electorate has produced everywhere a line of development which—though we cannot say what particular forms it will
take in any particular case—is clearly leading away from a liberal
social and political structure, to one which (in broad terms) may be
called ' managerial ' or ' technocratic '. The new pattern—more
advanced in some countries, for example Germany, than in others,
but everywhere coming into view—is a pattern of strict organisation
of social, economic and administrative activity. Everywhere, already,
the activity of the old-fashioned parties—relics of an age which is
past—has the appearance of ' shadow-boxing ' ; power, organized
on a mandatory basis by a highly technical party machinery, is

passing away from the electorate and from the politicians into the hands of administrators, the personal and individual retreating before the anonymous, impersonal group. You may call your state a 'welfare state' or a corporative state—and it may make a good deal of difference to the amenities and creature-comforts, to the amount of jam you are given to spread on your margarine—but the movement is universal. The differences between the position of the working-man in Communist Russia, business-dominated Germany, Franco Spain, and Great Britain under Attlee or Churchill or Eden, are doubtless very considerable. But all mark a departure from, a fundamental break with, the standards, values and practices of nineteenth-century liberalism.

*   *   *

These few observations must suffice. The question is : what conclusions are we to draw from them? And one thing is certain : any conclusions must be tentative and cautious. Nothing would be easier than to argue that the liberal parliamentary system which we have known is so closely bound up with the European inheritance that its collapse must necessarily mean the death of western civilisation. Nothing would be easier than to show that the ' revolt of the masses '—to use the expressive phrase of the Spaniard, Ortega y Gasset—is ' a great human flood ' battering down ' a civilisation whose pride it has been to affirm the greatness of human personality by the creation of strong aristocratic hierarchies '.[1] Nothing would be easier—did one take the time—than to illustrate the alleged ' decadence of Europe ', the ' disintegration of the bourgeois synthesis ', the ' bankruptcy of liberal humanism ', the alleged reaction against ' the tyranny of the intellect ', the ' faltering of morale ', ' the change from inherited optimism to introspective doubt ', and all the other cant phrases which are taken to imply the ' mortal sickness ' of European society. No doubt, all these things are partial observations of reality ; no doubt they reflect, one and all, ' disruptive forces ' at work in European society. But, as I insisted at the beginning of this lecture, the historian will hesitate long before he identifies a social transformation, which is certainly going on, with total disintegration. For anyone who looks objectively at the facts, there is, I think, no doubt that the various forms

[1] Thus E. Vermeil in *The European Inheritance* III (1954), 269.

of dictatorship between 1919 and 1939 awakened new energies—real and vital, if scarcely, by accepted standards, moral— in societies which seemed moribund ;[1] and the same is probably no less true in a different way of the so-called 'welfare state' of post-war England. You may not like those new energies any more than the English or Austrian or Prussian governments of 1793 and 1794 liked the new energies aroused by the French Revolution ; but that is no reason to deny their existence, and it seems to me that it is an unwarranted assumption to suppose that they must necessarily be negative or destructive. Disruptive forces there certainly are ; but there are constructive forces also. No one could maintain that there is in Europe to-day that gradual exhaustion of creative energy which was so obvious in the decline of the Roman Empire.[2]

What is obvious, on the other hand, is the dilemma of Europe— a dilemma which is nowhere more evident than in the contemporary projects for European union. If, as is commonly agreed, one of the prime causes of the decline of Europe is its lack of unity, then it seems too obvious for further discussion that the answer to that situation lies in federation. And yet the prospects of voluntary federation, so far as can be judged, are not very great, and I imagine most historians would be more impressed by the obstacles in the way of European union to-day than by the possibilities. To discuss those obstacles in detail is none of my business. But it is worth while—and, I think, important—to insist that they do not (as is too easily assumed) consist simply in a short-sighted, selfish inability to subordinate national interests to a greater, common good. No doubt, there are many such interests at play—not all of them lightly to be dismissed. But the real issue goes deeper, and it may perhaps best be put in the form of a comparison with Greece. In ancient Greece, in its greatest age, the independent city-states— Athens, Corinth, Sparta—were essential elements. Take away the independence of those city-states, and it is difficult, if not impossible, to see how what was of enduring value in Greek civilisation could have been secured. In other words, the independence of the city-states had the same roots as Greek civilisation itself ; it was ineradicable so long as that civilisation lasted.[3] May we not say the same of the European nations ? Or is it not at least a consideration

[1] Cf. Vermeil, op. cit., 252.   [2] Cf. Fischer, op. cit., 183.
[3] Ct. A. J. Toynbee, *Civilisation on Trial* (1948), 120.

which no serious, thoughtful person would simply dismiss? Back in 1924, in an address to an American audience, the Dutch historian, Jan Huizinga, a great European if ever there was one, put the position far better than I can. 'I do not know', he said,[1]

> whether Americans can fully realize the necessity there is for Europe of preserving its division into many nations, and the fervent desire of all and any of these to maintain their specific national existence. I do not mean this politically so much as culturally . . . It would be quite natural for you to say : why should not the European nations, after so many centuries of bitter strife, in the long run be merged into one vast unit ? . . . Still, political harmony and concord is not the one thing the world stands in need of. However indispensable to civilization peace and order may be, real civilization is not contained in them. They may even be a danger to it, should they be promoted by equalizing and levelling. What we envy you is your unity, not your uniformity. We Europeans feel too keenly that no nation, however prosperous or great, is fit to bear the burden of civilization alone. Each in his turn is called upon, in this wonderful world, to speak his word, and find a solution which just his particular spirit enabled him to express. Civilization is safeguarded by diversity. Even the smallest facets in the many-sided whole may sometimes catch the light and reflect it.

Those words of Huizinga—you may say that they are only one element of the story, but just for that reason they reveal what I have called the ' dilemma ' of Europe. On the one side, industrialisation—which in foreseeable time will not be checked or halted—seems, with its extending scale of operations, to demand and necessitate ever greater unification : unification, indeed, in which a European union, even if it embraced the whole of Europe, might still prove to be an inadequate economic unit. And with unification, standardisation and uniformity. On the other side, the maintenance of diversity, and what an English historian has called ' resistance ' to ' drab technological (or " technocratic ") universalism '.[2] And this is only one of the dilemmas with which Europe is faced. Europe's problem, it is often said, is that it has too much history ; it cannot escape from the toils of its own traditions, break away from the

[1] J. Huizinga, *Verzamelde Werken* II (1948), 282–3
[2] Sir Ernest Barker, *The European Inheritance* II, 348.

past, and make a new start. But, on the other hand, may it not be answered—and has it not often been said—that the alleged ' bankruptcy' of Europe is precisely due to the fact that European man has lost his historical roots, and become ' an exile from his own past '?[1] Here again—and I will not burden you with further examples— Europe is saddled with a dilemma which neither the U.S.A. nor the U.S.S.R. yet knows in the same intensity. It has rightly been said that, if Russia and America have forged ahead of Europe, it is not because either possesses greater political ability or political experience —on the contrary, they possess much less—but because political construction, and likewise economic construction, is easier in a new country on the fringes of a civilisation than in the old country at its centre. Evidently, the position in this and in other respects is far more complicated and difficult in Europe ; and this itself is a disadvantage from a political point of view. There is, in fact, no easy or right or correct solution of Europe's problems ; and that is an additional problem—perhaps the decisive problem. The self-confidence and directness of Russian policy and American policy, and their clear objectives, are impossible in Europe, because in Europe the objectives are not clear. We may put the European dilemma in a nutshell by saying that, if Europe does not preserve its traditions it will lose the spiritual forces, the belief in itself, the very anchorage, without which no civilisation can hope to survive, while if it maintains its traditions and the diversity and the values which those traditions have created, it will be at a disadvantage—probably at a fatal disadvantage—in a world where large-scale organisation, vast political and economic units, uniformity and standardisation, bring power and the right to have the last word.

In a sense, it might be argued that Europe still remains the centre of the world ; but that its position is now reversed.[2] Instead of being a centre from which energy and initiative radiate outwards, Europe has become a centre upon which non-European energy and initiative converge. Instead of the world being a theatre for the play of European activities and rivalries, Europe itself is an arena for the conflicts of extra-European powers. And yet even in this sense the position of Europe is in doubt. For the moment it would seem that the struggle for Europe, because of its great industrial

---

[1] Cf. Bruun, op. cit., 124, and *The World in the Twentieth Century* (1948), 697.
[2] Cf. Toynbee, *Civilisation on Trial*, 103–4.

potential, is the dominant theme in the relations of the two surviving great powers, Russia and the United States. But the series of conflicts in Korea, S.E. Asia and Formosa already indicates that the scene may be shifting, and that the sheer demographic weight of Asia—once the process of industrialisation fully activates it and makes its mobilization possible—may become the dominant factor, and in no far distant time leave Europe in a backwash. In any event, the traditional Europe—the Europe of our history books, the Europe of Louis XIV and Napoleon and Bismarck—is dead and beyond resurrection, and we may disabuse our minds of the illusion that there is any special relevance, from the point of view of contemporary affairs, in studying those neolithic figures. If you believe that the study of history has any relevance to current events, then you will gain more, in the present world, by studying the life and times of Alexander the Great, or Caesar and the Roman revolution. And it is perhaps fundamentally important to get this fact firmly in our minds, because there could be no more serious mistake in current policy than to suppose that a return to a Europe similar to that of the nineteenth century can be effected, or to direct political action to the restoration of what is fondly called ' the traditional order '.[1]

But if the traditional Europe has passed beyond recall, it does not follow with any rigour or logic of necessity that Europe has no future to look forward to. As Halecki says,[2] the ' passing ' of Europe does not mean that there will not, in the future, be a European history in the sense in which there was European history in Antiquity, when parts of Europe were joined with Asia Minor and North Africa in the Roman empire. The European community typical of the European age of history—a real unity in all its diversity, clearly distinct from any other part of the world—is disintegrating before our eyes. But individual European countries, or possibly different regions of Europe, will continue to play a role, which need not be inconsiderable, within larger, but not exclusively (or even predominantly) European communities, of which perhaps the so-called 'Atlantic Community ' is a forerunner.

Furthermore the ' passing ' of the traditional Europe does not mean that the system of values centring round the worth of human personality and the importance of the human individual, which has

[1] Holborn, op. cit., x.   [2] Op. cit., 47.

been built up in the course of European history, has ceased to count. It is true, I think, that these values are not ultimate, and must not be treated as ultimates. In the course of centuries eastern Christianity built up values with a different but no less real appreciation of the place of the individual in God's universe, and these values —and I say this, of course, without prejudice to the values of the other great religions, Islam, Buddhism, Confucianism—are not to be dismissed as less estimable or less valid than those of the west. Nevertheless western standards will survive, though doubtless shorn of many of the extravagances which marred them in the period of unbridled liberalism. But we must not expect the same implicit acceptance of those standards as in the past. We can see to-day that the acknowledgement of the system of values built up in the west as an ultimate standard in most parts of the world was, in large part, not a reflection of genuine belief in the validity of those values, but rather a result of the fact that they were the standards of a successful, expanding, forward-thrusting civilisation, and were therefore accepted, on pragmatic grounds, as one of the conditions of success. Now that European civilisation is on the defensive, the attitude of non-European peoples to European standards—as we can see very plainly in the case of India—is far more critical.

Nevertheless we need not fear that the values created and consolidated by European societies in the last 800 or 900 years will perish. They will not perish for two reasons. The first—and the more important—is that they reflect an approach to perennial human problems which is of too universal application to be neglected, a solution which the particular spirit of Europe—and that particular spirit alone—was able to express, but which, once expressed, has become the possession of mankind. And though a far too presumptuous insistence on the superiority of western standards has produced a very natural reaction, particularly against the unbridled individualism of western thought, we may be sure that that reaction in its turn will be followed by a counter-reaction, which will lead to a better appreciation of what is of enduring value in western traditions.

The second reason why European values, though they may be modified and re-assessed, will not perish, is that they are embedded both in Russian and in American civilisation. This is an important fact, provided that we do not misunderstand and misinterpret it;

and because of its importance I will say a few words in conclusion about it. As we are all aware, both Russia and America have drawn largely on western European thought—in particular, in both cases, on the thought of the eighteenth-century Enlightenment. But we must not conclude for that reason that, in either case, there has simply been a transportation of European civilisation—or of particular elements of European civilisation—into a new centre, and that in the new centre the old values and old culture continue essentially unchanged. In Russia the western strand came into contact with the eastern inheritance, also European, but derived from Byzantium, and thereby it was profoundly modified. But both in Russia and in America the decisive fact is that, in a new and different environment, the preconditions for the development of civilisation were totally different from those of the west. Both Russia and America are 'frontier' countries, with vast undeveloped territories behind them ; and there is no doubt that this frontier character has profoundly modified and transformed European institutions and the European inheritance.[1] The American historian, Eric Fischer, observed correctly of 'American civilisation' that it 'is part of western civilisation, but it has branched away from every European variety of that civilisation'.[2] And Halecki adds that, 'transferred to other continents and particularly to the Western hemisphere, the old civilisation of Europe is undergoing changes to such an extent that the cultural differences between the two continents . . . are greater than those between the various European nations'.[3]

To discuss these differences here and now would obviously be out of place. They are due evidently in part to the fact that what was taken over in each case was not an inheritance as a whole but part of an inheritance. The fact remains that both American and Russian civilisation to-day—though both contain many features which were

[1] Cf. above, pp. 148 sqq.

[2] Op. cit., 115. ' However greatly customs may differ in different parts of the territory of the United States ', he adds, ' the differences from European customs are yet more striking '. Cf. A. M. Schlesinger, *Amer. Hist. Review* XLVIII (1943), 244 : ' probably none of the traits is peculiar to the American people . . . , but the sum total represents a way of life unlike that of any other nation '. This requires emphasis in view of the plausible argument, now gaining currency, that American history ' is western history, moved by the same rhythms, stirred by the same impulses, inescapably involved in the same crises ' as European history (E. Mattingly, *The University and its World responsibilities*, 1946, 9–10). As I have indicated above (p. 172), this seems to me to be a misleading simplification of a very complicated issue ; and I hope on some future occasion to have an opportunity to discuss it at length.

[3] Op. cit., 57.

never found in Europe and could, for historical reasons, never have been found in Europe—are unthinkable without the European element. They are as unthinkable without it as Europe itself without the classical inheritance, which constantly stimulated, moulded, shaped, attracted, repelled, but—whatever its effects—never ceased to stir European thought and action, from Bede and Alcuin in Anglo-Saxon England through Petrarch and Erasmus of Rotterdam to Goethe and the two great luminaries of Basel, Burckhardt and Nietzsche. And that comparison is perhaps the aptest on which to end. Whatever the political future of Europe may be, the ideas it has contributed to the common stock—transformed, no doubt, misunderstood, garbled, and misapplied in inappropriate circumstances, just as the ideas of classical antiquity were misunderstood and misapplied in mediaeval Europe—but living nevertheless, a stimulus in men's minds, a guide to their actions, a consolation perhaps in a falling world (as Boethius drew consolation from the philosophy of Rome), and a spur to human endeavour : these at least will live. And it is with these, the lasting element in European history, and not with the din of battle and the strident notes of diplomacy, with kings and emperors and politicians, all as dead as the cohorts of Nineveh, that the wise man will concern himself to-day. Every age needs its own view of history ; and to-day we need a new view of the European past, adapted to the new perspectives in which the old Europe stands in a new age of global politics and global civilisation.

15. *What it is all about*

AS we sit here under the louring shadow of the atom-bomb[1]—
replete, well fed, with a conscientiously courageous smile on
our faces, but with inward foreboding, like convicts on the
morning of the day of execution—it is a good opportunity to take
stock of human history, and see what it is all about. Mankind has
been on earth I know not how many scores of thousands of years :
one authority, commendably cautious, says 'perhaps 500,000,
perhaps 250,000 years', so great is the margin of error. And less
than 10,000 years ago there began that phase in man's history which
we know generically as 'civilisation'. Five thousand years ago,
approximately, there was rising the great Sumerian civilisation of
Ur of the Chaldees ; more or less simultaneous were the civilisations
of the Nile valley and of the plains of the Indus. The area of ' civilisation' was expanding ; and from this time our knowledge of man's
history is sufficiently detailed, as a result of the labours of the
archaeologist and the anthropologist, of the historian and the pre-
historian, to be termed ' continuous '.

So we have behind us, as we face the future, approximately five
thousand years of experience ; for history, after all, is the record of
human experience. If we survey that experience, we should, if
the study of the past is worth anything, be able to discern trends
and movements, and even to 'extract from past experience the
lessons, the warnings and the inspiration which may serve as a light
to our feet to illuminate our path ' ; and that, I believe, is what the
ordinary man expects and demands of the professional historian.
Unhappily, the professional historian to-day, engrossed in his own
particular period or subject, is all too apt to shirk the reasonable
demands which an informed and intelligent public makes upon him ;
he finds research safer, less controversial, and less perilous than
interpretation, turning history (as Sir Maurice Powicke once said)

[1] This talk was originally written for a World Affairs Lunch-Hour Meeting held in
Sheffield in 1947, when the atom-bomb was still the terror and bogey of mankind.
To-day (unless perchance the cobalt-bomb is in secret preparation) it would be more
natural to speak of the hydrogen-bomb in this context.

into a ' pedantic chase after the insignificant ', and forgetting (in
the words of Philip Guedella) ' that the researcher's thread must
find its place one day in the historian's tapestry '. The idea that
history is a labour of bricks and mortar, manipulated by armies of
diligentlabourers amongrecords, is bringing th e historicalprofession
into disrepute with the public, which wants to know not the un-
related facts, but what it is all about. Not, of course, that we can
do without brick-makers ; but ' the edifice of history calls for an
architect as well ', who can see and follow the plan. And the danger
to-day is that the historian, overwhelmed by an ever accumulating
mass of intractable material, will fail to see, or even to seek, the plan.
Yet the craving for an interpretation of history is so deep-rooted
that, unless we have a constructive outlook over the past, we are
' drawn either to mysticism or to cynicism '.[1] The failure of the
historian to provide an interpretation of history, to say what it is
all about, is another example of the notorious ' trahison des clercs ',
of the refusal of the specialist to live up to his work ; and it is no
good his disclaiming the ability to interpret his work, because
(as Miss Wedgwood recently wrote) ' if the accurate, judicious and
highly-trained fail to draw the lessons of history, the unscrupulous
and unqualified will do it for them '.[2]

But I am afraid that is not the worst. Not only do historians as
a body signally fail to seek out the lessons of the past, but—in
subconscious or conscious justification of this attitude—they deny
that the past has any lessons to teach, or even any meaning. They
frown, and carp, and pick holes, when anyone tries to survey the
whole sweep of the past, severely criticizing such errors as they find
at those particular points where the writer, in his long journey
through space and time, happens to traverse their tiny allotment,
forgetting that in his attempt to interpret the whole life of mankind,
he is doing something which they would not dare to embark upon.
Or, if they widen their horizons to survey the whole, they deny
that the whole has any wholeness. ' One intellectual excitement has
. . . been denied me ', wrote H. A. L. Fisher, after completing his
History of Europe. ' Men wiser and more learned than I have discovered in history a plot, a rhythm, a predetermined pattern.
These harmonies are concealed from me. I can see only one emer-
gency following upon another, as wave follows upon wave, only

one great fact with respect to which, since it is unique, there can be no generalizations . . . the play of the contingent and the unforeseen.' Thus history seems to be no more than ' a tale, told by an idiot, full of sound and fury, signifying nothing '; and one is left wondering why so many men have expended so much time and effort on elucidating its course. ' The fallacy ', we are told, ' of any so-called philosophy of history lies in professing to discover certain immutable laws; for except the law of change, no other has ever existed or can exist.' And—a more contemptuous dismissal still —' speculations that have to do with primal causes and ultimate goals transcend the range of ordinary reason, and man is a baffled creature whenever he tries to go beyond the closed gates of his own limitations '.[1]

This attitude of contemptuous dismissal towards what is known as the ' philosophy of history '—that is to say, the attempt to perceive, behind the transient incidents, the drift, the motive forces, the continuity and the pattern of civilisation—is, of course, a reaction against the ' scientific ' history which flourished towards the end of the nineteenth century. Without any doubt we can trace back this ' scientific ' approach to history to the age of Newton and Descartes, to the ' scientific revolution ' of the seventeenth century, when technological progress, introducing a new spirit of enquiry in all branches of knowledge, led with revolutionary suddenness to the perfection and dissemination of a new cosmology and a new outlook on the world. Descartes' *Discourse on Method* was ' the project of a universal science which can elevate our nature to its highest degree of perfection '; while others (such as Hakewill) asserted the progress of man in social morality, as well as in material civilisation. This belief in a steady advance towards human perfection was put into more concrete form by the philosopher, Fontenelle, when he stated that ' the sound views of intellectual men in different generations will continually add up ', and concluded that progress is ' a natural and necessary effect of the constitution of the human mind '.[2]

From this time forward it is possible to trace the rise of the idea of progress as the determinative principle in human history; but it was not until the immense advance in natural science during

[1] L. Einstein, *Historical Change* (1946), 112, 120.
[2] Cf. J. B. Bury, *The Idea of Progress* (1920), 67, 92, 109, 126.

the nineteenth century, that the idea really took hold over popular imagination. A turning-point was the Great Exhibition of 1851, ' the first morning since the creation that all peoples have assembled from all parts of the world and done a common act '; and the instruments in popularizing the idea were Darwinianism and the theory of Evolution. Brought up in the ban of the great theory of Evolution, historians began to treat the subject-matter of history on an analogy with the natural sciences. ' The new history ', one wrote, ' is not a department of *belles-lettres* . . . but a branch of science '; and ' this science, like many other sciences, is largely the creation of the nineteenth century. It deals with the condition of masses of mankind living in a social state ', and ' seeks to discover the laws that govern these conditions '. This outlook was epitomized by J. B. Bury in a famous address.[1] ' History ', he insisted, ' is a science, no less, and no more '; and he went on to compare ' the facts of history ' with ' the facts of geology or astronomy '. The implication, quickly drawn, was that human history is ' a continuation of natural history '; in other words, that it is a continuous story from the time when man emerged, ' a rare animal ', ' the last great species ', living ' like any other beast of prey, a parasite on other creatures '.[2] The further implication was that the factors which enabled the human species to triumph over the other species, ' the forces that evolved us in the long succession of living beings ', the equipment through which man ' has succeeded in surviving and multiplying ', are still the active forces capable of raising mankind to ever higher perfection. And of these forces the decisive one is human reason, the faculty which differentiates man from the lower animals. Reason is the faculty which enables one generation to profit from another; it permits the accumulation of knowledge, and is thus the postulate behind the idea of human perfectibility.

Hence human history is seen as an upward curve, proceeding from the amoeba, via ' an infinite variety of lowly, jelly-like, shell-less and boneless creatures ' through the ' age of reptiles ', the monkeys and apes to Neanderthal man and primitive man, and thence to civilisation. The theme is ' up and up ', ' on and on '; even if there have been periods of regression, progress is real. ' No trough ' it was said, ' ever declines to the low level of the preceding one,

[1] J. B. Bury, ' The Science of History ', *Selected Essays*, 9, 22.
[2] V. G. Childe, *What Happened in History* (1942), 7, 22.

each crest out-tops its last precursor ' ; and ' even if temporarily fossilized ', ' the cultural capital accumulated in long ages ' is conserved and transmitted to new generations.[1] No generation starts off anew from the foundations ; a short view may show decline, such as intervened after the fall of the Roman Empire, but a long view of history shows mankind progressing, blindly (perhaps) and stumblingly but with inexorable logic, to better things. He is caught up in the march of evolution and carried forward in spite of himself.

This optimistic view of human history has its roots in the Christian and Jewish conception of the historical process as a progressive revelation of God's purpose (though this is certainly not the only interpretation consonant with Christian belief and theology),[2] but it was during the Enlightenment that it took on its modern garb, and in the nineteenth century, with the diffusion of popular education, that it became the dominant mode of thought. It underlay the outlook of Tennyson, with his belief in the coming ' Parliament of Man ' and ' Federation of the World '. It underlies equally—though translated into other terms—the powerful Marxist interpretation of history, which also sees the history of mankind passing through well-defined phases, culminating in a classless society, so perfect that the ugly contrivance of the state will ' wither away '. In literary garb the evolutionary conception of society was never more brilliantly expounded than in Bernard Shaw's dramatic cycle, *Back to Methuselah*, published in 1921. In historical form, it found its supreme expression in H. G. Wells's influential *Outline of History*, published in 1920. Both postulate that the development of intelligence is the work of ' natural selection ', and that the inexorable laws of natural selection will result in the replacement of the present imperfect society by one in which a finer humanity will inhabit a more perfect world.

The dates are significant : 1920 and 1921. The first world war and the impact of Wilsonian idealism had produced a belief that the shackles of the past—such things as national policies and secret diplomacy, sacrificing the common good to nefarious ends—had been cast off, and that mankind, conscious of the identity of its interests in all parts of the globe, would advance rapidly to a new

[1] Cf. Childe, op. cit., 250, 252.
[2] The orthodox or eastern Church has generally taken a different attitude ; for some further discussion cf. above, pp. 161, 164.

Q

social integration. To-day we know how deceptive these aspirations were. At the conclusion of a second world war, coming hard upon the heels of the first, we are less inclined (to put it mildly) than our predecessors thirty years ago to nail our flag to the mast of progress. And no thinkers were quicker than Shaw and Wells themselves to see the ominous signs of retrogression. Wells who in 1914 wrote *The World Set Free*, who earlier had always been ready with blue-prints of the new society, published after 1939 a series of despairing tracts with such expressive titles as *The Fate of Homo Sapiens, Babes in the Darkling Wood* and *Mind at the End of its Tether*. A few months before his death he faced up to the possibility ' that hard imaginative thinking has not increased so as to keep pace with the expansion and complication of human societies and organisation ', and concluded ' that Homo Sapiens, as he has been pleased to call himself, is in his present form played out '. He envisaged ' the death of Man ' and his ' replacement by the next Lord of Creation ', and went down expecting, though rebelling against, an imminent catastrophe in which mankind would give ' place to rats or unclean intrusive monsters equipped with streptococci for our undoing '.[1] Truly the great optimist had become the great pessimist ; the bubble of progress was pricked.

*   *   *

It will be sufficient to enumerate briefly one or two of the main fallacies vitiating the theory that the idea of progress provides the key to human history. The cardinal error is the false analogy from natural science to historical science, from natural to human history. The ideas of ' evolution ' and ' natural selection ' may be germane to the process by which the human species rose towering above the other animal species ; they are not germane to the history of man in civilized societies. The problem facing man is not that of contending with other animals for supremacy, or even of controlling his environment ; it is, from the dawn of civilisation, the problem of living together in societies. And it is neither proven, nor provable, nor even probable, that the qualities by which man triumphed over Dinosaurs and Ichthyosaurs, and out-distanced Pithecanthropus, are qualities which get us further in the problem of living together in civilized society. In other words, the attempt to trace a continuous upward line from man's earliest beginnings fails because it confuses

[1] Cf. H. G. Wells, *A Short History of the World* (revised ed., 1946), 290.

two totally different things when it represents the development of civilisation as a continuation of man's natural history, a further phase in the process by which he raised himself above the other animals. In fact, it only needs to be stated to be perfectly obvious that the problems of civilisation are totally different in character from anything that went before, and that our understanding of these problems is not furthered but rather befogged by analogies with a primitive state of nature. What it is important to know to-day is not whether mankind represents an advance on earlier forms of life—a proposition few of us would be inclined to deny—but whether, and in what ways, man has progressed since the advent of civilisation. The problem is not, in short, one of man but of societies, and not one of all societies, primitive or advanced, but of civilisations. We may believe, with Rousseau, that civilisation was itself a mistake, diminishing rather than increasing man's happiness and even his capacity for goodness ; but since we cannot of our own volition return to primitive society, such arguments are for all practical purposes beside the point. What we ask of history, and of the historian, is an answer to the question whether there is any unmistakeable advance, any progress, since the time of the earliest civilisations, and whether the course of history since that time provides any pointers to the future.

The answer at first glance seems obvious enough. If we take an early civilisation and compare it with our material state to-day, we shall unhesitatingly affirm the fact of progress. But immediately we come up against three points, each of cardinal importance for our understanding of the course of history. The first is that, if we make comparisons, we must take care to compare comparables. It is, for example, beside the point to take a civilisation in its early phases, and compare it with the advanced state of our civilisation to-day ; rather our comparison should, for example, be with the Rome of Caesar. And straight away the contention of progress becomes more controversial. Certainly, Rome had no motor-cars and turbine-engines, no electricity, no machine-guns, no atom-bombs ; nor did its techniques and institutions and ideas extend so far over the globe as those which we regard as characteristic of what we call western European civilisation to-day. But the question is whether these things are the essential differentiating factors.

With that question we come to the second point : namely, our

standard of comparison. In this respect we may recall the words of
Bernard Shaw, in *Man and Superman*, when he wrote that ' those who
admire modern civilisation ' and are convinced of the fact of progress, are those who identify civilisation ' with the steam-engine and
the electric telegraph '. No doubt we are far ahead of Greece and
Rome in scientific knowledge and in the technical exploitation of
this knowledge ; but—apart from the very real possibility that, like
the Chinese, who made so many of the basic scientific discoveries,
the Greeks and Romans may simply not have been interested in
exploiting science (and not, as it is so often assumed, merely incapable of exploiting it)—it is only too obvious that ' all our marvel-
lous inventions are as powerful for evil as they are for good '.
Technical and material advance certainly brings increase of pressure
in life ; but it is another question whether it brings a general advance
in either happiness or in social aptitudes. In any case, as Arnold
Toynbee has said, ' civilisations are not, in spite of the perverted
notions of modern materialism, built of such bricks as these ; they
are not built of sewing-machines and tobacco and rifles, nor even
of alphabets and numerals '. In short, the real question is whether
the assumption made in the Age of Reason is correct, that man has
progressed in social morality, as well as in knowledge and technical
ability. And the same consideration applies to the argument that
the spread of western techniques throughout the world, to India
and Africa, to China and Japan, represents a substantial advance ;
for there again we are faced with the fact that, although ' it is the
easiest thing in the world for commerce to export a new western
technique ', ' it is infinitely harder ' (to quote Toynbee again) ' for
a western poet or saint to kindle in a non-western soul the spiritual
flame that is alight in his own '.[1]

Therewith we come to the third point that is germane to our
argument. It is the question of the truth of the assumption that
' the sound views of intellectual men in different generations will
continually add up '. It is one of the most plausible arguments in
favour of progress, with its picture of one generation building on
the work of another, one civilisation profiting from the discoveries
and experience of its predecessors. But when we come to examine
in detail the handing on of ' the torch of civilisation ' from one
culture-group to another, we are in deep and perilous water. Every

---

[1] A. J. Toynbee, *A Study of History*, abridged edition by D. C. Somervell (1946), **40**.

historian, when he turns to the scanty survivals of the past, is at once aware of the immense difficulty—some would say impossibility —of thinking himself into the thought of the past, and re-living in his own mind and experience the life of the past generation he wishes to re-create; and yet he is aware that, without such an imaginative re-creation of the past, he cannot properly interpret the few remaining survivals which lie to his hand, whether they consist of art and architecture, of documents and literature, or of shards and ploughshares. The same difficulty besets us when we face up to the problem of continuity in civilisation, of the transmission of ideas and achievements from one civilisation to another. It is easy to speak of the Renaissance, for example, as the rediscovery of Greece and Rome ; and it is certainly true that what they thought was Greek and Roman was a powerful external stimulus in the minds of men of the Renaissance. But did they rediscover and take over as an inheritance the spirit of classical antiquity? One simple example— the history of handwriting—precisely because it is simple and factual and uncontroversial, will serve to clarify the situation. Revolting against mediaeval ' barbarism ', the Humanists of the Renaissance deliberately revived, in the belief that it was the handwriting of classical antiquity, the script of the ninth century, because that was the script in which the bulk of ancient classical texts they were intent upon studying, was written. What are we to think of a ' classicism ' so superficial that it committed this palpable error?[1] Or let us take one more example, this time from the field of the transmission of ideas. No one doubts that the rediscovery of Aristotle was, from the thirteenth century onwards, one of the most potent influences on political and other speculation. But two points stand out. First, the new Aristotelianism was not the thought of Aristotle but an interpretation of Aristotle's writings, altered, adapted, often misinterpreted, by men whose minds, at a far different level, worked in a far different way.[2] Secondly, though the stimulus

[1] The same point was made in a different context by N. Berdyaev, *The Meaning of History* (1936), 138-9 : ' The affinity between the ancient and the Renaissance worlds has been exaggerated. Renaissance art fails to reproduce antique perfection. . . . Renaissance Platonism bears but a slight resemblance to that of the ancient world. The same is true of the attempts to set up artificial political forms on the model of the antiquity which they do not at all resemble. Such resemblances as exist are merely superficial and illusory.'

[2] J. W. Allen (*Mediaeval Contributions to Modern Civilisation*, ed. Hearnshaw, 259) doubted whether ' the schoolmen of the thirteenth century . . . ever understood Aristotle '.

provided by Aristotelianism is undoubted, who can say that, if it
had not been Aristotle, it would not have been something ·else?
The decisive fact, in other words, was not the accidental rediscovery
of Aristotle through the intermediacy of Arab civilisation, but the
fact—which could be illustrated in a hundred ways, did space
permit—that the development of western society had reached a stage
at which it was ready to grasp at any theoretical justification for a
new political system (the system of· the national state) which was
already far advanced in evolution. The impact of Aristotelianism
happened conveniently; but it did not create a new political outlook;
it only provided a convenient peg upon which to hang it.

*   *   *

What I have been trying to indicate, as I hope you will have seen,
is that the external stimulus exerted upon one civilisation by another
does not constitute the passing on of an inheritance; the driving
forces come from within, the spirit is within. As one historian has
said, ' continuity is by no means the most conspicuous feature of
history '; ' the connexion of one civilisation with another is often
obscure ', ' a matter of faith rather· than of sight '.[1] It is one thing
to talk of progress within a civilisation, another to talk of progress
from one civilisation to another civilisation. What we see, rather,
is a number of civilisations, each inspired by a different spirit and
each pursuing different aims, but each passing through specific
phases; and it is impossible to describe one as ' progressive ' by
comparison with the other, because we have no standards by which
to affirm that the spirit of one civilisation is more ' advanced ' than
that of another—no reason to place our western civilisation with its
dominating sense of infinite space and depth, of the soul and its
destiny, above classical civilisation—a civilisation ' at home in the
body '—with its acute perception of the moment and its ideal of
concrete, finite perfection.[2]

Nor can we say that one is ' progressive ' in the sense that one
has ' succeeded '; for in fact all have failed to solve the problems
of their internal tensions and contradictions, save our own, and it
has yet to be demonstrated that our own will succeed where the
others have failed. All history has to show is a rise and fall, an
upward surge, a grappling with problems, an exhaustion, and a slow,

[1] Cf. above, p. 35.   [2] Cf. above, p. 48.

steady decline, a stiffening of the fibres of society after the dying-down of creative forces. Or rather, though I have used the word 'all', it is the wrong word; for it creates an impression of pointless, wasted striving, whereas if we cast our mind back over past civilisations, we see such a diversity of valuable effort, touching perfection at so many points, that—far from evoking pessimism—history is the most exhilarating testimony to the creative vigour, to the splendid variety, of the human spirit. But the achievements of different civilisations do not add up. The extraordinarily impressive portrait head of Yarim-Lim, king of Alalakh in the eighteenth century B.C., the Hermes of Praxiteles, and Raphael's Sistine Madonna, are not stages in a continuous development towards artistic perfection; each is the expression of a distinct civilisation, Hittite, Greek and European, and can be understood only in terms of that civilisation and what it was setting out to do. If they stand in any relation to each other, it is not as links in a chain, but as representing parallel achievements in parallel cycles of development.

It is the same in regard to the different civilisations themselves. It is unfair and unprofitable to blame the Greeks and the Egyptians, the Chinese and the Indians, for having failed to achieve what *we* have achieved, for there is no reason to suppose that they set out to achieve what seems to us desirable. What is profitable is to examine the reasons for their failure to achieve what *they* set out to achieve, for in that way, working by parallels, we may get some inkling of the causes underlying the rise and fall of civilisations, and of the process of civilisation itself. To begin with, we must banish completely from our minds the old parochial division of history into 'ancient—mediaeval—and modern'—a meaningless time-scheme which makes nonsense of the past;[1] we must abolish also the more fashionable time-scheme which divides history into ages, the 'Copper Age', the 'Bronze Age', the 'Iron Age', and is supposed to culminate to-day in the 'Machine Age'. And in the second place we must be clear—a matter about which the most diverse views are still held—what we mean by a 'civilisation'. We shall, for example, befog our minds if we speak of French civilisation, or English civilisation, or Italian civilisation, as comparable entities, instead of elements within one European civilisation;[2] and if we take a purely geographical basis and speak of everything which has happened in

[1] Cf. above, p. 57.   [2] Cf. above, p. 49.

Italy, for example, from the beginning of time as part of one and the same civilisation, we shall make confusion still more confused. Similarly we shall never understand classical civilisation, if we regard Greece and Rome as two distinct cultures, instead of phases within the framework of a single civilisation.

All that is part of the essential groundwork which it is the business of the professional historian to work out in detail. In fact, it has not yet been worked out in anything like final detail, owing in no small degree to the fact that our knowledge of the earlier civilisations and of many oriental civilisations is severely limited. But making all due allowance for that, the basic fact remains that we can perceive, and many historians to-day are increasingly accepting, the cyclic nature of civilisation. We see history no longer as an upward curve, marred by certain unfortunate drops in the graph, but as the story of a number of cultures, each rising to a height, each falling into a trough and petering out when its creative powers are used up. About this view of history itself there is nothing new ; it was the orthodox belief of the ancient world, held by Platonists, Pythagoreans and Stoics alike, and it was propagated in the eighteenth century by the Italian thinker, Giambattista Vico, though in all these cases the cycles were to our way of thinking capricious, unhistoric and unnaturally rigid. Still, it is well to realize that the ' cyclic theory ' (as it is sometimes called) is not merely a transient fashionable novelty put forward in our own generation by Spengler and Toynbee; on the contrary, the transient novelty was the overweening belief in progress which it is superseding.

Grasp of the fact that the story of civilisation is the story of civilisations gives at once an intelligible field of enquiry to the historian and to all others who are concerned to know ' what it is all about '. The first requisite is to view history comparatively, to establish a time-sheet showing the parallel phases in each civilisation, and thus to establish which events are ' contemporary '. ' I designate as " contemporary ",' says Spengler,[1] ' two historical facts that occur in exactly the same relative positions in their respective cultures, and therefore possess equivalent importance.' In this sense, the Ionic and the Baroque ' ran their course contemporaneously. Polygnotus pairs in time with Rembrandt, Polycletus with Bach ' ; and we can establish the correspondence, item by item, of the Trojan

[1] O. Spengler, The Decline of the West I, 112 ; cf. also p. 27.

War and the Crusades, Homer and Beowulf, the Greek city-state and the European national states from the Reformation to the French Revolution, the Dionysian movement and the Renaissance, Athens and Paris, Aristotle and Kant, London and Rome, New York and Alexandria, Alexander and Napoleon, the Wars of Hannibal and the First World War—perhaps even we may compare the Third Punic War and the Carthaginian Peace that followed with the struggle from which we have just emerged.

Such a comparative time-sheet is basic to the study of civilisations. It is certainly not easy to establish on a basis which is assured of general agreement ; and there are bound to be many disagreements between experts before an acceptable chronology is obtained.[1] Only when it is established, can we safely proceed to the next step ; and that is to seek out the causes influencing the observable rhythm of civilisations. In classical civilisation, for example, we can see how the exhaustion and ravages of the Punic Wars undermined the existing economy, how the dispossessed peasantry drifted into the towns to swell the urban proletariat ; we can see the consequent social conflicts, the attempt of the Gracchi to impose a radical (it might even be called a ' socialist ') solution, its failure and the emergence of the Empire under Caesar and Augustus. . . . I cannot pause to pursue the story further ; indeed, I cannot pursue it at all ; but he from whose eyes the blinkers of a false historiography have fallen, will best be in a position to perceive the why and the wherefore.

*   *   *

The question remains : what does it all mean to us to-day? To answer that question we must see our own civilisation comparatively, fixing the parallel events and turning-points in the civilisations which have preceded our own, and assessing them in intelligent anticipation. We must observe in each case how inspiration has given way to purely intellectual creativeness, and note how and when this latter reached its zenith. We must note, again, how and when faith and optimism and firm belief in the future have been superseded by a phase of world-weariness and scepticism, in which the worthwhileness of life itself becomes problematical. We must watch intently the fate of social movements, the transformation of the fine

---

[1] One of the cardinal weaknesses of A. J. Toynbee's work, as it seems to me, is the failure to construct a rigorous chronology. To this point I hope to return ; meanwhile cf. my criticisms in *The Listener*, October 14th, 1954.

hope of world democracy into the ' tyranny of the masses ', the
failure to carry out the Marxian dream of a ' new society ' and instead
(as Burnham has already prognosticated) the substitution of new
masters for old. We must observe, in brief—and that is the crux
of the matter—the failure to overcome the inherent conflicts within
society and its economic contradictions ; for it is this twofold failure
which has brought down all preceding civilisations, however different in spirit each has been from the other and no matter what their
material achievements. All these are lessons of history which have
relevance to-day. What we have to do is to apply them dispassionately, step by step and stage by stage, to our own civilisation, from
its genesis back in the time of the ' barbarian invasions ' and its first
crystallization in the empire of Charlemagne, down to to-day. The
parallelism is there ; it is for us to see it and interpret it. All I can
do in conclusion is to point out, as I see them, one or two guiding
lines :—

    1. The first is that we can see pretty plainly the relative stage
which our own civilisation has reached. We can see that we are nearing
the end of a phase parallel to that in Classical civilisation which ran
from Alexander to Caesar. We are in a period like that of the two
Gracchi, Tiberius and Gaius, when Rome was getting her food more
and more from abroad, and when cheaper and more abundant wheat
was coming in from Sicily and Egypt. Tiberius set out to stop the
rot, to encourage home production, not merely as an economic but
as a social measure ; faced by the opposition of the bourgeoisie,
of commercial and financial interests, he failed. His brother Gaius
passed laws establishing a system of wheat-purchase by the state,
to secure the poor against famine and high prices ; he arranged for
a lease of the taxes of the province of Asia to financial companies ;
but he again failed. ' The Senators ', it has been said, ' saw clearly
enough that his continuance in power meant the end of their rule ' ;
and the outcome was his violent death. But the old ruling classes
could no longer rule ; the old constitution was creaking. Not only
was there social strife at home ; further afield, the conquered pro-
vinces were intensely discontented with their lot. Italy revolted
against Rome, by which it was exploited ; and simultaneously Asia
rose too. The pure colonial phase was over. The failure of the old
governing class led to the rise of new men, dictators of the right and
left. Of them it has been said : ' The Gracchi were men of ideas ;

Marius was a man indeed ', but ' Sulla concerns us no more than any other reactionary who for a while is successful '. Yet all ' play their part in bringing about the great change from republic to empire ' ; and that movement itself is more momentous than any of them. It culminates—the product of unresolved social tension— with Caesar and Augustus, and therewith begins a new phase : the Empire.

2. What I am suggesting is that we to-day stand on the verge, like the Romans of 100 B.C., of the imperial phase. We can see already the inadequacy of national economies, but clinging to outworn sovereignties, cannot overcome it. We can also see the need for a radical redistribution of purchasing power to provide new life for an economy in which the classical device of exploitation of the external market is played out; but how far will our modern Gracchi, our radicals and reformers, be able to bring about the modification of the social structure without which there can be no enduring increase in the purchasing power of the working classes? We can see, to whatever political party we belong, the inadequacy of in-herited political institutions to the tasks of the present; but can the necessary readjustment be made in the face of vested opposition from both right and left?

3. It is easy, and it is fashionable, to give the answer ' Yes '. Toynbee ends his *Study of History* with ' a message of encouragement for us children of the western civilisation, as we drift to-day alone, with none but stricken civilisations around us '.[1] ' No known law of historical determinism ', he says, ' compels us to leap out of the intolerable frying-pan of our time of troubles into the slow and steady fire of a universal state, where we shall in due course be reduced to dust and ashes '. ' The divine spark of creative power is still alive in us, and if we have the grace to kindle it into flame, then the stars in their courses cannot defeat our efforts to attain the goal of human endeavour '. It is finely put ; but it can be put more concisely in the old, trite saying, ' where there's a will there's a way '. But the more fundamental question still remains : is there a will? Is ' the divine spark of creative power ' still alive in us, despite what Toynbee calls ' the spiritual inadequacy ' of our eighteenth-century

---

[1] Cf. A. J. Toynbee, *A Study of History, Abridgement of Volumes* I–VI, by D. C. Somervell (1946), 254, 553. These pages were, of course, written before the appearance in 1954, of vols. VII–X of the *Study*.

Enlightenment? We are much preoccupied to-day with economic problems; but we must remember, as Toynbee says, that 'the economic explanation of the decay of the Ancient World must be rejected completely', because it was simply the outcome of a preceding spiritual decay, because already 'society . . . had gone to pieces'.[1] And there is another point as well. It is easy to talk of our 'will', but (in Spengler's words) 'no culture is at liberty to choose the path and conduct' it will follow. Our actions are conditioned by our environment; and it is evident that the broad pattern of the post-war world, much as we may dislike it, has already been set, in part by the inexorable development of American industrial potential between 1939 and 1945, in part by the failure of statesmen of all countries after 1945 to cast off the blighting shadow of supposed national interests and come to grips with realities. These are the facts; and whether or not the stars in their courses can defeat our efforts to attain the goal of human endeavour, it is pretty clear that the combined efforts of Mr. Molotov and Mr. Dulles, and the off-stage sniping of General Chiang Kai-shek, can.

4. Therefore I find it hard to assimilate the fashionable optimism; but I do not think the alternative is pessimism. On the contrary, I think the crude alternative: 'optimism—pessimism', puts the whole issue in a false perspective. Those who see the course of history as 'cyclic' are commonly denounced as pessimists, because they are supposed to regard the whole of human destiny as subject to mechanical 'laws'. In fact, nothing could be more mistaken. If you wish for an analogy to illustrate the position more vividly, then it is not to the laws of mechanics that you should turn, but to the rhythm of human life; and I do not think that any of us are pessimistic because we know that youth will give way to maturity, passion to calm, activity to serenity, because we know that our creative powers will not last, though our intellects may remain untarnished, and because we are conscious that death will ensue.

5. There is much exaggeration to-day in the depicting of our crisis. People talk of the 'fate of man' being at stake, but it is only the fate of one civilisation that is at stake—and only our egocentricity makes us think that the whole of mankind is involved. H. G. Wells's fearful prediction of the supersession of man by a new species of 'unclean intrusive monsters' lacks all basis in fact—it is mere

[1] Ibid., 256, 553.

fantasy—and however destructive a war conducted with hydrogen-bombs might be, there is no reason to think that it would wipe mankind off the face of the earth. What we can see, if we have eyes to see, is the dim shape of the coming civilisation which will super-sede our own, just as a Roman with eyes to see might have perceived the shape of things to come when, in 113 B.C., Teutons and Cimbrians moved forward on a broad front and came ' over the Alps in a huge migration '. But even the sight of our own successors growing up side by side with us, as the empire of Charlemagne grew up side by side with the empire of Rome, which survived in Constantinople, should not dismay. History does not move in cataclysms ; Rome in 113 B.C. still had five centuries of existence before it, even in the west ; and as we stand on the verge of a new universal state, we shall do well to recall Gibbon's famous judgement that the peoples of Europe were never happier than under the imperial regime of the Antonines.

6. Hence there is still much to look forward to in western civilisa-tion, provided we realize (as Spengler said) that ' we are civilized, not Gothic or Rococo people ', and provided that we ' reckon with the hard cold facts of a late life, to which the parallel is to be found not in Pericles' Athens, but in Caesar's Rome '.[1] Of great painting and great music there can, no doubt, no longer be any question ; our architectural possibilities have been exhausted for a hundred and fifty years, and we are destined to monster buildings like the Colosseum and the baths of Caraculla. Yet for a sound and vigorous generation that knows its limitations, there is much worth doing to be done. If effort which will go down into the dust seems to us vain and wearisome, if we are only prepared to strive under the illusion of perpetuity, the fault is in us, and not in the world around us; the rose is no less worth growing and tending because it fades to-morrow and withers next week. It is for us to grasp this cardinal fact in relation to ourselves and to our own civilisation. ' What is important in life ', said Goethe, ' is life and not the result of life ', and if we make that belief our own, we shall see no cause for pessi-mism in a society which is not governed by a law of progress. On the contrary, the fact—as I hinted earlier—that there is not one single line of development, all deviations from which are cast aside as worthless waste-efforts, adds to the richness of life. For at once

[1] *Decline of the West* I, 40.

' there emerges an astonishing wealth of actual forms ', and ' in place of that empty figment of one linear history, which can only be kept up by shutting one's eyes to the overwhelming multitude of facts ', we see unfolding before us ' the drama of a number of mighty cultures ', each springing with primitive strength from the soil of different regions ; each stamping its material in its own image ; each having its own idea, its own passions, its own life, will and feeling, its own death.[1] Here indeed are colours, lights and movements ; for each civilisation has its own possibilities of self-expression which arise, mature, decay and never return. The pitiful fantasy of an ' ageing Mankind ', petering out in senile decay, until finally dispatched by a mythical ' Superman ', is gone ; and in its place we have a picture, fresh and exhilarating, of endless formations and transformations, of achievement without end, of waxing and waning. Though our own spring and summer may have passed, we can look forward to a new spring and a new summer, and know, as we move into our September, that—however different—the spring and summer that will assuredly come, will be just as fair and no less inspiring than the last.

[1] Cf. Spengler, op. cit. I, 21.

INDEX